MORLEY LIBRARY

3 0112 1061 9569 3

42.00

MORLEY LIBRARY
184 PHELPS STREET
PAINESVILLE, OHIO 44077
(440) 352-3383

D1288539

Colonial
America
Primary Sources

Colonial
America
Primary Sources

PEGGY SARRI

Julie Carnagie, Editor

AN IMPRINT OF THE GALE GROUP

DETROIT · SAN FRANCISCO · LONDON
BOSTON · WOODBRIDGE, CT

Colonial America: Primary Sources

Peggy Saari

Staff

Julie L. Carnagie, *U•X•L Editor*
Carol DeKane Nagel, *U•X•L Managing Editor*
Thomas L. Romig, *U•X•L Publisher*

Shalice Shah-Caldwell, *Permissions Associate*

Rita Wimberley, *Senior Buyer*
Evi Seoud, *Assistant Production Manager*
Dorothy Maki, *Manufacturing Manager*

Pamela A. E. Galbreath, *Senior Art Director*
Cynthia Baldwin, *Product Design Manager*

LM Design, *Typesetting*

Cover photographs (from top to bottom): Olaudah Equiano reproduced by permission of the New York Historical Society; Anne Dudley Bradstreet reproduced by permission of the vicar and church wardens of St. Boloph's Church, Boston, Lincolnshire; Benjamin Franklin reproduced by permission of The Library of Congress.

Library of Congress Cataloging-in-Publication Data

Saari, Peggy.
    Colonial America: primary sources / Peggy Saari.
    p.   cm.
    Includes bibliographical references and indexes.
    Summary: Presents the historical events and social issues of colonial America through twenty-four primary documents, including diary entries, poems, and personal narratives.
    ISBN 0-7876-3766-1
    1. United States-History-Colonial period, ca. 1600-1700 Sources Juvenile literature.   [1. United States-History-Colonial period, ca. 1600-1775 Sources.]   I. Title.
    E187.S23   1999
    973.2-dc21   99-34460
                                                                                            CIP

This publication is a creative work fully protected by all applicable copyright laws, as well as by misappropriation, trade secret, unfair competition, and other applicable laws. The editors of this work have added value to the underlying factual material herein through one or more of the following: unique and original selection, coordination, expression, arrangement, and classification of the information. All rights to this publication will be vigorously defended.

Copyright © 2000
U•X•L, an Imprint of The Gale Group
27500 Drake Rd.
Farmington Hills, MI 48331-3535

All rights reserved, including the right of reproduction in whole or in part in any form.

Printed in the United States of America

10 9 8 7 6 5 4 3 2 1

Contents

Reader's Guide

Colonial America: Primary Sources presents 24 excerpted documents written by people who lived during America's colonial period. The autobiographical essays, diary entries, poems, trial testimonies, and letters in this volume reflect the experiences of Native Americans, explorers, colonists, and slaves. Some entries, such as John Smith's "The Founding of Jamestown" and William Bradford's "The Pilgrims' Landing and First Winter," relay the harsh conditions and struggles that Europeans faced as they settled in the New World. Other excerpts, including Cotton Mather, Ezekiel Cheever, and Samuel Sewell's Account of the Salem Witch Trials and Robert Beverley's "Servants and Slaves and Virginia," detail the oppressive treatment of both women and Africans in the colonies. Personal stories of colonial determination and heroism are featured as well, for example Sarah Kemble Knight's *The Journal of Madame Knight* and Mary Rowlandson's *A Narrative of the Captivity and Restauration of Mrs. Mary Rowlandson.*

Format

Colonial America: Primary Sources is divided into three chapters. Each chapter focuses on a specific theme: European Exploration and Settlement, Social Issues, and Personal Narratives. All three chapters open with an historical overview, followed by six to nine document excerpts.

Each excerpt is divided into six sections:

• **Introductory material** places the document and its author in an historical context

• **Things to remember** offers readers important background information about the featured text

• **Excerpt** presents the document in its original format

• **What happened next** discusses the impact of the document on both the speaker and his or her audience

• **Did you know** provides interesting facts about each document and its author

• **For more information** presents sources for more information on documents and speakers

Additional Features

Many of the *Colonial America: Primary Sources* contain sidebar boxes examining related excerpts, events, and issues, while 60 black-and-white illustrations help illuminate the text. Each excerpt is accompanied by a glossary running alongside the primary document that defines terms, people, and ideas discussed within the document. Also included within the volume is a timeline of important events and a subject index of the topics discussed in *Colonial America: Primary Sources*.

Advsory Board

Special thanks are due for the invaluable comments and suggestions provided by U•X•L's Colonial America Reference Library advisors:

• Katherine L. Bailey, Library Media Specialist, Seabreeze High School, Daytona Beach, Florida

• Jonathan Betz-Zall, Children's Librarian, Sno-Isle Regional Library System, Edmonds, Washington

- Deborah Hammer, Manager of the Social Sciences Division, Queens Borough Public Library, New Hyde Park, New York

- Fannie Louden, Fifth Grade History Teacher, B. F. Yancey Elementary School, Esmont, Virginia

Timeline of Events in Colonial America

1492 Italian explorer **Christopher Columbus**, sailing for Spain, reaches North America. Upon returning to Spain he reports to King Ferdinand and Queen Isabella that he has discovered "the Indies."

1588 **Thomas Harriot**, an English surveyor and Roanoke colonist, publishes *A Brief and True Report of the New Found Land of Virginia*. It contains one of the first descriptions of Native Americans written in English.

1607 **John Smith** gives an account of building the fort at Jamestown, the first permanent English settlement in North America. He publishes his account in *The Generall Historie of Virginia* (1624).

1517
Martin Luther
posts his 95
theses

1558
Elizabethan
age begins

1603
Samuel de
Champlain explores
St. Lawrence River

| 1500 | 1540 | 1580 | 1620 |

1621	In "The Pilgrims' Landing and First Winter" **William Bradford** describes the perilous experience of settling the Plymouth Colony in Massachusetts. The narrative appears in his history of Plymouth, *Of Plymouth Plantation* (1856).
1627	Massachusetts colonist **Thomas Morton** enrages Pilgrims with a May Day celebration at his trading post in Merry Mount. Morton publishes his version of the incident in *New English Canaan* (1637).
1634	Spanish Franciscan friar **Alonso de Benavides** sends a lengthy report to Spain, giving glowing evidence that the Pueblos of New Mexico have been successfully converted to Christianity.
1637	In *John Winthrop's Christian Experience* Massachusetts Bay governor **John Winthrop** writes a spiritual autobiography that chronicles his life-long struggle to be a model Christian.
1637	At a trial before the Massachusetts general court **Anne Hutchinson** is found guilty of heresy and banished from the colony. The official transcript of the trial shows an obstinate Hutchinson, who refuses to give in to the Puritan judges' charges.
1666	Massachusetts housewife **Anne Dudley Bradstreet** continues to write poetry after earning fame as the first published poet in America with *The Tenth Muse Lately Sprung Up in America* (1650).
1673	French-Canadian explorer Louis Jolliet and French Jesuit missionary **Jacques Marquette** are the first Europeans to travel down the Mississippi River. Marquette writes the official account of the expedition.
1674	In *A Relacion of the Indyan Warre* Rhode Island colonist **John Easton** describes a meeting in which New Englanders and Wampanoag chief Metacom try to prevent the bloody conflict that becomes King Philip's War (1675-76).

1630
Lemonade is invented
in Paris, France

1640
Portugal wins
independence
from Spain

1657
First fountain pens
manufactured

1625   1640   1655   1670

1676 Connecticut colonist **Mary Rowlandson** and her children are taken captive by Native Americans during King Philip's War. Her published account of the experience, *The Narrative of the Captivity and Restauration of Mrs. Mary Rowlandson,* becomes a best seller upon publication in 1682.

1676 In a letter to her sister, **Elizabeth Bacon** claims Virginians fully support the rebellion that Nathaniel Bacon, her husband, is leading against royal governor William Berkeley.

1676 Virginia colonist **William Sherwood,** in "A Narrative of Bacon's Rebellion by William Sherwood," charges Nathaniel Bacon with instigating colonists to break laws.

1681 In *The Propriety of Pennsylvania* English Quaker **William Penn** advertises his Pennsylvania colony, which he founds the following year to promote religious tolerance and political freedom.

1692 Puritan leaders **Cotton Mather, Ezekiel Cheever,** and **Samuel Sewall** write a transcript of the witch trials at Salem, Massachusetts, showing that spectral evidence is the basis for determining the guilt or innocence of accused witches.

Early 1700s New Jersey colonist **Elizabeth Ashbridge** is abused by her husband because she has become a Quaker. The account of her ordeal appears in her autobiography, *Some Account of the Early Part of the Life of Elizabeth Ashbridge, . . . Written by Herself,* which is published in 1807.

1704 Boston business woman **Sarah Kemble Knight** keeps a detailed journal during her trip from Boston to New Haven, Connecticut. Published in 1825, *The Journal of Madame Knight* becomes one of the most famous works of American travel literature.

1682
Peter the Great
becomes czar
of Russia

1692
Aesop's Fables is
published

1701–14
War of
Spanish Succession

1675   1685   1695   1705

1705 Virginia planter **Robert Beverley** promotes the benefits of being an indentured servant in "Servants and Slaves in Virginia," which is published later that year in *The History and Present State of Virginia.*

1724 Seventeen-year-old Boston native **Benjamin Franklin** starts a new life in Philadelphia, Pennsylvania. An account of his experience appears in his famous *Benjamin Franklin: A Biography in His Own Words,* which is published in 1868.

1735 New York newspaper publisher **John Peter Zenger** is found not guilty in a libel trial, achieving the first victory for freedom of the press in America. An account of the trial is published in 1736.

1741 The Tlingits of Southeast Alaska encounter Europeans for the first time. "The Coming of the First White Man," written down in 1786, records the traditional Tlingit story about the event.

1750 In *Impressions of New Jersey and New York* Swedish travel writer **Per (Peter) Kalm** describes a diverse society in New York and New Jersey.

1754 Quaker preacher **John Woolman** publishes *Some Considerations on the Keeping of Negroes,* an argument against holding slaves, which spurs a Quaker abolitionist movement.

1758 Future U.S. president **John Adams** decides to become a lawyer after graduating from Harvard College. His account of overcoming the obstacle of being an outsider in the elite Boston legal world appears in *The Diary and Autobiography of John Adams.*

1726
Gulliver's Travels
published

1738
Treaty of
Vienna ratified

1750
Westminster
Bridge opens

1715   1730   1745   1760

European Exploration and Settlement

Explorers and settlers from four European nations—Spain, France, the Netherlands, and England—arrived in North America during the early stages of the colonial period. From the outset, the presence of Europeans had a devastating impact on Native Americans who had been living on the continent since 30,000 B.C "**The Coming of the First White Man**" is a Tlingit story that gives a vivid description of the confusion and fear Native Americans experienced upon encountering Europeans. Although the story dates from the 1700s, it is considered the earliest Native American account of meeting white settlers for the first time.

Italian explorer **Christopher Columbus** opened the way for European exploration of the New World. His report to Spanish monarchs Ferdinand and Isabella is the official record of Columbus's accidental discovery of a group of islands in the Caribbean Sea, which he thought were the "Indies." Within a half century the Spanish had moved into North America. Along with explorers came Roman Catholic missionaries such as Franciscan friar **Alonso de Benavides**, who converted the Pueblos of New Mexico. An excerpt from a report written by

Benavides, gives modern readers an insight into Spanish attitudes toward the "heathen" native peoples.

While the Spanish were settling the Southwest and Southeast, the French had founded Quebec in present-day Canada and sent explorers into the region that became the United States. Among them were French-Canadian explorer Louis Jolliet and Jesuit missionary **Jacques Marquette**, who became the first Europeans to travel down the Mississippi River. "Jolliet and Marquette Travel the Mississippi" is Marquette's official account of the expedition. In the meantime, the English had made three failed attempts to settle on Roanoke Island. Surveyor **Thomas Harriot** was a member of the first expedition to Roanoke. He later published *A Brief and True Report of the New Found Land of Virginia*. It is considered the first description of Native American customs written in English.

The English finally established Jamestown, the first permanent English settlement in North America. Excerpts from *The Generall Historie of Virginia* provide **John Smith**'s famous account of the early months at Jamestown. This successful venture inspired other English colonists to move to North America. The story of the Pilgrims in the Plymouth Colony is told by **William Bradford** in his book *Of Plymouth Plantation*. Excerpts from the book include the Pilgrims' accidental landing in Massachusetts, their signing of the Mayflower Compact, and their celebration of the first Thanksgiving with Native Americans who helped them survive the winter. The Pilgrims were seeking religious freedom when they came to the New World. Likewise, **William Penn** founded the colony of Pennsylvania as a refuge for Quakers and other religious and political minorities. *The Propriety of Pennsylvania* was Penn's promotional literature, in which he stressed the attractions of North America and outlined his plans for a free society. Excerpts from the book are especially notable for Penn's liberal policies toward Native Americans. Penn also remarked on the diverse culture he encountered in the mid-Atlantic region. His depictions were echoed by Swedish travel writer **Per (Peter) Kalm**'s "Impressions of New Jersey and New York," which presents Kalm's observations on life among the Dutch and Germans.

"The Coming of the First White Man"

Told by George R. Betts and translated by Nora Dauenhauer
Reprinted in *American Literature: A Prentice Hall Anthology*
Published in 1987
Edited by Emory Elliot

According to some scholars, native peoples arrived in North America from Asia via the Bering Sea Land Bridge around 30,000 B.C. In about A.D. 986 the Thule Inuit in Greenland were the first Native Americans to come in contact with Europeans. Inuit hunters encountered the Norse (inhabitants of present-day Scandinavia; also called Vikings) expedition led by Eric the Red, who founded a settlement in Greenland. Inuit, Beothuk, and Micmac peoples are said to have met him and members of his party along the eastern coast of North America. In 1002 Eric's son, Leif Ericsson, made one of the first documented European contacts with Native Americans. According to the "Saga of Eric the Red" (contained in a collection of Norse sagas titled *Hauksbok,*) Leif Ericsson spent the winter of 1002 in a place called "Vinland." Historians disagree about the exact location of Vinland, though many speculate it could have been Nova Scotia (a peninsula on the coast of eastern Canada) or northern New England (the northeast part of modern-day United States). Yet the Native Americans maintained their own way of life.

The situation changed dramatically, however, when a Spanish expedition led by Italian explorer Christopher Colum-

"Next/They told everything./After that,/ they all went out on their canoes./This was the very first time the white man came ashore,/through Lituya Bay;"

bus (see "Christopher Columbus Reports to Ferdinand and Isabella") landed on an island in the Bahamas in the Caribbean Sea (south of Florida) in 1492. From that time onward, Europeans came to establish settlements in North America.

According to some scholars, in the 1490s the native population of North America north of the Rio Grande (a river that runs along the border between present-day Texas and Mexico) was estimated as seven million to ten million. These native peoples made up approximately six hundred tribes and spoke numerous languages, perhaps more than one thousand different dialects (some estimates reach as high as two thousand). Although native groups had distinct social and cultural characteristics, they were all focused on the family, clan, and village. Life was tied to the cycles of nature, and their religions revolved around the belief that nature was alive, pulsating with spiritual power.

In the area that is now the United States, Native Americans encountered European explorers and colonists in three distinct regions—the Southwest (New Mexico, Arizona, and Texas), the Southeast (Florida, Louisiana, Georgia, the Carolinas, Maryland, and Virginia), and the Northeast (New England, New York, and Pennsylvania). The earliest Europeans in these regions were the Spanish, French, English, Dutch, and Germans, who arrived in increasing numbers over the next 250 years. At the same time the French were settling in eastern Canada around present-day Quebec and Montreal. By the late 1700s Europeans, including settlers from Russia, were moving into southeastern Alaska.

From the late 1500s onward, Europeans wrote detailed reports of their contacts with Native Americans. They described native peoples and customs, kept records of treaties, and transcribed the speeches of great chiefs. Many Europeans also interviewed Native Americans about their reactions to explorers and colonizers, then recorded translations in letters or reports. Known as contact stories, these interviews often took place two hundred years after the arrival of Europeans. For instance, in the late eighteenth century John Heckewelder (1743–1823), an English missionary, recorded a contact story that had been passed down by generations of Delawares in present-day New York State. The tale describes the Delawares' traumatic first encounter with Europeans, which occurred in

1609 when English explorer Henry Hudson (1565–1611) anchored his ship *Half Moon* off the coast of Manhattan island. The Native Americans thought the ship was a large fish or animal, perhaps even a house in which Mannitto (the Supreme Being) lived. Overwhelmed by the prospect that one of the Englishmen—the first white men they had ever seen—might be Mannitto himself, the Delawares hastily made elaborate preparations to greet Hudson and his crew.

Yet the Delaware story was not written down by Native Americans themselves. In fact, the tale was recorded in European narrative prose. (Narrative prose involves telling a story in paragraph form with description of action and dialogue.) The reason most contact stories were written down by Europeans was because native peoples did not maintain written records. Instead, they relied on oral traditions (stories told by a speaker to a group of listeners) that were passed down from generation to generation within close-knit tribes or clans. Native American orators (storytellers) took pride in showing

An engraving of Henry Hudson's ship *Half-Moon* on the Hudson River in 1609. Hudson and his crew were the first Europeans that the Delaware tribe had encountered. *Reproduced by permission of The Granger Collection.*

In 1741, Danish navigator Vitus Jonassen Bering and his expedition were the first known Europeans to come in contact with Tlingit Native Americans. *Reproduced by permission of the Corbis Corporation (Bellevue).*

their skills at council meetings, religious ceremonies, and conferences with other tribes. During the twentieth century scholars began reconstructing the history of native peoples in North America, in part by studying Native American oral traditions. Translators attempted to reproduce the tales in the simple, direct style used by native orators. The resulting form often resembles poetry (words used to convey images that are arranged in separate lines) instead of prose. An example is "The Coming of the First White Man," a contact story that has been passed down for centuries among Tlingit tribes in Southeast Alaska.

Things to Remember While Reading "The Coming of the First White Man":

• The Tlingits (also spelled Tlinget, Tlinkit, and Tlinket) are a related group of fourteen tribes who once lived along the coast of Southeast Alaska and on islands that fringe the coast. Separate tribes include the Chilkats, the Yakutats, the Stikines, the Sitkas, the Auks, and the Hunas. The earliest known Tlingit contact with Europeans took place in 1741, after the arrival of a Russian expedition led by Danish navigator Vitus Bering (1681–1741) and Russian explorer Aleksey Chirikov (1703–1748). Numerous versions of "The Coming of the First White Man" have been told throughout Tlingit country since the eighteenth century. Some stories refer to the white men as Russians, while others mention only Europeans.

• The eighteenth-century European settlement of Southeast Alaska is generally excluded from the history of the colonial period. Living on the other side of the North American continent, the Tlingits were far removed from the most heavily colonized territories along the Atlantic coast and around the Gulf of Mexico. Nevertheless the Tlingit contact story is valuable as a distinctly Native American description of a first encounter with Europeans. "The Coming of the First White Man" relates an experience that was representative of Native Americans, from New Mexico to New England to New France.

- The story was translated into English in 1987. The translator was presented with a challenge in trying to capture word meanings, not only across the centuries but also across cultures. Similarly, the reader is presented with a challenge; as part of an oral tradition, "The Coming of the First White Man" was meant to be spoken, not read. Consequently, the audience addressed by the storyteller played an important role in giving shape and meaning to the presentation. Native American listeners had heard the story many times before, and that provided them with an understanding of events and background passed from generation to generation. Modern readers may not share these insights, yet they can gain a better understanding of the impact of European culture on native life.

- Keep in mind that the storyteller is speaking about the past, and that he or she has become accustomed to European items such as ships, anchors, galleys, mirrors, rice, and brandy. At the time of the first encounter with Europeans, however, the Tlingit had no names for these things. Consequently, they thought of rice as worms and sugar as sand. The Tlingits explained unusual occurrences like the arrival of the Europeans in terms of their religious teachings (the Raven created the world), which required them to observe certain rituals (viewing the ship—possibly the Raven himself—through a plant stalk) in order to avoid disaster (being turned to stone).

"The Coming of the First White Man"

People lived in Lituya Bay
loooong ago.
Smoke houses and other houses were there.
There was a deserted place called Lituya Bay before the white man
migrated *in from the sea.*
At one point one morning

Migrated: Traveled

a person went outside.
Then there was a white object that could be seen way out on the sea
bouncing on the waves
and rocked by the waves.
At one point it was coming closer to the people.
"What's that?"
"What's that, what's that?"
"It's something different!"
"It's something different!"
"Is it Raven?"
"Maybe that's what it is."
"I think that's what it is—
Raven who created the world.
He said he would come back again."
Some dangerous thing was happening.
(Lituya Bay
lay like a lake.
There was a current;
salt water flowed in when the tide was coming in.
But when the tide was going out
the sea water would also drain out.)
So the thing went right on in with the flood tide.
Then the people of the village ran scared right into the forest,
all of them;
the children too,
were taken to the forest.
They watched from the forest.
At one point
they heard strange sounds.
Actually it was the anchor that was thrown in the water.
"Don't look at it!"
they told the children.
"Don't anybody look at it.
If you look at it, you'll turn to stone.
That's Raven, he's come by boat."
"Oh! People are running around on it!"
Things are moving around on it.
*Actually it was the sailors climbing around the **mast**.*
At one point after they had watched for a loooong time,
*they took blue **hellebore***
and broke the stalks,
blue hellebore.

Mast: A vertical pole that rises
from a ship to hold the sails

Hellebore: A poisonous plant

They poked holes though them
so that they wouldn't turn to stone;
they watched through them.
When no one turned to stone while watching,
someone said,
"Let's go out there.
We'll go out there."
"What's that?"
Then there were two young men;
from the woods
a canoe
(the kind of canoe called "seet")
was pulled down to the beach.
They quickly went aboard.
They quickly went out to it, paddled out to it.
When they got out to it,
a rope ladder was lowered.
Then they were beckoned to go aboard,
they were beckoned over by the crewmen's fingers,
the crewmen's fingers.
Then they went up there.
They examined it; they had not seen anything like it.
Actually it was a huge sail boat.
When the crew took them inside the cabin,
they saw-
they saw themselves.
Actually it was a huge mirror inside there,
a huge mirror.
They gave this name then,
to the thing an image of people could be seen on.
Then they were taken to the cook's **galley.**
There they were given food.
Worms were cooked for them,
worms.
They stared at it.
White sand
was put in front of them.
Then they spooned this white sand into the rice.
Actually it was sugar.
What they thought were worms, was rice.
This was what they had just been staring at.
At what point was it one of them took a spoonful?

Galley: The kitchen of a ship

The first encounter between Europeans and Native Americans described by the Tlignit story *The Coming of the First White Man* set the stage for future meetings like the one pictured here.

Reproduced by permission of Corbis-Bettmann.

Maggot: A larva of a fly

"Hey! Look!
Go ahead! Taste it!"
"It might be good."
So the other took a spoonful.
Just as he did, he said "This is good food,
these worms,
maggots,
this is good food."
After they were fed all kinds of food,
then they were given alcohol
alcohol
perhaps it was brandy.
Then they began to feel very strange.
Never before... ...
"Why am I beginning to feel this way?
Look! I'm beginning to feel strange!"
And "I'm beginning to feel happiness settling through my body too,"
they said.

After they had taken them through the whole ship,
they took them to the railing.
They gave them some things.
Rice
and sugar
*and **pilot bread***
were given to them to take along.
They were told how to cook them.
Now I wonder what it was cooked on.
You know, people didn't have pots then. . . .
There was no cooking pot for it.
When they got ashore
they told everyone:
"There are many people in there.
Strange things are in there too.
A box of our images,
this looking glass,
a box of out images;
we could just see ourselves.
Next
they cooked maggots for us to eat."
They told everything.
After that,
they all went out on their canoes.
This was the very first time the white man came ashore,
through Lituya Bay;
Ltu.áa is called Lituya Bay
in Alaska.
Well! This is all of my story.

Pilot bread: A saltless, hard biscuit, bread or cracker

What happened next . . .

Culture, climate, location, and timing determined the nature of a native group's contact with Europeans—but usually the results were devastating. Scholars estimate that within a century after Columbus's arrival the Native American population had been reduced by nearly fifty percent. Several factors contributed to this dramatic decline. European weapons and warfare devastated native peoples. Native Americans routinely died as a result of mistreatment, especially slavery. Population loss also occurred when Native American farming and hunting methods were disrupted and starvation resulted. Disease was even more damaging. In virtually every encounter with Europeans, Native Americans succumbed rapidly to diseases caused by microbes (tiny organisms) the Europeans carried into North America.

Life for native peoples throughout North America was also severely affected by trade. In a relatively brief time European items that had been novelties became an essential part of native culture. Land became a crucial medium of exchange during trade negotiations between Native Americans and Europeans. Immediately, disputes regarding land ownership led to misunderstandings and conflicts. When colonists followed the European practice of drawing up legal contracts, Native Americans responded according to their own traditions and assumed they were signing peace treaties. Soon the Europeans were acquiring vast stretches of territory throughout North America. The fate of Native Americans was finally sealed when European colonists began to claim the best land for their own use. They then set aside undesirable lands (called reservations) and forced native peoples to live there. By the late nineteenth century all Native Americans, including the Tlingits, were living on reservations.

Did you know . . .

- Around A.D. 986 the Thule Inuits (Eskimos) in Greenland were the first Native Americans to come in contact with Europeans. Inuit hunters encountered the Norse (inhabitants of present-day Scandinavia; also called Vikings) expedition led by Eric the Red, who established a settlement in Greenland. (The settlement died out around 1500.) In 1002 Eric's son, Leif Ericsson, made one of the first documented European contacts with Native Americans. According to the "Saga of Eric the Red" (contained in a collection of Norse sagas titled *Hauksbok*), Leif Ericsson spent the winter of 1002 in a place called "Vinland." Historians disagree about the exact location of Vinland, though many speculate it could have been Nova Scotia or northern New England. Leif Ericsson and his men met members of a

Native American tribe, whom they called "Skraelings." After a heated battle the Skraelings drove the Norsemen back to Greenland.

- Alcohol was by far the most destructive aspect of European trade for native peoples. Before 1500, Native Americans had had virtually no exposure to alcohol. Consequently, they were as vulnerable to alcoholism as they were to European diseases. As "The Coming of the First White Man" shows, by the late seventeenth century brandy and rum were important trade items. Since many Native Americans found liquor highly addictive, they would do anything to obtain it. The demand for alcohol caused breakdowns in the native economy, as Native American hunters would trade skins for alcohol, then go into debt for goods that had become necessities. In order to claim land, Europeans eventually took advantage of Native Americans' addiction. They began to use so-called whiskey treaties, agreements that were signed while Native Americans were under the influence of alcohol.

For more information

Adler, Bill, ed. *The American Indian: The First Victim.* New York: Morrow, 1972.

Elliot, Emory, and others, eds. *American Literature: A Prentice Hall Anthology.* Englewood Cliffs, N.J., 1991.

The Mayas. http://www.indians.org/welker/mayamenu.htm Available September 30, 1999.

National Geographic Society. *The World of the American Indian.* Revised edition. Washington, D.C.: National Geographic Society. 1993.

Sherman, Josepha. *The First Americans: Spirit of the Land and People.* New York: Smithmark, 1996.

Tlingit Culture. http:/www.geocities.com/Athens/Atlantis/4513/ Available September 30, 1999.

Christopher Columbus

"Christopher Columbus Reports to Ferdinand and Isabella"
Reprinted in *Major Problems of American Colonial History*
Published in 1993
Edited by Karen Ordahl Kupperman

Exploration and settlement of the United States began in the late fifteenth century as a direct outcome of events in Europe, the Middle East, and Africa. One of the most significant reasons was the Crusades (1099–1272), an unsuccessful Christian campaign to recapture the Holy Land (a region in the Middle East comprising parts of modern Israel, Jordan, and Egypt; today known as Palestine) from the Muslims (followers of the Islamic religion).

During four hundred years of interaction with Middle Eastern cultures Europeans were able to make significant advances in exploration based on information the Muslims provided. For instance, European civilizations drafted more accurate maps of the known world, built swifter ships, and charted sea routes by observing the Sun. Another important development was the discovery of luxury goods such as silks and spices that came from China and the East Indies (India and adjacent lands and islands in the Far East), which created a thriving market in Europe.

Motivated by greed, adventurers were willing to take risks to search for trade routes to previously unknown lands. At

"...I promise, that with a little assistance afforded me by our most invincible sovereigns, I will procure them as much gold as they need, as great a quantity of spices, of cotton,...and as many men for the service of the navy as their Majesties may require."

that time the only way for Europeans to reach the Far East was to sail south along the western coast of Africa and then east into the Indian Ocean. The most direct route was through the Mediterranean Sea, but the eastern end of that waterway was controlled by Turkey, a Muslim foe of the Europeans. Portugal was the first country to send explorers eastward. Financed by merchants, they traveled down the African coast in search of gold and ivory. The Portuguese also became involved in the small but lucrative business of buying African slaves from Muslim traders. Soon Spain entered into competition with Portugal to find the best trade routes. The Spanish were the principal defenders of Roman Catholicism throughout the world, and they seized the opportunity to gain converts to Christianity in the newly conquered lands. (Roman Catholicism is a branch of Christianity that is based in Rome, Italy, and headed by a pope who is considered infallible.) Thus the stage was set for the discovery of the New World (the European term for North America and South America) by Italian explorer Christopher Columbus (1451–1506).

Born in Genoa, Italy, Columbus began his career as a sailor on merchant and war ships in the Mediterranean. In 1476 he went to Lisbon, Portugal, where he learned mathematics and astronomy (study of the stars), subjects that were vital for navigation. He made several voyages, including one to Iceland (an island between the North Atlantic and Arctic Oceans) with other explorers. In the early 1480s Columbus sought a sponsor for his own voyage of exploration. He wanted to prove his theory that China and the East Indies could be reached more easily by sailing west across the Atlantic Ocean than by going around Africa to the Indian Ocean. If he succeeded, he would also confirm a long-held European belief that the world was round. Educated Europeans of the fifteenth century knew the Earth was a sphere, but no one had yet determined its size. Columbus also contended that by taking the Atlantic route, he could make an accurate measurement of the distance between Europe and China.

For several years Columbus had failed in his attempts to enlist the king of Portugal in this quest, primarily because Portuguese explorer Bartolomeu Dias (c.1450–1500) had found the sea passage from Europe to India, which was considered the best route at the time. Not to be discouraged, Columbus decided to try his luck in Spain. He first met with Queen Isabella I (1451–1504) in 1486, but it wasn't until April 1492, that Isabella and her husband, King Ferdinand V (1452–1516) agreed to finance an expedition. As part of the deal, Columbus would be named admiral, become governor of any territory he discovered, and receive a share of any riches he found.

On August 3, 1492, Columbus set sail from Cadiz, Spain, with three ships—the *Santa Maria* (with Columbus as captain), the *Niña,* and the *Pinta.* Initially, the expedition made rapid progress. By October 10, however, the crew had turned mutinous (rebellious) because they had not seen land for months. Luckily for Columbus, two days later they spotted a small island in the present-day Bahamas (a group of islands south of Florida). After going ashore Columbus spent several weeks meeting the native peoples and exploring the islands. On December 25, 1492, he established the first European settlement in the Americas. Called La Navidad ("the birth"; in commemoration of being founded on Christmas Day), it stood on the site of present-day Limonade-Bord-de-Mer, Haiti. Columbus returned to Spain in early 1493, leaving twenty-two men at La Navidad. He wrote the report on his triumphant voyage on March 14, 1493.

Christopher Columbus finally persuaded King Ferdinand V and Queen Isabella I to finance his first expeditions to the New World. *Reproduced by permission of the Corbis Corporation (Bellevue).*

Things to Remember While Reading "Christopher Columbus Reports to Ferdinand and Isabella":

- When Columbus went ashore in the Bahamas, he mistakenly assumed he had reached the East Indies. For instance, in his report he mentioned "a certain island called Charis, which is the second from Española [now Haiti] on the side towards India." Columbus therefore gave the name "Indians" to the Native Americans—members of the Taino tribe—who greeted him. When the Tainos directed Columbus southward to a larger island, which he named Juana, he assumed it must be part of Cathay (the European term for China). In fact, the island is today known as Cuba.

- The Tainos thought Columbus and his crew were gods, or "beings of a celestial [heavenly] race." This was a common reaction among native peoples upon meeting Europeans for the first time (see "The Coming of the First White Man.") They usually made elaborate preparations to greet these supreme beings. During the early years of exploration and settlement, Native Americans welcomed Europeans to their land, even after they learned that white men were also ordinary humans and not gods.

- Columbus's voyage was tremendously expensive, and he was expected to find riches that would bring great profits for the Spanish monarchs and merchants. In his report he took every advantage to make a case for returning immediately to Hispaniola. For instance, he made extravagant promises of bringing back gold, cotton, spices, drugs, and even navy recruits from future voyages to the New World.

- Columbus mentioned that the Native Americans, "like idiots," traded valuable commodities such as gold and cotton for ordinary European-made items. Keep in mind that although Columbus quickly prohibited "unjust" trading between his men and the Native Americans, he was not motivated by good will toward the "Indians." Instead he wanted to cast the Spanish in the best light and encourage friendly relations that would work to Spain's advantage. He was also preparing the way for Roman Catholic missionaries, making it easier for them to convert the native peoples to Christianity.

"Christopher Columbus Reports to Ferdinand and Isabella"

First Voyage, 1492–1493

Knowing that it will afford you pleasure to learn that I have brought in undertaking to a successful termination, I have decided upon writing you this letter to acquaint you with all the events which have occurred in my voyage, and the discoveries which have resulted from it. *Thirty-three days after my departure from Cadiz I reached the Indian sea, where I discovered many islands, thickly peopled, of which I took possession without resistance in the name of our most illustrious Monarch, by public proclamation and with **unfurled** banners. To the first of these islands, which is called by the Indians Guanahani, I gave the name of the blessed Saviour (San Salvador), relying upon whose protection I had reached this as well as the other islands; to each of these I also gave a name, ordering that one should be called Santa Maria de la Concepcion, another Fernandina, the third Isabella, the fourth Juana, and so with all the rest respectively. As soon as we arrived at that, which as I have said was named Juana, I proceeded along its coast a short distance westward, and found it to be so large and apparently without termination, that I could not suppose it to be an island, but the continental province of Cathay [China]. Seeing, how-ever, no towns or populous places on the sea coast, but only a few detached houses and cottages, with whose inhabitants I was unable to communicate, because they fled as soon as they saw us, I went fur-ther on, thinking that in my progress I should certainly find some city or village. . . . I afterwards dispatched two of our men to ascertain whether there were a king or any cities in that province. These men **reconnoitred** the country for three days, and found a most numerous population, and great numbers of houses, though small, and built without any regard to order: with which information they returned to us. In the mean time I had learned from some Indians whom I had seized, that that country was certainly an island: and therefore I sailed towards the east, coasting to the distance of three hundred and twenty-two miles, which brought us to the extremity of it; from this point I saw lying eastwards another island, fifty-four miles distant from Juana, to which I gave the name of Española [Hispaniola]: . . . In that island also which I have before said we named Española, there are mountains of very great size and beauty, vast plains, groves, and very fruitful fields, admirably adapted for **tillage**, pasture, and habitation. The convenience and excellence of the harbours in this island, and the abundance of the rivers, so indispensable to the health of man, sur-pass anything that would be believed by one who had not seen it. The trees, **herbage**, and fruits of Española are very different from those of Juana, and moreover it abounds in various kinds of spices, gold, and other metals. The inhabitants of both sexes in this island, and in all the others which I have seen, or of which I have received information, go always naked as they were born, with the exception of some of the women, who use the covering of a leaf, or small bough, or an apron of cotton which they prepare for that purpose. None of them, as I have*

Unfurled: Unfolded

Reconnoitred: Made an exploratory survey

Tillage: Cultivated land

Herbage: Vegetation often used for grazing animals

*already said, are possessed of any iron, neither have they weapons, being unacquainted with, and indeed incompetent to use them, not from any deformity of body (for they are well-formed), but because they are timid and full of fear. They carry however **in lieu of** arms, canes dried in the sun, on the ends of which they fix heads of dried wood sharpened to a point, and even these they dare not use habitually; for it has often occurred when I have sent two or three of my men to any of the villages to speak with the natives, that they have come out in a disorderly troop, and have fled in such haste at the approach of our men, that the fathers **forsook** their children and the children their fathers. This timidity did not arise from any loss or injury that they had received from us; for, on the contrary, I gave to all I approached whatever articles I had about me, such as cloth and many other things, taking nothing of theirs in return: but they are naturally timid and fearful. As soon however as they see that they are safe, and have laid aside all fear, they are very simple and honest, and exceedingly liberal with all they have; none of them refusing any thing he may possess when he is asked for it, but on the contrary inviting us to ask them. They exhibit great love towards all others in preference to themselves: they also give objects of great value for **trifles**, and content themselves with very little or nothing in return. I however forbad that these trifles and articles of no value (such as pieces of dishes, plates, and glass, keys, and leather straps) should be given to them, although if they could obtain them, they imagined themselves to be possessed of the most beautiful trinkets in the world. It even happened that a sailor received for a leather strap as much gold as was worth three golden nobles, and for things of more trifling value offered by our men, especially newly coined **blancas**, or any gold coins, the Indians would give whatever the seller required; as, for instance, an ounce and a half or two ounces of gold, or thirty or forty pounds of cotton, with which commodity they were already acquainted.*

*Thus they **bartered**, like idiots, cotton and gold for fragments of bows, glasses, bottles, and jars; which I forbad as being unjust, and myself gave them many beautiful and acceptable articles which I had brought with me, taking nothing from them in return; I did this in order that I might the more easily **conciliate** them, that they might be led to become Christians, and be inclined to entertain a regard for the King and Queen, our Princes and all Spaniards, and that I might induce them to take an interest in seeking out, and collecting, and delivering to us things as they possessed ion abundance, but which we greatly needed. They practise no kind of **idolatry**, but have a firm belief that all strength and power, and indeed all good things, are in*

In lieu of: Instead of

Forsook: Renounced

Trifles: Objects of little value

Blancas: Spanish coins

Bartered: Traded by exchanging one object for another

Conciliate: To gain by pleasing acts

Idolatry: Worship of a physical object as a god

Celestial: Heavenly

Cannibals: People who eat the flesh of other humans

Deference: Respect; esteem

Colonial America: Primary Sources

heaven, and that I had descended from thence with these ships and sailors, and under this impression was I received after they had thrown aside their fears. Nor are they slow or stupid, but of very clear understanding; and those men who have crossed to the neighbouring islands give an admirable description of everything they observed; but they never saw any people clothed, nor any ships like ours. On my arrival at that sea, I had taken some Indians by force from the first island that I came to, in order that they might learn our language, and communicate to us what they knew respecting the country; which plan succeeded excellently, and was a great advantage to us, for in a short time, either by gestures and signs, or by words, we were enabled to understand each other. These men are still travelling with me, and although they have been with us now a long time, they continue to entertain the idea that I have descended from heaven; and on our arrival at any new place they

Christopher Columbus mistakenly thought that he had reached the East Indies when he landed in the Bahamas. As a result, he gave Native Americans the name "Indians." *Reproduced by permission of The Library of Congress.*

published this, crying out immediately with a loud voice to the other Indians, "Come, come and look upon beings of a **celestial** race": upon which both women and men, children and adults, young men and old, when they got rid of the fear they at first entertained, would come out in throngs, crowding the roads to see us, some bringing food, others drink, with astonishing affection and kindness. . . . I could not clearly understand whether the people possess any private property, for I observed that one man had the charge of distributing various things to the rest, but especially meat and provisions and the like. I did not find, as some of us had expected, any **cannibals** amongst them, but on the contrary men of great **deference** and kindness. Neither are they black, like the **Ethiopians** their hair is smooth and straight: for they do not dwell where the rays of the sun strike most vividly,—and the sun has intense power there, the distance from the **equinoctial** line being, it appears, but six-and-twenty degrees. On the tops of the mountains the cold is very great, but the effect of this upon the Indians is lessened by their being accustomed to the climate, and by their frequently indulging in the use of very hot meats and drinks.

Ethiopians: Inhabitants of Ethiopia, an ancient country in northeast Africa

Equinoctial: The time of equal day and night

Ferocious: Fierce or violent

Javelins: Light weapons thrown as spears in hunting or war

Sovereigns: People who have supreme authority over a state, especially a king and queen

Mastic: A pasty material secreted by a mastic tree

Chios: An island in the Aegean Sea off the coast of Turkey

Rhubarb: An edible plant then used in China and Tibet as a cure for stomach disorders

Tarried: Waited

Wont: Accustomed to

Precepts: Orders intended as general rules

Conjectures: Guesses

*Thus, as I have already said, I saw no cannibals, nor did I hear of any, except in a certain island called Charis, which is the second from Española on the side towards India, where dwell a people who are considered by the neighbouring islanders as most **ferocious** and these feed upon human flesh. The same people have many kinds of canoes, in which they cross to all the surrounding islands and rob and plunder wherever they can; they are not different from the other islanders, except that they wear their hair long, like women, and make use of the bows and **javelins** of cane, with sharpened spear-points fixed on the thickest end, which I have before described, and therefore they are looked upon as ferocious, and regarded by the other Indians with unbounded fear; but I think no more of them than of the rest. . . . Finally, to compress into few words the entire summary of my voyage and speedy return, and of the advantages derivable therefrom, I promise, that with a little assistance afforded me by our most invincible **sovereigns**, I will procure them as much gold as they need, as great a quantity of spices, of cotton, and of **mastic** (which is only found in **Chios**), and as many men for the service of the navy as their Majesties may require. I promise also **rhubarb** and other sorts of drugs, which I am persuaded the men whom I have left in the aforesaid fortress have found already and will continue to find; for I myself have **tarried** no where longer than I was compelled to do by the winds, except in the city of Navidad, while I provided for the building of the fortress, and took the necessary precautions for the perfect security of the men I left there. Although all I have related may appear to be wonderful and unheard of, yet the results of my voyage would have been more astonishing if I had had at my disposal such ships as I required. But these great and marvellous results are not to be attributed to any merit of mine, but to the holy Christian faith, and to the piety and religion of our Sovereigns; for that which the unaided intellect of men could not compass, the spirit of God has granted to human exertions, for God is **wont** to hear the prayers of his servants who love his **precepts** even to the performance of apparent impossibilities. Thus it has happened to me in the present instance, who have accomplished a task to which the powers of mortal men had never hitherto attained; for if there have been those who have anywhere written or spoken of these islands, they have done so with doubts and **conjectures,** and no one has ever asserted that he has seen them, on which account their writings have been looked upon as little else than fables. Therefore let the king and queen, our princes and their most happy kingdoms, and all the other provinces of **Christendom**, render* *thanks to our Lord and Saviour Jesus Christ, who has granted us so great a victory and such prosperity. Let processions be made, and sacred feasts be held, and the temples be adorned with festive boughs. Let Christ rejoice on earth, as he rejoices in heaven in the prospect of the salvation of the souls of so many nations hitherto lost. Let us also rejoice, as well on account of the exaltation of our faith, as on account of the increase of our **temporal** prosperity, of which not only Spain, but all Christendom will be partakers.*

Such are the events which I have briefly described. Farewell.

Lisbon, the 14th of March.

Christopher Columbus,

Admiral of the Fleet of the Ocean

Christendom: A part of the world in which Christianity prevails

Temporal: Of or relating to earthly life

What happened next . . .

With promises of untold riches, Columbus had no difficulty persuading Ferdinand and Isabella to sponsor a second voyage. This time the monarchs rewarded the admiral with seventeen ships and sent along a thousand colonists to live in the new Spanish settlement. When the expedition reached La Navidad in November 1493, however, they found the settlement in ruins. Unburied Spaniard corpses were scattered everywhere. Either the Native Americans had turned against the Europeans, or the Spaniards had fought among themselves—no one had survived to tell the story. Columbus decided to move seventy-five miles east, where he started building a settlement called Isabela. Immediately he sent a party of men in search of gold while he explored the nearby islands.

When Columbus returned to Isabela in late September 1494, he learned that his men had found very little gold. He also encountered mounting tensions between the Native Americans and the Spaniards. Having been mistreated by the colonists, the Native Americans were organizing an army to try to drive the Europeans off the island. The Spanish took drastic measures, which led to the near extermination of the inhabitants of Hispaniola. During the next three years Columbus ruled harshly, imposing heavy taxes on the Native Americans and forcing them into slavery. Native American offenses against the Spanish were often punished with death, using such methods as burning at the stake or beheading. Colonists often attacked or killed native men, women, and children on a whim. Native Americans also died of diseases the Europeans brought with them.

Soon shocking reports about conditions on Hispaniola were reaching Spain. Ferdinand and Isabella were already displeased because they were receiving little gold from the New World, and very few Native Americans had been converted to Catholicism. No longer confident of Columbus's ability to govern the colony, the monarchs recalled him to Spain in 1496. Within two years, however, he had persuaded the king and queen to send him back to Hispaniola. On this third voyage Columbus sailed along the coast of Venezuela, thus becoming the first European to view the continent of South America.

When Columbus returned to Spain he left his brother Bartholomeo in charge at Isabela. In the meantime, Bartholomeo had moved the settlement to the south side of the island to a place called Santo Domingo. Upon reaching Santo Domingo in August 1498, Columbus was beset by numerous problems. The Spaniards found gold only in small quantities, and there weren't enough native workers. Friction had also continued between the surviving Native Americans and the colonists. Death and sickness were rampant, supplies were scarce, and living conditions were poor. It was not long before the Spanish colonists were openly challenging Columbus.

Finally Ferdinand and Isabella sent Francisco de Bobadilla (d. 1502) to replace Columbus as governor. When de Bobadilla arrived in Santo Domingo in 1500, he found the colony in chaos. The bodies of seven rebel Spaniards were hanging in the town square, and Columbus's brother Diego was planning to hang five others. Columbus himself was trying to put down a rebellion on another part of the island, and Bartholomeo was making similar efforts elsewhere. After arresting all three men, Bobadilla ordered that they be put in chains and sent back to Spain for trial. Although Columbus subsequently lost all of his titles except admiral, during his years in Hispaniola he had become a wealthy man. In 1502 he set out on a fourth voyage to the Caribbean, but the trip ended

Spanish abuses of Natives

Bartolome de Las Casas (1474–1566), a Spanish missionary, witnessed many horrible abuses of Native Americans on Hispaniola. He reported that Spaniards "made bets as to who would slit a man in two, or cut off his head at one blow. . . . They tore the babes from their mother's breast by their feet, and dashed their heads against the rocks. . . . They spitted [held like meat over a fire] the bodies of other babes, together with their mothers and all who were before them, on their swords." He also described the psychological impact of the mistreatment: "In this time, the greatest outrages and slaughterings of people were perpetrated, whole villages being depopulated. . . . The Indians saw that without any offence on their part they were despoiled [robbed] of their kingdoms, their lands and liberties and of their lives, their wives, and homes. As they saw themselves each day perishing by the cruel and inhuman treatment of the Spaniards, crushed to the earth by the horses, cut in pieces by swords, eaten and torn by dogs, many buried alive and suffering all kinds of exquisite [extreme] tortures, some of the Princes . . . decided to abandon themselves

Bartolome de Las Casas witnessed the horrible abuses that Columbus and his men caused the Native Americans. *Reproduced by permission of The Library of Congress.*

to their unhappy fate with no further struggles, placing themselves in the hands of their enemies that they might do with them as they liked. There were still those people who fled to the mountains."

Source: Sale, Kirkpatrick. The Conquest of Paradise: Christopher Columbus and the Columbian Legacy. New York: Knopf, 1990, p. 157.

in humiliation: He actually had to be rescued after spending a year marooned (stranded) on the island of Jamaica. Ferdinand refused to send Columbus on another expedition, so the defeated explorer spent the last three years of his life in splendid retirement at Valladolid, Spain.

Did you know . . .

- While Columbus was exploring the islands around Isabela in 1496, he assembled his men and made them take an oath that they had been sailing along the mainland of Asia, not the coast of an island. Apparently he was still convinced—or was trying to convince himself—that he had found the "Indies." If he suspected he had made a geographical error, he did not want the news to come from his men.

- From 1496 to 1498 Columbus tried to persuade Ferdinand and Isabella to send him on a third voyage to Hispaniola. During that time he wore the coarse dress of a Franciscan friar (member of the Roman Catholic monastic order of Saint Francis). His strange attire has never been completely understood. Some historians speculate that he may have adopted it to express regret for wrongdoing, to show humility, or to use as a disguise.

- The Portuguese introduced African slavery to North America. Soon after the Spanish arrived in the Caribbean, the Native Americans began to die of European diseases. Consequently the Spanish did not have enough slave workers. They found an alternative labor supply in 1510, however, when the Portuguese sent the first shipment of African slaves to Hispaniola.

For more information

Columbus and the Age of Discovery. http://www.millersv.edu/~columbus/mainmenu.html Available September 30, 1999.

Columbus, Christopher. *The Voyage of Christopher Columbus: Columbus's Own Journal of Discovery.* John Cummins, translator. New York: St. Martin's Press, 1992.

Kupperman, Karen Ordahl, ed. *Major Problems in American Colonial History.* Lexington, Mass.: D. C. Heath, 1993, pp. 4–7.

Sale, Kirkpatrick. *The Conquest of Paradise: Christopher Columbus and the Columbian Legacy.* New York: Knopf, 1990.

Wilford, John Noble. *The Mysterious History of Columbus: An Exploration of the Man, the Myth, the Legacy.* New York: Knopf, distributed by Random House, 1991.

Yewell, John, and others, eds. *Confronting Columbus: An Anthology.* Jefferson, N.C.: McFarland and Company, 1992.

Alonso de Benavides

"Fray Alonso de Benavides Reports New Mexico
Indians Eager for Conversion"
Reprinted in *Major Problems in American Colonial History*
Published in 1993
Edited by Karen Ordahl Kupperman

Italian explorer Christopher Columbus paved the way for the European conquest of North America after his 1492 journey to the Bahamas. During the early 1500s the Spanish established settlements on other Caribbean islands—present-day Puerto Rico, Jamaica, and Cuba—that had been visited by Columbus. While Columbus's wild promises of huge deposits of gold and other riches failed to materialize, the Spanish still managed to make comfortable profits from tobacco, sugar, and ranching in the Caribbean. Soon they moved onto the mainland of South America and set up trading posts in Venezuela and Colombia. Then in 1519 Hernán Cortés (1485–1547) led an expedition into Mexico in Central America, brutally conquering the Aztec empire headed by Emperor Montezuma II (1466–1520). In Mexico the Spaniards found advanced civilizations that had perfected sophisticated architectural and agricultural techniques. They also discovered an abundance of gold and silver, which enticed other Spanish conquistadors (conquerors) to prepare expeditions to the continent. When Francisco de Pizarro (c.1475–1541) invaded Peru (a country in South America) and conquered the Incas in 1531, Spain became a major world power.

> "...here, where scarcely thirty years earlier all was idolatry and worship of the devil, without any vestige of civilization, today they all worship our true God and Lord."

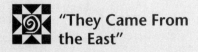

"They Came From the East"

The following poem was written by the Mayas in 1541, after the Spanish brutally conquered the native peoples of Central America.

They came from the east when they arrived.

Then Christianity also began.

The fulfillment of its prophecy is ascribed to [comes from] the east . . .

Then with the true God, the true Dios,

came the beginning of our misery.

It was the beginning of tribute [a form of taxation],

the beginning of church dues,

the beginning of strife with purse-snatching,

the beginning of strife with blow-guns [European weapons];

the beginning of strife of trampling people,

the beginning of robbery with violence,

the beginning of forced debts,

the beginning of debts enforced by false testimony,

the beginning of individual strife,

a beginning of vexation [worry].

Reprinted in: Elliott, Emory, and others, eds. *American Literature: A Prentice Hall Anthology.* Englewood Cliffs, N.J.: 1991, p. 25.

During the 1530s Spanish explorers crossed the Rio Grande into southwestern North America in search of the fabulously wealthy "Seven Cities of Cibola." In 1540 Francisco Vásquez de Coronado (c.1510–1554), the governor of New Galicia (a Spanish province northwest of present-day Mexico City), headed a large expedition that had been organized to find the golden cities and claim their treasures for Spain. During a two-year quest for riches Coronado explored the Rio Grande valley and parts of present-day Texas and Kansas. Finally he realized that he had been misled: The "Seven Cities" were in fact the apartment-like villages of the Pueblos (several interrelated Southwest Native American tribes)—and they contained neither gold nor silver. Although Coronado returned to Mexico empty-handed, he paved the way for Spanish settlement of the Southwest. It is for this reason that many historians regard him as one of the great European explorers.

While the conquistadors were colonizing Peru, Mexico, and New Mexico, the Spanish had had little success in advancing farther into the North American continent. In 1513 Juan Ponce de León (1460–1521) briefly explored the coast of Florida (called La Florida by the Spanish), but was driven out by local Native Americans. More than two decades later Hernando de Soto (c.1500–1542) was drawn to the region by the same tales of fabulously rich cities that had enthralled Coronado. In 1539 de Soto led an expedition into the Mississippi River valley and along the western coast of La Florida. Like Coronado, he found no gold or silver, but he did open the way for European colonization. By the 1560s the French were competing with the

Franciso Vasquez de Coronado on horseback in search of the "Seven Cities." *Reproduced by permission of Corbis-Bettmann.*

Spanish to establish permanent colonies on the Atlantic coast. Responding to these threats in 1565, Spanish naval officer Pedro Menéndez de Avilés (1519–1574) claimed La Florida for Spain. The following spring he and his men built a town called Saint Augustine, which became the first permanent European settlement in North America. Later they constructed a massive stone fort that enabled the Spanish to keep the French out of La Florida. Nevertheless, Spanish settlement was confined to Florida throughout the colonial period.

By the 1600s Spaniards had made great progress in colonizing the Southwest. They were also fulfilling their goal of spreading Christianity among the "pagans"(people who worship more than one god) and "heathens" of the New World (European term for North America and South America). Military leaders created Nuevo México (New Mexico), and Franciscan friars (members of a Roman Catholic religious order) founded missions (religious centers with schools and churches) for the conversion of the Pueblo peoples. "Fray

Alonso de Benavides Reports New Mexico Indians Eager for Conversion" provides a vivid description of the Catholic friars' encounter with traditional Pueblo beliefs.

The Pueblos initially accepted the Spanish presence without resistance, even adopting European innovations (new ideas or methods) in cooking, architecture, and town planning. Some also offered the Franciscans the same respect they gave their own spiritual leaders because they considered the white friars to be assistants of their gods. The Pueblos were so accepting because religion was already the center of their culture, which was headed by spiritual leaders (priests; sometimes called medicine men) who were brought to earth by the gods. Having received instructions directly from the gods, the priests conducted rituals that enabled the Pueblos to live in harmony with nature.

Things to Remember While Reading "Fray Alonso de Benavides Reports New Mexico Indians Eager for Conversion":

- Benavides believed that Spanish friars could find many converts among the Pueblos and Apaches. (The Apaches are six culturally related Native American groups who lived in New Mexico and present-day Arizona. The enemies of the Pueblos, the Apaches were known as fierce fighters.) Benavides wrote his report in an effort to convince Spanish authorities to concentrate their colonization efforts on New Mexico.

- The Apaches successfully resisted Spanish colonization, so the Catholic friars had the most interaction with the Pueblos. Traditional beliefs, such as the Pueblo creation myth (a story that explains the beginning of the world), influenced their general acceptance of Catholicism. According to the myth, the Pueblos had once lived in the center of the Earth (the middle level of the cosmos, or universe) with their mother and all living creatures. When it was time to leave, their mother gave them corn to take the place of her nourishment and appointed a priest to care for them. Helped by the birds, insects, and animals, the people and their gods climbed up to the surface of the Earth (the second level of the cosmos) and entered the White House. From the White

St. Augustine, Florida. Established by the Spanish, it was the first permanent European colony in the New World. *Reproduced by permission of the Corbis Corporation (Bellevue).*

House they could view the sky. In the sky were two sisters who were competing to see who was the stronger. It was a tie, so one sister went to the east and became the mother of white people, while the other became the mother of the Native Americans. The Pueblos remained at the White House with their gods, who taught them how to farm. They were also taught how to honor the gods by performing sacred rituals and ceremonies that integrated humans into the forces of the universe. Then the people left the White House and established their own villages.

- The *kiva*, a circular room located underground, was the most sacred place in a Pueblo village. Representing the hole through which they came to the surface of the earth, the *kiva* extended down to the underworld (the first level of the cosmos). Through the *kiva* the Pueblo people could communicate with their mother and the gods. The *kiva* was the center of each village, and the point from which all aspects of the village—apartments, fields, boundaries—

were measured. All of the important ceremonies took place in the *kiva*. Next to it was a room where sacred masks (worn by the priests) and other religious objects were stored. A chief priest, aided by trained assistants, took care of this room and oversaw the rituals.

- At first the Pueblos had no difficulty incorporating Catholicism into their traditional religion because they considered the white friars to be the priests or assistants of the eastern sister (the mother of the white people). Therefore the Christian god had a place with their gods. In fact, the Pueblos added Catholic practices such as kneeling in prayer and chanting to their own rituals. They included chalices (cups used for drinking wine during the Catholic communion service) among the objects in their sacred warehouse. In addition they found similarities between Catholic crucifixes (crosses bearing the image of the cruci-fied Jesus of Nazareth, also called Christ) and their own prayer sticks, and the use of incense (a material used to produce a fragrant odor when burned) in Catholic worship services resembled their smoking rituals. The friars wel-comed this blending of traditions and even formed Pueblo boys' choirs to perfect their chanting.

- Although Native Americans were initially willing to become Christians, even in the early period of Spanish colonization they had conflicts with the friars. For instance, Benavides's report opens with an account of the Pueblos driving Fray (friar) Martín de Arvide out of their village and refusing to accept other Spanish missionaries for several years. Bena-vides continued with a description of Franciscan efforts to convert the Apaches after converting the Pueblos.

"Fray Alonso de Benavides Reports New Mexico Indians Eager for Conversion"

*. . . Father Fray Martín de Arvide, who had spent many years in preaching the divine word in New Mexico [suffered **martyrdom**]. The*

Martyrdom: The suffering of death on account of adherence to a cause, such as one's religious faith

great **pueblo** of Picuries had fallen to his lot. Here he converted more than two hundred Indians, suffering great hardships and personal dangers, as these people are the most **indomitable** of that kingdom. He founded a church and **convent** large enough to minister to all the **baptized**. Among the newly converted, there was a young man, a son of one of the principal **sorcerers**. On a certain occasion, the latter undertook to pervert his son and dissuade him from what the **padre** taught. When the **father** was informed of it, he left the convent with a **crucifix** in his hands and, filled with **apostolic** spirit, he went to the place where the **infernal** minister was perverting that soul and began to **remonstrate** with him, saying, "Is it not sufficient that you yourself want to go to hell without desiring to take your son also?" Addressing the young man, he said, "Son, I am more your father and I love you more than he, for he wants to take you with him to the suffering of hell, while I wish you to enjoy the blessings of being a Christian." With divine zeal, he advanced these and other arguments. The old sorcerer arose, grasped a large club near by, and struck the blessed father such a blow on the head that he felled him and then he and others dragged him around the plaza and ill-treated him cruelly. Miraculously he escaped from their hands; although very eager to offer his life to its Giver, God preserved him for a later occasion.

As a result of this the Indians rebelled, so that for several years that pueblo refused to receive a friar who might preach our holy Catholic faith to them. This situation continued until the year 1628 when I stationed there Father Andréde Zea, who converted many people. . . .

. . . All the Indians are now converted, baptized, and very well ministered to, with thirty-three convents and churches in the principal pueblos and more than one hundred and fifty churches throughout the other pueblos; here, where scarcely thirty years earlier all was **idolatry** and worship of the devil, without any **vestige** of civilization, today they all worship our true God and Lord. The whole land is dotted with churches, convents, and crosses along the roads. The people are so well taught that they now live like perfect Christians. They are skilled in all the **refinements** of life, especially in the singing of organ chants, with which they enhance the **solemnity** of the divine service.

All these nations settled in this most northerly region in order to escape the intolerable cold and to find there a milder climate, but they met with opposition and resistance from the native inhabitants of this whole land, that is, from the huge Apache nation. In fact, the Apaches surround the abovementioned nations on all sides and have continuous wars with them.

Pueblo: A Native American village consisting of multistory apartment-like dwellings with many rooms

Indomitable: Incapable of being subdued

Convent: A place where members of a religious order live

Baptized: Spiritually purified or cleansed, usually with water, in a Christian religious service

Sorcerers: Wizards

Padre: The Spanish word for priest

Father: Priest

Crucifix: A cross bearing the image of the crucified Jesus of Nazareth (also called Christ)

Apostolic: Of, relating to, or conforming to the teachings of the New Testament

Infernal: Demonic; hellish

Remonstrate: To protest

Idolatry: The worship of a physical object as a god

Vestige: Trace or sign left by something vanished or lost

Refinements: Moral characters

Solemnity: Seriousness

Thus, since we had converted all these nations, we endeavored to convert the Apaches, who alone are more numerous than all the others together, and even more numerous than the people of New Spain. These Indians are very spirited and **belligerent.** They are a people of a clearer and more subtle understanding, and as such they laugh at the other nations because they worship idols of wood and stone. The Apaches worship only the sun and the moon. They wear clothing, and although their chief **sustenance** is derived from hunting, they also plant much corn. Their houses are modest, but adequate for protection against the cold spells of that region. In this nation only, the husband often has as many wives as he can support. This also depends on rank, for it is a mark of prestige to have numerous wives. They cut off the nose and ears of the woman taken in **adultery.** They pride themselves on never lying but on always speaking the truth. The people of this nation are countless, for they occupy the whole of New Mexico. Thus, armies of more than thirty thousand have been seen on the way to war against each other, the fields swarming with them. They have no one king who governs them, in general, but in each district or province they allow themselves to be ruled by one who is famous for some brave deed. The neighboring provinces, however, always heed and have respect for someone from a larger province. . . .

Starting, then, with that portion of this nation nearest to the Pira [Piro] nation, which is the first we meet on reaching New Mexico, there is, on the opposite bank of the Rio del Norte to the west, the province and tribe of the Xila Apaches. It is fourteen **leagues** from the pueblo of San Antonio Senecú, where their chief captain, called Sanaba, oftentimes comes to gamble. After he had heard me preach to the Piros several times, he became inclined to our holy Catholic faith and confided his thoughts to me; and when I had satisfied him in regard to certain difficulties that he had encountered, he determined to become a Christian and said that he wanted to go and tell his people in order that they too should become Christians. This he did, and within a few days he returned to see me, with some of his people already converted by what he had told them. Confirming them in their good intentions, I persuaded them, since they were the chief lords, that, as a good beginning to their Christianity, they should at once erect a cross in the center of the plaza of their pueblo so that I could find and worship it when I came to visit them. They promised me to do this and departed very happy. And, although I, because of the demands of my office and the lack of friars, could not go there that year, **withal** I learned that Captain Sanaba was an apostolic preacher and desired that all of his tribe should be converted, and he had already prepared them for it.

Belligerent: Aggressive or hostile

Sustenance: The means of support, maintenance, or subsistence

Adultery: Married women or men who have sexual relations with someone other than their husband or wife

Leagues: Any of various units of distance from about 2.4 to 4.6 statute miles

Withal: Nevertheless

Chamois: A type of leather

The Spanish established many missions like the one pictured here in their efforts to convert Native Americans to Christianity. *Reproduced by permission of The Granger Collection.*

*After the lapse of a few days, I returned there to ascertain the state of that conversion. When Captain Sanaba heard that I had arrived at San Antonio Senecú, he came those fourteen to see me, accompanied by many of his people. After I had welcomed him with honor in the presence of all, he presented me with a folded **chamois**, which is a dressed deerskin. It is customary among these people, when going to visit someone, to bring a gift. I accepted it to gratify him, although I told him that I did not want anything from him except* *that he and all his people should become Christians. He asked me to unfold the chamois and see what was painted on it. This I did and saw that it had been decorated with the sun and the moon, and above each a cross, and although the symbolism was apparent to me, I asked him about it. He responded in these formal words: "Father, until now we have not known any benefactors as great as the sun and the moon, because the sun lights us by day, warms us, and makes our plants grow; the moon lights us by night. Thus we worship them as our gods. But, now that you have taught us who God, the creator of all things is, and that the sun and the moon are His creatures, in order that you might know that we now worship only God, I had these crosses, which are the emblem of God, painted above the sun and the moon. We have also erected one in the plaza, as you commanded."*

*Only one who has worked in these conversions can appreciate the joy that such happenings bring to a **friar** when he sees the results of his preaching. Recognizing this gift as the fruit of the divine word, I took the chamois and placed it on the high altar as a banner won from the enemy and as evidence of the high intelligence of this nation, for I do not know what more any of the ancient philosophers could have done. With this I bade farewell to him and his people, who were very happy. Within a few days he came more than sixty leagues to see me, rejoicing that all of his people had decided to become Christians. In his own name and in behalf of all of them he rendered obedience to me in the name of our holy mother, the church. With this good start, I founded that conversion in their pueblo of Xila, placing it in charge of Father Fray Martín del Espíritu Santo, who administered it with great courage during the year 1628.*

Friar: A member of a religious order who engages in missionary activity

What happened next. . .

The Spaniards profoundly disturbed the local ecology (pattern of relations between organisms and their environment) in New Mexico. For instance, they brought cattle and sheep that grazed on the land, consuming large amounts of prairie grasses. Spanish baking ovens greatly increased the need for firewood, depleting local supplies. To expand the existing network of irrigation canals, the Spanish forced native peoples to work as laborers. When the Acoma Pueblo finally

The Founding of Saint Augustine, Florida

Francisco López De Mendoza Grajales, a member of the Spanish force led by Pedro Menéndez de Avilés, gave the following account of the founding of Saint Augustine, Florida. The first permanent European settlement in North America, it is the oldest city in the United States.

On Monday, August 27, while near the entrance to the Bahama Channel, god showed to us a miracle from heaven. About nine o'clock in the evening a comet appeared, which showed itself directly above us, a little eastward, giving so much light that it might have been taken for the sun. It went towards the west,—that is, towards Florida,—and its brightness lasted long enough to repeat two Credos [Catholic oaths]. According to the sailors, this was a good omen [sign].

Wednesday morning, September 5, at sunrise, so great a storm arose that we feared we should be shipwrecked. The same evening, about sunset, we perceived a sail afar off, which we supposed was one of our galleys [ships], and which was a great subject of rejoicing; but, as the ship approached, we discovered it was the French flagship Trinity *we had fired at the night before. At first we thought she was going to attack us; but she did not dare to do it, and anchored between us and the shore, about a league from us. That night the pilots of our other ships came on board, to consult with the Admiral. The next morning, being fully persuaded that the storm had made a wreck of our galley, or that, at least, she had been driven a hundred leagues out to sea, we decided that so soon as daylight came we would weigh anchor and withdraw to a river which was below the French colony, and there disembark, and construct a fort, which we would defend until assistance came to us.*

Our fort is at a distance of about fifteen leagues from that of the enemy. The energy and talents of these two brave captains, joined to the efforts of their brave soldiers, who had no tools with which to work the earth, accomplished the construction of this fortress of defence; and, when the general disembarked, he was quite surprised with what had been done.

Reprinted in: Colbert, David, ed. Eyewitness to America. New York: Pantheon Books, 1997, pp. 9–10.

refused to submit to the intruders, hundreds of Native Americans were killed or enslaved, which produced a legacy of resentment. Never finding the gold or silver they had hoped for, the Spanish struggled economically and maintained an uneasy peace with their neighbors.

Native Americans in the Southwest became increasingly resentful of the missionaries. In 1680, after eighty-two years of Spanish occupation, the Pueblo revolutionary leader Popé (c.1625–c. 1692) led a revolt against Catholicism. Defying Spanish laws, Popé urged the Pueblos to return to their traditional religion and way of life. Organizing a massive force of followers at Santa Fe, New Mexico, he led a siege in which four hundred Spanish missionaries and colonists were killed. The survivors fled hundreds of miles to the south, into Mexico. As the new leader of the Pueblos, Popé removed all traces of Spanish influence; most significantly, he outlawed the Spanish language, destroyed Catholic churches, and cleansed the people who had been baptized by missionaries. Within a decade, however, Popé's power was weakened by Apache raids, internal Pueblo dissension, and his own harsh rule. In 1692, less than two years after Popé's death, the Spaniards once again conquered the Pueblos.

Did you know . . .

- The Pueblo revolt coincided with a series of droughts that had been afflicting the Southwest for several years. Popé used fear to get people to follow him when he asserted that the droughts were caused by the Pueblo gods were offended and were punishing the Pueblos for accepting Christianity.

- Popé eventually lost support because the Pueblos had become accustomed to European goods. In addition, the Pueblos were attacked by Apaches, who seized their horses and brought them into contact with other native cultures.

- When the Spanish returned to New Mexico in 1692, the humbled Franciscans allowed the Native Americans to continue their traditional religious practices.

For more information

Guiterrez, Ramon A. *When Jesus Came, the Corn Mothers Went Away.* Stanford, Calif.: Stanford University Press, 1991.

Knaut, Andrew L. *The Pueblo Revolt of 1680: Conquest and Resistance in Seventeenth-Century New Mexico.* Norman, Okla.: University of Oklahoma Press, 1995.

Kupperman, Karen Ordahl, ed. *Major Problems in American Colonial History.* Lexington, Mass.: D. C. Heath, 1993, pp. 42–45.

Sando, Joe S. *Pueblo Profiles: Cultural Identity through Centuries of Change.* Santa Fe: Clear Light, 1995.

Jacques Marquette

"Jolliet and Marquette Travel the Mississippi"

Reprinted in *Eyewitness to America*
Published in 1997
Edited by David Colbert

The Spanish dominated southwestern and southeastern North America until the late seventeenth century. While Franciscan friars colonized New Mexico, other members of their order began a large-scale missionary effort in Florida in 1595. By 1655 they had created a chain of thirty-eight missions from south of Saint Augustine, northward to South Carolina, and westward to Alabama. Within twenty years, however, Spanish influence declined as a result of English expansion into South Carolina and Georgia. Native Americans came to rely on English trade goods and formed alliances with the English against the Spanish.

During this time the Spanish were also threatened by the French, who initially launched exploratory missions from settlements in Canada (then known as New France). French explorers were attracted to the New World (European term for North and South America) by promises of a profitable fur trade in the Great Lakes region of Canada and the present-day United States (territory bordering a chain of five lakes: Superior, Michigan, Huron, Erie, and Ontario). Like the Spanish, the French were also seeking to spread Roman Catholicism (a

"As we were descending the river we saw high rock with hideous monsters painted on them, and upon which the bravest Indians dare not look."

Like their Spanish counterparts, French missionaries, such as Jesuit priest Jean de Brébeuf, were seeking to spread Roman Catholicism to Native Americans.
Reproduced by permission of Archive Photos, Inc.

Christian religion based in Rome, Italy, headed by a pope who has absolute authority) among the "pagan" (believing in more than one god) tribes—in this case the Hurons, a mighty nation of thirty thousand who inhabited the region around lakes Huron, Erie, and Ontario. The Hurons produced large surpluses of corn and had developed a vast trading network long before the arrival of the Europeans. Leading the conversion effort were the Jesuits (members of the Society of Jesus), who arrived in Canada in 1625. They were known throughout the world for their ability to adapt to foreign cultures in order to draw converts to Catholicism. Attired in distinctive black tunics, the priests were called the "Black Robes" by the Hurons. The Jesuits ministered to French settlers and the Hurons until the fall of Quebec, the main settlement in New France, four years later. The French then moved south into territory that is now the United States. (The province of New France was restored in 1632.)

When the French started to migrate southward, however, they encountered strong opposition from the Spanish and the English. Spreading Christianity therefore became less important than expanding French territory and protecting trade routes. The Jesuits also met resistance from several Huron and Iroquois groups who did not want to adopt European customs. In 1647 the Jesuits relaxed their requirements for baptism (initiation into Christianity through anointment with water) and became more tolerant of traditional Native American religious practices in response to this opposition. To gain more favor with the Huron and Iroquois groups the missionaries took advantage of the natives' belief in the supernatural. For instance, the priests claimed the Catholic crucifix had the power to heal simple diseases. They also made a great show of their ability to read and write and predict solar eclipses, which seemed magical to the Native Americans.

"These are our Fathers"

In 1632 the French reacquired New France in a treaty with the English. Samuel de Champlain (c. 1567–1635), the governor and founder of the New France, had visions of establishing a French empire in North America. He realized, however, that he would first have to form an alliance with the Hurons against the Iroquois, bitter enemies of the Hurons. To achieve this goal Champlain turned to the Jesuits, who could speak the Huron language and knew the native customs. Father Paul le Jeune, a Jesuit priest, wrote an account of a series of council meetings at which Champlain took the first step toward an alliance. Following is a description of one of the meetings.

> Thereupon Sieur de Champlain began to speak, and told them [the Hurons] that he had always loved them, that he wished very much to have them as his brothers, and, having been sent in behalf of our great King [Louis XIII] to protect them, he would do it very willingly; that he had sent to meet them a bark and a shallop [small open boat propelled by oars], and that the Iroquois had treacherously [in violation of an allegiance] killed two or three of our men; that he did not lose heart on that account, that the French feared nothing, and that they cherished their friends very dearly. . . . He added that our Fathers [the Jesuits] were going to see them in their country, as a proof of the affection which we bore them, telling marvelous things in our favor.

> "These are our Fathers," said he, "we love them more than our children or ourselves; they are held in very high esteem in France; it is neither hunger nor want that brings them to this country; they do not want to come to see you for your property or your furs. . . . If you love the French people, as you say you do, then love these Fathers; honor them, and they will teach you the way to Heaven. . . ."

> The conclusion of the council was that Father [Jean de] Brébeuf told them, in their language, that we were going with them to live and to die in their country; that they would be our brothers, that hereafter we would be of their people. . . . All the savages, according to their custom evinced [expressed] their satisfaction by their profound aspiration: ho, ho, ho, ho! Then they surrounded Father Brébeuf, each one wanting to carry him in his boat. Some came to me and touched my hand, saying to each other: "See how much they look alike," speaking of the Father and me. . . .

Reprinted in: Stiles, T. J., ed. In Their Own Words: The Colonizers. New York: Berkeley Publishing, 1998, p. 125.

As the French concentrated on expanding their empire and spreading religion, some of the Jesuits became explorers themselves. One of the most prominent was Father Jacques Marquette (1637–1675), who had settled in New France in 1666. Proficient in six Native American languages, he founded a mission at Saint Ignace (in present-day Michigan) in 1671. The fol-

Marquette and Jolliet's being greeted by the Illinois Indians during their exploration of the Mississippi River.
Reproduced by permission of The Granger Collection.

lowing year the governor of New France, Louis de Buade (1622-1698; also known as the Count of Frontenac), announced plans to send an expedition through Native American country to discover the "South Sea [Gulf of Mexico]" and to explore "the great river they call Mississippi, which is believed to discharge into the sea of California [Gulf of California]."

Frontenac chose Marquette to accompany the leader of the expedition, the French-Canadian explorer Louis Jolliet (1645–1700). Jolliet had studied for the Jesuit priesthood in France, but by 1671 he had returned to New France and entered the fur trade. Jolliet's party, which included five Native American guides, left Quebec on October 4, 1672. By early December they reached Saint Ignace, where they were joined by Marquette. The following May the seven men embarked in two canoes, going westward along the north shore of Lake Michigan to present-day Green Bay, Wisconsin, then up the Fox River. From there they portaged (carried boats overland) to the Wisconsin River and descended to the Mississippi on June 15, 1673.

During the voyage Jolliet and Marquette traveled down the Mississippi past the Missouri and Ohio Rivers. They stopped at the mouth of the Arkansas River, about 450 miles south of the mouth of the Ohio. This point is just north of the present boundary between Arkansas and Louisiana. Here they stayed among the Quapaw tribe until they heard reports of the Spanish approaching from the west. Fearing the Spanish and concluding that the Mississippi must run into the Gulf of Mexico, not the Gulf of California, the explorers turned back without having reached the mouth of the Mississippi. As a result, they had explored only the northern portion of the river.

Things to Remember While Reading "Jolliet and Marquette Travel the Mississippi":

- Over a century earlier, in 1541, Hernando de Soto (c. 1500–1542) and his party were the first Europeans to view the Mississippi River. The Spanish were primarily interested in finding the gold and silver rumored to be in the Ozark Mountains, however, so they did not spend any time tracing the course of the great river. By exploring the Mississippi, the French were hoping to find more direct water routes, which would facilitate their fur trade and expand their empire.

- Although Jolliet and Marquette were sent to explore the area, the French remained committed to converting Native Americans to Christianity. Therefore, Marquette's role was to preach to native groups along the route down the Mississippi. He also kept a detailed journal, which provided an invaluable first-person account of the expedition and a description of life along the river. "Jolliet and Marquette Travel the Mississippi" is an excerpt from the journal.

- Marquette wrote that he and Jolliet decided not to travel to the mouth of the Mississippi because they were afraid of falling "into the hands of the Spaniards, from whom we could expect no other treatment than death or slavery." This was a well-founded fear: The Spanish conducted raids along the Atlantic coast and into the interior, selling Native Americans and other captives into slavery in the Caribbean.

"Jolliet and Marquette Travel the Mississippi"

June 10–17, 1673

Father Jacques Marquette

*This bay is about thirty **leagues** long, and eight broad in its greatest breadth, for it grows narrower and forms a cone at the extremity. It has tides that **ebb** as regular as the sea. We left this bay to go to a river [the Fox River] that discharges itself therein. . . . It flows very gently. . . . We next came to a village of the Maskoutens [a Native American tribe] or nation of fire. . . .*

The next day, being the 10th of June, the two guides [from the Miami tribe] embarked with us in sight of all the village, who were astonished at our attempting so dangerous an expedition. We were informed that at three leagues from the Maskoutens, we should find a river which runs into the Mississippi, and that we were to go to the west-south-west to find it, but there were so many marshes and lakes, that if it had not been for our guides we could not have found it.

*The river upon which we rowed and had to carry our canoes from one to the other, looked more like a corn-field than a river, insomuch that we could hardly find its **channel**. As our guides had been frequently at this **portage**, they knew the way, and helped us to carry our canoes overland into the other river, distant about two miles and a half; from whence they returned home, leaving us in an unknown country, having nothing to rely upon by **Divine Providence**. We now left the waters which extend to Quebec, about five or six hundred leagues, to take those which would lead us hereafter into strange lands.*

*Before embarking we all offered up prayers to the **Holy Virgin**, which we continued to do every morning, placing ourselves and the events of the journey under her protection, and after having encouraged each other, we got into our canoes. The river upon which we embarked is called Mesconsin [Wisconsin]; the river is very wide, but the sand bars make it very difficult to navigate, which is increased by numerous islands covered with grape vines.*

*The country through which it flows is beautiful; the **groves** are so dispersed in the prairies that it makes a noble prospect; and the fruit*

Leagues: Various units of distance from about 2.4 to 4.6 miles

Ebb: The decline of the tide

Channel: The narrow sea between two close landmasses

Portage: The carrying of boats or goods overland from one body of water to another

Divine Providence: The goodwill of God

Holy Virgin: Virgin Mary, the mother of Jesus of Nazareth, founder of Christianity

Groves: A planting of fruit or nut trees

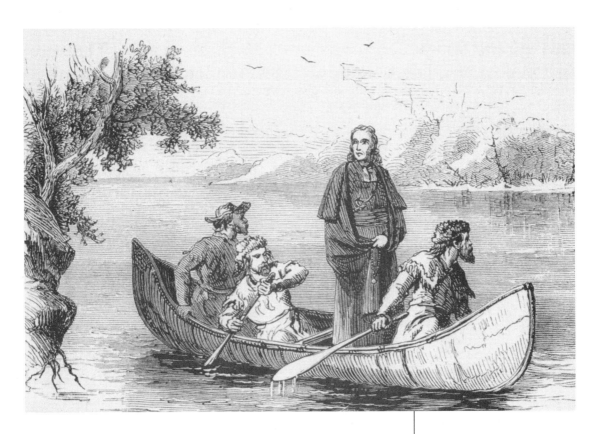

of the trees shows a fertile soil. These groves are full of walnut, oak, and other trees unknown to us in Europe. We saw neither game nor fish, but **roebuck** and buffaloes in great numbers. After having navigated thirty leagues we discovered some iron mines, and one of our company who had seen such mines before, said these were very rich in ore. They are covered with about three feet of soil, and situate near a chain of rocks, whose base is covered with fine timber. After having rowed ten leagues further, making forty leagues from the place where we had embarked, we came into the Mississippi on the 17th of June.

Behold us, then, upon this celebrated river, whose **singularities** I have attentively studied. The Mississippi takes its rise in several lakes in the North. Its channel is very narrow at the mouth of the Mesconsin, and runs south until it is affected by very high hills. Its current is slow, because of its depth. In sounding we found nineteen **fathoms** of water. A little further on it widens nearly three-quarters of a league, and the width continues to be more equal. We slowly followed its course to the south and south-east to the **42° N. lat.** Here we perceived the country change its appearance. There were scarcely any

An engraving of Marquette descending the Mississippi River. *Reproduced by permission of Archive Photos, Inc.*

Roebuck: The male roe deer

Singularities: Unusual behavior

Fathoms: A unit of length equal to six feet used for measuring water

42° N. lat.: Forty-two degrees north latitude; a measurement indicating distance north of the equator

*more woods or mountains. The islands are covered with fine trees, but we could not see any more roebucks, buffaloes, **bustards**, swans.*

We met from time to time monstrous fish, which struck so violently against our canoes, that at first we took them to be large trees, which threatened to upset us. We saw also a hideous monster; his head was like that of a tiger, his nose was sharp, and somewhat resembled a wildcat; his beard was long; his ears stood upright; the color of his head was gray; and his neck black. He looked upon us for some time, but as we came near him our oars frightened him away.

*When we threw our nets into the water we caught an abundance of **sturgeons**, and another kind of fish like our trout, except that the eyes and nose are much smaller, and they have near the nose a bone like a woman's **busk**, three inches broad and a foot and a half long, the end of which is flat and broad, and when it leaps out of the water the weight of it throws it on its back.*

Having descended the river as far as 41°28' we found that turkeys took the place of game, and the Pisikious that of other animals. We called the Pisikious wild buffaloes, because they very much resemble our domestic oxen; they are not so long, but twice as large. We shot one of them, and it was as much as thirteen men could do to drag him from the place where he fell.

About the end of June, we embarked in presence of all the village, who admired our birch canoes, as they had never before seen anything like them. We descended the river, looking for another called Pekitanoni [the Missouri] which runs from the north-west into the Mississippi, of which I will speak more hereafter.

As we were descending the river we saw high rocks with hideous monsters painted on them, and upon which the bravest Indians dare not look. They are as large as a calf, with head and horns like a goat; their eyes red; beard like a tiger's; and a face like a man's. Their tails are so long that they pass over their heads and between their fore legs, under their belly, and ending like a fish's tail. They are painted red, green, and black. They are so well drawn that I cannot believe they were drawn by the Indians. And for what purpose they were made seems to me a great mystery.

*As we fell down the river, and while we were **discoursing** upon these monsters, we heard a great rushing and bubbling of waters, and small islands of floating trees coming from the mouth of the Pekitanoni [Missouri], with such rapidity that we could not drink it. It so discolors the Mississippi as to make the navigation of it dangerous.*

Bustards: Any of a family of large terrestrial Old World and Australian game birds

Sturgeon: Any of the family of large, elongated freshwater bony fishes

Busk: Tight-fitting undergarment wore by women that is hooked and laced and that extends from above or below the bust or from the waist to below the hips

Discoursing: Discussing

This river comes from the north-west, and empties into the Mississippi, and on its banks are situated a number of Indian villages. We judged by the compass, that the Mississippi discharged itself into the Gulf of Mexico.

Having satisfied ourselves, we resolved to return home. We considered that the advantage of our travels would be altogether lost to our nation if we fell into the hands of the Spaniards, from whom we could expect no other treatment than death or slavery.

What happened next . . .

In mid-July 1674 Jolliet and Marquette began the return trip up the Mississippi to the Illinois River. They parted at the Saint Francis Xavier mission at Green Bay. Jolliet continued on to Montreal to report on their discoveries, but Marquette became ill and stayed at the mission. He died the following year. Over the next twenty-five years Jolliet had a successful career in the fur and fish trades and headed several other expeditions.

The Jolliet-Marquette voyage established French claims to the northern Mississippi valley region. The explorers also were the first Europeans to determine that the river empties into the Gulf of Mexico instead of the Gulf of California. In 1682 French explorer Robert Cavelier, Sieur de La Salle (1643–1687) became the first European to sail down the Mississippi River to its mouth at the Gulf of Mexico. Claiming the territory along the southern part of the river and around the gulf, he gave it the name Louisiana in honor of the French king, Louis XIV (1638–1715).

The Mississippi valley region was now opened to French settlement. The most prosperous area was the Illinois country (*le pays des Illinois*), which stretched from Cahokia (across the river from Saint Louis, Missouri) 50 miles downriver to Kaskaskia. Cahokia was founded in 1699 as a mission for the conversion of Native Americans, and Kaskaskia was a fort established in 1703. Both settlements attracted *coureurs de bois* (woods runners), French trappers and traders who lived among the Native Americans. In 1718 the region began to prosper as a result of the French Gulf Coast settlements that provided them with a market for wheat, beef, and pork.

Settlement of Louisiana progressed slowly as the French were unable to invest money or people in a new colony. Louisiana became a province in 1718, and over the next half century it served as a penal colony (settlement for convicted criminals), a temporary home for indentured servants (laborers contracted to work for a master for a specified length of time), and a slave import center.

Did you know . . .

- By the summer of 1674 Marquette had recovered from his illness and set out to fulfill a promise to build a mission in present-day Illinois. However, falling ill again, he could not resume his journey until the following spring. Although he was near death, he preached his last sermon on the Thursday before Easter, 1675, to a gathering of two thousand members of the Illinois nation. He then tried to reach his home at Saint Ignace, but he died along the way. Marquette was buried at the mouth of the river that was named for him, on the site of present-day Ludington, Michigan.

- Jolliet spent the winter of 1673–74 at Sault Sainte Marie (in the Upper Peninsula of Michigan), working on his journal and making maps. Unfortunately, he later lost all of his papers when his canoe overturned on the Lachine Rapids near Montreal. After this mishap Jolliet reached Quebec in the fall of 1674. He wrote another report on the trip entirely from memory. His narrative corresponds with Marquette's description, which is considered the official account of the journey.

- In 1683 La Salle was involved in a plan to seize valuable mines in New Mexico and New Spain (Mexico). He purposely falsified his discoveries, making a map that incorrectly showed the Mississippi River emptying into the Gulf of Mexico from Texas rather than from Louisiana. Two years later La Salle constructed a fort at the mouth of the Lavaca River in present-day Texas, establishing the only

French colony in the Southwest. In 1687 he was killed in cold blood by several of his own men because of the misery he had caused them. His body was left to be eaten by wild animals.

For more information

Colbert, David, ed. *Eyewitness to America*. New York: Pantheon Books, 1997, pp. 30–32.

Coulter, Tony. *La Salle and the Explorers of the Mississippi*. New York: Chelsea House, 1991.

Eccles, W. J. *France in America*. Revised edition. Markham, Ontario: Fitzhenry & Whiteside, 1990.

Father Jacques Marquette National Memorial and Museum. http://www.uptravel.com/uptravel/attractions/3.htm Available September 30, 1999.

Giovanni Verrazano. http://www.greencastle.k12.in.us/stark/verrazano.htm Available September 30, 1999.

Jacques Cartier. http://www.win.tue.nl/cs/fm/engels/discovery/cartier.html Available September 30, 1999.

Kent, Zachary. *Jacques Marquette and Louis Jolliet*. Chicago: Children's Press, 1994.

La Salle Ship Sighted. http://www.he.net/~archaeol/9601/newsbriefs/lasalle.html Available September 30, 1999.

René-Robert Cavelier, sieur de La Salle. http: www.knight.org/advent/cathen/09009b.htm Available September 30, 1999.

Thomas Harriot

A Brief and True Report of the New Found Land of Virginia
Reprinted in *Major Problems in American Colonial History*
Published in 1999
Edited by Karen Ordahl Kupperman

E nglish exploration of North America began with the voyages of Italian-born navigator John Cabot (c.1450–c.1499), who reached the region that eventually became known as New England in 1497. By 1502 fishermen were sending cod (a type of fish used for food) from Labrador, Canada, and New England to the port of Bristol, England. As early as 1508–1509 Cabot's son Sebastian (c. 1476–1557) had explored the Atlantic coast, but the English did not establish a permanent presence on the continent for another hundred years. Although Bartholomew Gosnold (d. 1607) briefly attempted to colonize New England in 1602, the English settlers were not prepared for life in the New World. Nevertheless published reports of Gosnold's venture described North America as "the goodliest continent that ever we saw, promising more by farre than we any way did expect." Eager investors formed business ventures in the hopes of exploiting the bountiful resources in the wilderness.

English explorers were also trying to find a northwest passage, a natural waterway between the Atlantic Ocean and the Pacific Ocean, which would provide more direct access to

> "...some people could not tell whether to think us gods or men..."

John Cabot's voyages opened the doors for other English exploration of the New World.
Reproduced by permission of The Library of Congress.

Asia. In 1576 Martin Frobisher (c.1535–1594) undertook a series of voyages to Greenland to search for a water route, but each time his ships were stopped by ice in the Canadian Arctic. In 1578 English navigator Humphrey Gilbert (c.1539–1583) was given a patent (contract granting specific rights) by Queen Elizabeth I (1533–1603) to explore and colonize North America. On his second expedition, in 1585, he reached Newfoundland and claimed the region for England. Discovering some fishermen living on the site of present-day St. John's, Gilbert appointed himself governor of the settlement. According to a few scholars, Gilbert established the first English colony in the New World, although most historians give that distinction to Jamestown, Virginia (see "The Founding of Jamestown").

During the return trip to England, Gilbert was lost at sea. The North America patent was then transferred to his half brother, Walter Raleigh (1554–1618), who secured the support of influential noblemen and navigators for another attempt to establish a settlement. In 1584 Raleigh appointed Philip Amadas (1550–1618) and Arthur Barlowe to head an expedition to explore the mid-Atlantic coast of North America. Reaching the outer banks of present-day North Carolina, the expedition party came in contact with the Roanokes, Native Americans who inhabited Roanoke Island and the surrounding region. After a brief stay the Englishmen took two Native Americans, Manteo and Wachese, back to England. Amadas and Barlowe gave enthusiastic reports about Roanoke, claiming the island offered favorable trading prospects and an excellent location for a military fort. Impressed by the success of the mission, Elizabeth I knighted Raleigh and named the region Virginia in honor of herself (she was called the "Virgin Queen" because she refused to marry).

Raleigh immediately organized a venture to establish a permanent colony at Roanoke. He assembled five ships and two boats, which he placed under the command of English navigator Richard Grenville (1542–1591). Among the party of 108 men—mainly soldiers and servants—was Thomas Harriot (1560–1621), a mathematician and Raleigh's tutor, who was given the task of surveying Virginia. (Surveying is a branch of mathematics that involves determining the area of any portion of the Earth's surface, the lengths and directions of bounding lines, and the contour of the surface.) Manteo and Wachese were to serve as interpreters, and artist John White (?–1593) planned to make drawings of animal and plant life in North America. Upon arriving at Roanoke in July 1585, the expedition got off to a bad start. First, Grenville determined that the island was not appropriate for a permanent military base. Then he ordered the burning of a Native American village when he discovered a silver cup was missing.

Walter Raleigh organized the venture to establish the Roanoke Colony in Virginia of which Thomas Harriot wrote. *Reproduced by permission of The Library of Congress.*

Later the next month Grenville departed Roanoke for the Caribbean. Before leaving he placed colonist Ralph Lane (1530–1603) in charge of one hundred men. He then ordered the men to find a better site for the settlement and construct a fort and other buildings. In spite of Grenville's earlier aggression toward the Native Americans, the Englishmen had a good relationship with the Roanoke (also called Wiroan) people and their chief, Wingina. Lane freely explored the area, White sketched plants and animals, and Harriot conducted a detailed survey of the land. Harriot also recorded his observations of Native American life, language, and customs. As spring approached, the colonists ran out of food, so Lane took the drastic step of demanding corn from Wingina. Although the chief offered some land and seeds, Lane overlooked his generosity and concluded that the Native Americans were planning an attack. Lane therefore decided to strike first, and in the conflict Wingina and several of his people were killed.

The murder of Wingina and other Roanokes only made the food shortage at Roanoke worse because neighboring Native American groups avoided contact with the Europeans. The struggling colony was in desperate straits by June 1586, when English seaman Francis Drake (1540?–1596) paid a surprise visit on his way back from the Caribbean. Anxious to go home, all but three of the settlers boarded Drake's ship and set sail for England. About a year after their return Harriot published *A Brief and True Report of the New Found Land of Virginia.*

Things to Remember While Reading *A Brief and True Report of the New Found Land of Virginia:*

- Harriot published *A Brief and True Report of the New Found Land of Virginia* primarily to encourage English colonization in North America. Many consider it to be the first description of Native Americans to be written in English. In the report Harriot also included a survey of the geographic features of Roanoke, nearby islands, and portions of the mainland. It is one of the earliest known statistical land surveys.

- When the English initially organized the Roanoke expeditions they were motivated by the prospect of making profits on precious metals and trade in North America. Nevertheless, like the Spanish and French, they were also intent on converting Native American "savages" to Christianity (see "New Mexico Indians Eager for Conversion" and "Jolliet and Marquette Explore the Mississippi"). Note Harriot's statement that "Some religion they [Native Americans] have already, which although it be far from the truth, yet being as it is, there is hope it may be the easier and sooner reformed." Later he observed that the Native Americans kept no written records. This was because they had a rich oral tradition, whereby master storytellers passed myths and legends down from generation to generation (see "The Coming of the First White Man").

- Harriot commented that "some of the people [the Wiroans] could not tell whether to think us gods or men." Compare the Wiroans' confusion to the reactions of the Tlingits of Southeast Alaska (see "The Coming of the First White Man") and the Tainos in the Caribbean (see "Christopher Columbus Reports to Ferdinand and Isabella") upon meeting Europeans for the first time.

- Historians maintain that Harriot showed unusual insight into problems that would eventually develop between Native Americans and European colonists. For instance, he wrote that native peoples "are not to be feared, but that they shall have cause both to fear and love us, that shall inhabit with them." Later he observed, "If there fall out any wars between us & them," the English would have "advantages against them in so many manner of ways."

- Harriot described the friendly relations the English enjoyed with Wingina and the Wiroans. Although the situation changed drastically after Lane initiated the attack that resulted in the deaths of the chief and several other Wiroans.

- The Wiroans died in great numbers after the Englishmen visited their towns, a "marvelous accident" that puzzled both Harriot and the Wiroans. Since none of the Englishmen were stricken, the deaths were undoubtedly caused by diseases they had carried with them from Europe. Disease was a major factor in the near-extermination of the Native American population during the seventeenth and eighteenth centuries.

- Keep in mind that Harriot wrote *A Brief and True Report* for a sixteenth-century audience. Since his language and writing style are unfamiliar to twentieth-century readers, explanatory notes are included in the following excerpts from the document.

A Brief and True Report of the New Found Land of Virginia

Harriot opened his report with a detailed description of the appearance and customs of Native Americans, whom he called "natural inhabitants." He remarked that native peoples did not have sophisticated tools, nor did they have any weapons except bows and arrows for fighting against the English settlers ("to offend us withal"):

It resteth I [I pause to] speak a word or two of the natural inhabitants, their natures and manners, . . as that you know, how that they in respect of troubling our inhabiting and planting, are not to be feared, [they pose no threat to our settlement] but that they shall have cause both to fear and love us, that shall inhabit with them.

*They are a people clothed with loose **mantles** made of Deer skins, & aprons of the same round about their middles; all else naked; . . having no edge tools or weapons of iron or steel to offend us withal, neither know they how to make any: those weapons that they have,*

Mantles: Cloaks

*are only bows made of **Witch hazel**, & arrows of reeds, flat edged **truncheons** also of wood about a yard long, neither have they anything to defend themselves but targets made of barks, and some **armours** made of sticks **wickered** together with thread. . . .*

Harriot observed that the Native Americans admired English customs ("our manner of knowledges and crafts"), which they found superior to their own. Consequently they wanted to please and cooperate with the English ("and have greater respect for pleasing and obeying us"). He went on to describe Native Americans' wars with one another, observing that battle strategy ("set battles") was rare, except when there happened to be ("it fall out") fighting in the forest. At this point Harriot made his prediction about the Native Americans' lack of preparation for wars with Europeans. Since they could not defend themselves against superior battle plans and weaponry, they could be expected to run away from confrontation. Yet he praised their "excellence of wit," and he predicted that the English could eventually civilize them and convert them to Christianity (the "true religion"):

*Their manner of wars amongst themselves is either by sudden surprising one another most commonly about the dawning of the day, or moonlight, or else by **ambushes**, or some subtle devices [secretive methods]. Set battles are very rare, except it fall out where there are many trees, where either part may have some hope of defence, after the delivery of every arrow, in leaping behind some [tree] or other.*

*If there fall out any wars between us & them, what their fight is likely to be, we having advantages against them so many manner of ways, as by our discipline, our strange weapons and devices else [other devices], especially by **ordinance** great and small, it may be easily imagined; by the experience we have had in some places, the turning up of their heels against us in running away was their best defence. In respect of us they are a people poor, and for want of skill and judgment in the knowledge and use of our things, do esteem our **trifles** before things of greater value: Notwithstanding in their proper manner considering the want of such means as we have [in spite of not having our advantages], they seem very **ingenious**; For although they have no such tools, nor any such crafts, sciences and arts as we . . . they should desire our friendships & love, and have the greater respect for pleasing and obeying us. Whereby may be hoped if means of good government be used, [if we govern them properly] that they may in short time be brought to civility and embracing of true religion.*

Witch hazel: Shrub or tree with slender-petaled yellow flowers borne in late fall or early spring

Truncheons: Clubs

Armours: Hand-held weapons

Wickered: Woven

Ambushes: Surprise attacks

Ordinance: Weapons and ammunition

Trifles: Things of little value

Ingenious: Clever, resourceful

Von der ankunfft der Engellender zu Virginia. II.

DJe Port oder Meerhafen der Landschafft Virginia ist voll Inseln / die da verursachen / daß man gar beschwerlichen in dieselben kommen kan. Dann wiewol sie an vielen orten weit von einander gescheiden sind / vnd sich ansehen lässet / als solte man dadurch leichtlich können hinein kommen / so haben wir dannoch mit vnserm grossen schaden erfahren / daß dieselben offte Plätz voll Sandes sind. Deßwegen haben wir niemals können hinein kommen / biß so lang wir an vielen vnnd mancherley örtern mit einem kleinen Schiff die sach versucht haben. Zuletzt haben wir einen Paß gefunden / auff einem sonderlichen ort / der vnsern Engelländern wol bekannt ist. Als wir nun hinein kommen / vnd eine zeitlang darinn on vnterlaß geschifft hatten / sind wir eines grossen fliessenden Wassers gewar worden / dessen außgang gegen der Inseln / von welcher wir gesagt haben / sich erstrecket. Dieweil aber der Inngang zu demselbigen Wasser deß Sandes halben zu klein war / haben wir denselben verlassen / vn seyn weiter fort geschifft / biß daß wir an eine grosse Inseln kommen sind / deren Einwohner / nach dem sie vnser gewar worden / haben alsbald mit lauter vnd schrecklicher stimm zu ruffen angefangen / dieweil sie zuvor keine Menschen / die vns gleich weren / beschawet hatten. Deßwegen sie sich auch auff die Flucht begeben haben / vnnd nicht anders dann als Wölffe vnd vnsinnige Leut / alles mit ihrem heulen erfüllt. Da wir ihnen aber freundtlich nachgeruffen / vnd sie widerumb zu vns gelocket / auch ihnen vnsere Wahr / als da sind Spiegel / Messer / Puppen / vnd ander geringe Krämerey (an welchen wir vermeyneten sie einen lust haben solten) fürgestellt hatten / sind sie stehen blibe. Vnd nach dem sie vnsern guten willen vnd freundtschafft gespürt / haben sie vns gute Wort geben / vnnd zu vnser ankunfft glück gewündschet. Darnach haben sie vns in ihre Statt / Roanoac genannt / ja daß noch mehr ist / zu ihrem Weroans oder Oberherrn geführet / der vns freundtlich empfangen hat / wiewol er ersilich sich ab vns entsetzte. Also ist es vns ergangen in vnser ersten ankunfft der newen Welt / so wir Virginiam nennten. Was nun für Leiber / Kleydung / art zu leben / Feste vnd Gastereyen die Einwohner daselbst haben / das will ich stück für stück nach einander einem jeden vor die Augen stellen / wie nachfolget.

An early map of the Roanoke Colony in Virginia. *Reproduced by permission of The Library of Congress.*

Harriot reported that the Native Americans believed in an eternal god who created other gods. Nevertheless he dismissed their views as simply "some religion" that was "far from the truth" and would make the task of conversion easier for the English. Notice that Native Americans, like Christians, believed in immortality, heaven, and hell:

Some religion they have already, which although it be far from the truth, yet being as it is, there is hope it may be the easier and sooner reformed.

They believe that there are many Gods which they call Montóac, but of different sorts and degrees; one only chief and great God, which hath been from all eternity. Who as they affirm when he purposed to make the world, made first other gods of a principal order to be as means and instruments to be used in the creation and government to follow; and after the Sun, Moon, and Stars as petty gods. . . . First they say were made waters, out of which by the gods was made all diversity of creatures that are visible or invisible.

For mankind they say a woman was made first, which by the working of one of the gods, conceived and brought forth children: And in such sort [in this manner] they say they had their beginning. But how many years or ages have passed since, they say they can make no relation, having no letters nor other such means as we to keep records of the particularities of times past, but only tradition from father to son. . . .

*They believe also the **immortality** of the soul, that after this life as soon as the soul is departed from the body, according to the works it hath done, it is either carried to heaven the **habitacle** of gods, there to enjoy perpetual bliss and happiness, or else to a great pit or hole, which they think to be in the furthest parts of their part of the world toward the sunset, there to burn continually: the place they call Popogusso. . . .*

In this final excerpt Harriot described the Wiroans' reactions to Christianity. They accepted the Englishmen's faith, eventually rejecting their own. They grew to fear the Christian God. For instance, the Wiroans blamed illness or crop failure on the wrath of the Englishmen's god. In fact, whenever the Englishmen encountered hostility or resentment in Native American villages, the inhabitants began dying within a few days after they left. Both Harriot and the Wiroans seemed to make a connection between the mysterious deaths

Immortality: The state of being free from death

Habitacle: Dwelling place

and offenses toward the Englishmen. The Wiroans therefore concluded that the Englishmen were gods, especially since they had no women with them. (The earliest Virginia expeditions were comprised only of men.) The true reason for the illnesses, however, was that the Native Americans were not immune to the diseases that the Europeans often carried.

Wiroans with whom we dwelt called Wingina, *and many of his people would be glad many times to be with us at our prayers, and many times call upon us both in his own town, as also in others whither he sometimes accompanied us, to pray and sing **Psalms;** hoping thereby to be partaker of the same effects which we by that means also expected [hoping to gain the same benefits from our religion].*

*Twice this Wiroans [Wingina] was so **grievously** sick that he was like to die, and as he lay **languishing,** doubting of any help by his own priests, and thinking he was in such danger for offending [because he had offended] us and thereby our god, sent for some of us to pray and be a means [connection] to our God that it would please him either that he [Wingina] might live, or after death dwell with him [God] in bliss, so likewise were the requests of many others in the like case.*

*On a time also when their corn began to wither by reason of a **drought** which happened extraordinarily, fearing [they feared] that it had come to pass by reason that in something they had displeased us, many would come to us & desire us to pray to our God of England, that he would preserve their corn, promising that when it was ripe we also should be partakers of the fruit.*

*There could at no time happen any strange sickness, losses, hurts, or any other cross [misfortune] unto them, but that they would **impute** to us the cause or means thereof for offending or not pleasing us. . . .*

There was no town where we had any subtle device practiced against us [the inhabitants showed hostility], we leaving it unpunished or not revenged (because we sought by all means possible to win them by gentleness) but that within a few days after our departure from every such town, the people began to die very fast, and many in short space; in some towns about twenty, in some forty, in some sixty, & in one six score [one hundred twenty], which in truth was very many in respect of their numbers. This happened in no place that we could learn but where we had been where they used some practice against us, and after such time; The disease also was so

Psalms: A book in the Old Testament containing sacred songs and poems

Grievously: Terribly

Languishing: Suffering

Drought: A period of prolonged dryness that causes extensive damage to crops or prevents their successful growth

Impute: Attribute

strange, that they neither knew what it was, nor how to cure it; the like by report of the oldest men in the country never happened before, time out of mind. A thing specially observed by us, as also by the natural inhabitants themselves. . . .

This marvelous accident in all the country wrought so strange opinions of us, that some people could not tell whether to think us gods or men . . . because . . . there was no man of ours known to die, or that was especially sick: they noted also that we had no women among us, neither that we did care for any of theirs.

*Some therefore were of opinion that we were not born of women, and therefore not **mortal**, but that we were men of an old generation many years past then risen again to immortality.*

Mortal: Human

What happened next . . .

Soon after the departure of the colonists Grenville returned to Roanoke with a new load of supplies and six hundred additional men. He found the colony deserted—no one knows what happened to the three men who had remained on the island. Eventually Grenville decided to return to England and recruit more settlers. He left fifteen men at Roanoke to plant crops and build dwellings in preparation for the new colonists. By that time, however, Raleigh had lost interest in colonizing Virginia. John White, the artist who accompanied Grenville in 1585, therefore took over the project and acquired the backing of several investors for another expedition.

White's plan was to start a new colony called the City of Raleigh, which would be located north of Roanoke in the Chesapeake Bay area. White would be the governor of the new colony. Since this settlement would be devoted to families and farming instead of military defense, the party included seventeen women, nine children, and ninety-four men. When the ships reached North America in late 1587, the pilot refused to go any farther than Roanoke. Forced to remain at the old settlement, the colonists discovered that the fifteen men left by Grenville were gone, possibly driven out by Native Americans. Consequently crops had not been planted and there was no

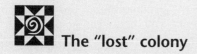

The "lost" colony

After a three-year absence John White returned from England in 1591, only to find Roanoke deserted. The fate of the inhabitants of the "lost colony" remains a mystery. These excerpts from White's journal describe what he found at the site.

August 17 . . . we espied [spied] toward the north end of the island the light of a great fire through the woods, to which we presently rode. When we came right over against it, we let fall our grapnel [anchor] near the shore and sounded with a trumpet a call, and afterwards many familiar English tunes of songs, and called to them friendly. But we had no answer. We therefore landed at daybreak, and coming to the fire, we found the grass and sundry [numerous] rotten trees burned about the place....

In all this way we saw in the sand the print of the savages' feet of two or three sorts trodden the night, and as we entered up the sandy bank, upon a tree, in the very brow thereof, were curiously carved these fair Roman letters CRO; which letters presently we knew to signify the place where I should find the planters seated, according to a secret token agreed upon between them and me at my last

departure from them, which was that they should not fail to write or carve on the tree or posts of the doors the name of the place where they should be seated; for at my coming away they were prepared to remove from Roanoke 50 miles in the main.

Therefore at my departure from them in 1587 I willed them that if they should happen to be distressed in any of those places, that then they should carve over the letters or name a cross; but we found no such sign of distress. And having well considered of this, we passed towards the place where they were left in sundry houses, but we found the houses taken down, and the place very strongly enclosed with a high palisade [fence] of great trees . . . and one of the chief trees or posts at the right side of the entrance had the bark taken off, and five foot from the ground in fair capital letters was graven [carved] CROATOAN without any cross or sign of distress. . . .

This could be no other but the deed of the savages our enemies.

Reprinted in: Colbert, David, ed. Eyewitness to America. *New York: Pantheon Books, 1997, pp. 11–12.*

suitable housing. The only solution was for White to go back to England for more supplies and additional men. Before departing he told the colonists to move to another location if they had any problems and to leave a message telling him where to find them.

In the meantime, war had been brewing between England and Spain. When the conflict erupted in 1588—as White was about to sail from England back to North America—contact between England and Roanoke was cut off. In 1591, after the English defeated the Spanish Armada, White was finally able to return to Roanoke. By that time the settlers had all vanished without a trace, and White found only two clues to their whereabouts: the word "Croatan" carved on a fence post and the letters "Cro" etched into a tree trunk. The English suspected that the colonists' disappearance was somehow linked with the Croatoans, a friendly Native American tribe who lived on Croatoan Island about fifty miles south of Roanoke.

The Roanoke settlers were never found, and the fate of the "lost colony" remains a mystery. Numerous theories about their disappearance have evolved over the centuries. They could have died as the result of a natural disaster such as disease, starvation, hurricane, flood, or tornado. They could have tried to return to England and their ship sank at sea. More outlandish explanations include pirates coming ashore and kidnapping all the inhabitants. The most reassuring conclusion is that the colonists joined a nearby Native American tribe, with whom they intermarried and prospered.

After the dismal failure of the Roanoke colony the English made no other attempts to colonize North America for nearly twenty years. They realized they had neither the skills nor the money to establish permanent settlements in a strange and hostile land. One modern historian has noted that venturing into the wilderness of North America in the sixteenth century was similar to landing on the moon in the twentieth century. Moreover, the English, like the Spanish, were primarily interested in conquering Native American empires that would yield instant wealth with such treasures as precious metals and jewelry. Yet by the late 1590s Europeans had seized most of the available riches in the New World.

Did you know . . .

- *A Brief and True Report of the New Found Land of Virginia* was immensely popular among Englishmen who entertained visions of an exciting and prosperous life in the New World. By 1610 the book had been reprinted seventeen times.

- Harriot may have performed some of the earliest scientific experiments in North America. In addition to conducting a survey of Virginia, he helped another member of the 1585 expedition, German scientist Joachim Ganz, search for copper and other precious metals. Archaeologists excavating the Roanoke site have found equipment that Harriot and Ganz probably used to test metals and ores.

- John White was the grandfather of Virginia Dare (1587–?), the first European reported to be born in America. Nine days before White's departure from Roanoke, Virginia was born to his daughter Eleanor and his son-in-law Ananais Dare. All three Dares disappeared with the other Roanoke colonists, and White died without ever knowing what happened to his family.

- Evidence discovered in 1998 has led historians to speculate that the Roanoke colonists may have been driven out by a drought (a period of prolonged dryness that causes damage to crops). Scientists studying the rings of a bald cypress in southeastern Virginia found that a seven-year drought was occurring at the same time the second group of settlers arrived at Roanoke in 1587. In fact, it was the most severe period of dryness in more than eight hundred years. Thus a food shortage could have forced the colonists to seek another location for their community.

For more information

"The Cabot Dilemma: John Cabot's 1497 Voyage & the Limits of Historiography" in *Documents Relevant to the United States Before 1700*. http://www.geocities.com/Athens/Forum/9061/USA/colonial/bef1700.html Available September 30, 1999.

Campbell, Elizabeth A. *The Carving in the Tree*. New York: Little, Brown, 1968.

Kupperman, Karen Ordahl, ed. *Major Problems in American Colonial History*. Lexington, Mass.: D. C. Heath, 1993, pp. 12–15.

Middleton, Richard. *Colonial America: A History, 1585–1776*. Second edition. Malden, Mass.: Blackwell Publishers, 1996, pp. 9–12.

Quinn, David Beers. *Set Fair for Roanoke: Voyages and Colonies, 1584–1606*. Chapel Hill, N.C.: University of North Carolina Press, 1985.

Steven, William K. "Drought May Have Doomed the Lost Colony." *The New York Times*. April 14, 1998, pp. A1, A14.

John Smith

"The Founding of Jamestown," an excerpt from **The Generall Historie of Virginia**

Reprinted in *Eyewitness to America*
Published in 1997
Edited by David Colbert

England again turned its attention to North America in 1604, after signing a peace treaty with Spain. Freed from the threat of war, the government now had funds that could be used for colonization and trade. Since the failure of the Roanoke settlement sixteen years earlier, English investors had come to realize that North America offered more than gold, silver, and other precious metals. As the Spanish had proven in the Caribbean, sizable profits could be made from plantations that produced cotton, sugar, tobacco, and coffee. Fishing was also a source of potential wealth. Speculating on new opportunities overseas, several investors received a charter for the "Virginia Company of London and of Plymouth" in 1606. The charter gave them the rights to land stretching northward along the Atlantic coast from the Cape Fear River in North Carolina to present-day Bangor, Maine. This vast territory was divided into two colonies: the northern colony, named Plymouth, was granted to the Plymouth Company; the southern, called Virginia, was given to the London Company. Each was to be governed by a council in America that took its orders from a royal council in England. The charter also provided that all colonists and their descendants would enjoy the full rights of Englishmen.

"Now fell every man to work, the Council contrive the Fort, the rest cut down trees to make a place to pitch their tents;"

Although initially hostile toward the settlers, Native American leader Powhatan eventually offered the Jamestown colonists food and other assistance.

Reproduced by permission of Archive Photos/American Stock.

The London Company was the first to organize an expedition. The plan was to build the capital of the Virginia colony on a site that would provide access for sea trade yet give protection against Spanish attack. Under the temporary leadership of Christopher Newport (1565?–1617), three vessels carrying 105 settlers—all of them men—embarked from England in December 1606. The expedition ran into the first of many problems that would nearly doom the venture. Winds prevented the ships from making any progress, and for a full six weeks they stayed within sight of England. Arriving on the shore of Virginia more than four months later, Newport led the party fifty miles inland along the James River. He spotted an apparently suitable location for a fort and town—a small peninsula surrounded by a marsh—then he claimed the land for King James I (1566–1625) and named the new settlement Jamestown.

For a time the situation seemed ideal as the settlers cleared the land and built a town. They erected a fort and high fence, constructed one- and two-room cottages inside the fence, and prepared nearby fields for crops. They also made friends with the Powhatans, the local Native Americans, who were initially hostile to the Europeans. Within a few days, however, Powhatan (c. 1550–1618), the principal Native American leader in the Chesapeake region, had given the settlers food and offered them other assistance. A substantial number of the Englishmen were exploring the surrounding countryside in search of gold. Although the Virginia project was devoted to agriculture and trade, the English government and private investors were still hoping to find instant wealth in the New World.

Before the settlers departed from England, the London Company had appointed a seven-member council to govern the colony. The names of the councilmen were to be kept secret, however, until the ships reached their destination. By the time the colonists landed in North America, the seven men on the committee despised one another. The ablest member of the group was John Smith (1580–1631), but Newport had placed him under arrest for an unspecified charge. No doubt unaware that Smith was one of the councilmen, Newport had imprisoned him for the majority of the voyage.

Smith was a colorful Englishman who began a career in the foreign military service at age sixteen and was known for his often fantastic adventures. Although historians doubt some of his claims, he apparently did receive the title of captain after a hand-to-hand combat victory in Hungary. Smith was seeking new adventures when he joined the Jamestown expedition, and during his two-year stay in Virginia he had experiences that would have defeated a lesser man: for instance, he was captured by Native Americans; survived starvation and disease; explored rivers; mapped previously unknown territory; and ran the colony. He also kept detailed notes that formed the basis of his *The Generall Historie of Virginia* (1624), an informative and entertaining book that is still widely read today. "The Founding of Jamestown," in which Smith described the early months of the Jamestown settlement, is an excerpt from *The Generall Historie of Virginia*.

Things to Remember While Reading "The Founding of Jamestown":

- Throughout "The Founding of Jamestown" Smith referred to himself as "Captain John Smith" or "Captain Smith."

- Smith stated that Bartholomew Gosnold (d. 1607; also spelled Gosnoll) was "one of the first movers of this plantation." The leader of the Jamestown expedition, Gosnold was an early promoter of English exploration and colonization in North America. In 1602 he conducted a voyage along the Atlantic coast from Maine to Narragansett Bay. He named Cape Cod and several islands and built a fort at Cuttyhunk, one of the Elizabeth islands.

- In the opening paragraph of the excerpt from "The Founding of Jamestown" Smith described Gosnold's two-year effort to organize a more ambitious venture to Virginia. Gosnold finally gained the support of "the nobility, gentry, and merchants" (among them Smith, Edward Maria Wingfield, and Robert Hunt), and King James I ("his Majesty") approved the project with a company charter ("letters patent"). James granted the settlers the right to form a government that was overseen by a council in England ("gave commission for establishing councils to direct here; and to govern, and to execute there"). The first colonies in America—Jamestown, Plymouth, Massachusetts Bay, Rhode Island, and Connecticut—all had company or private charters that allowed some independence from English rule. Similarly, proprietary charters gave considerable freedom to individual founders of Maryland, Carolina, and Pennsylvania. As Englishmen continued leaving for America in increasing numbers, however, the monarchy tightened its control over colonial governments because the colonies had turned out to be a source of huge revenues. By the 1660s the Crown (monarchy) ruled all thirteen colonies under royal charters, which mandated an imperial system headed by a governor and a council appointed by the king.

- After the party reached Virginia (Cape Henry) on April 26, 1607, thirty men went ashore and were attacked by Native Americans. They were the Powhatans, who were initially suspicious of the Englishmen because they had had negative experiences with Europeans in the past. As time went on, however, the Powhatans and the colonists became friendly and Powhatan in fact saved the Englishmen from starvation.

- Once Smith was revealed to be one of the seven councilors, the settlers debated whether he should be allowed to serve in light of his imprisonment during the voyage. Smith referred to this situation in the fourth paragraph, on the selection of the Jamestown site and the swearing-in of the council about: "an oration [was] made, why Captain Smith was not admitted of the Council as the rest." Nevertheless he was officially a councilor and within only a few months he became the head of the settlement.

- In the fifth paragraph Smith hinted at further conflict: Wingfield, the president, would not permit the settlers to use their weapons in skirmishes with the Native Americans ("The Presidents overweening jealousy [excessive need for power] would admit no exercise at arms"). Wingfield also would not approve the building of a strong fort ("fortification [was] but the boughs [branches] of trees cast [tied] together in a half moon [an unclosed circle]"). Smith indicated that some men worked harder than others by citing the "extraordinary pains and diligence of Captain Kendall."

- In the next paragraph Smith provides an account of an exploring expedition by ship inland along the James River. He and his party reached the Powhatan village, which is the site of present-day Richmond, Virginia. The Englishmen were well treated ("kindly entreated") by the Native Americans, but while they were returning to Jamestown they met with some hostility ("till being returned within twenty miles of James town, they gave just cause of jealousy"). Then Smith told how the settlers narrowly escaped being massacred ("but had God not blessed the discoverers otherwise than those at the Fort"). As the exploring party approached Jamestown they discovered the settlement was being attacked by Native Americans, who had already injured seventeen men and killed a boy. Smith noted that the warriors were scared away only by chance, when a crossbar on the Englishmen's ship broke a tree limb as it was sailing into the harbor. This was a stroke of luck because the Englishmen on land were working and, in keeping with Wingfield's ban on carrying firearms, had no weapons to defend themselves.

- The near-massacre forced Wingfield to change his mind about weapons, and about fencing the fort: Smith reported that Wingfield decided "the Fort should be palisaded [fenced], the ordnance mounted [heavy weapons and ammunition prepared], his men armed and exercised [trained]." The Native Americans staged other attacks, and Englishmen were still hurt because of poor discipline ("their disorderly straggling"), which prevented them from moving as quickly as the warriors.

"The Founding of Jamestown"

Captain Bartholomew Gosnoll, one of the first movers of this ***plantation****, having many years solicited many of his friends, but found small assistants; at last prevailed with some gentlemen, as*

Plantation: A settlement in a new country or region

John Smith, leader of the Jamestown settlement, who enabled the colony to survive the rigors of the New World as the first permanent English settlement in North America. *Reproduced by permission of The National Portrait Gallery/Smithsonian Institution.*

Apprehended: Learned about

Gentry: Class whose members are entitled to bear a coat of arms though not of noble rank

Mariner: A person who navigates a ship

Recreating: Refreshing

Captain John Smith, Master Edward-Maria Wingfield, Master Robert Hunt, and many others, who depended a year upon his projects, but nothing could be effected, till by their great charge and industries it came to be **apprehended** by certain of the nobility, **gentry,** and merchants, so that his Majesty by his letters patents, gave commission for establishing councils, to direct here; and to govern, and to execute there. To effect this, was spent another year, and by that, three ships were provided, one of 100 tons, another of 40, and a pinnace of 20. The transportation of the company was committed to Captain Christopher Newport, a **mariner** well practiced for [familiar with] the western parts of America. But their orders for government were put in a box, not to be opened, nor the governors known until they arrived in Virginia.

The first land they made they called Cape Henry; where thirty of them **recreating** themselves on shore, were assaulted by five savages [Native Americans], who hurt two of the English very dangerously.

That night was the box opened, and the orders read, in which Bartholomew Gosnoll, John Smith, Edward Wingfield, Christopher Newport, John Ratliffe, John Martin, and George Kendall, were named to be the Council, and to choose a President amongst them for a year, who with the Council should govern. Matters of **moment** were to be examined by a jury, but determined by the major part of the Council, in which the President had two **voices.**

Until the 13 of May they sought a place to plant in; them the Council was sworn, Master Wingfield was chosen President, and an **oration** made, why Captain Smith was not admitted of the Council as the rest.

Now fell every man to work, the Council **contrive** the Fort, the rest cut down trees to make place to pitch their tents; some provide **clapboard** to **relade** the ships, some make gardens, some nets, etc. The savages often visited us kindly. The Presidents **overweening** jealousy would admit no **exercise at arms,** or fortification but the **boughs** of trees cast together in the form of a half moon by the extraordinary pains and **diligence** of Captain Kendall. ˈ

Newport, Smith, and twenty others, were sent to discover the head of the river: by **divers** small habitants they passed, in six days they arrived at a town called Powhatan, consisting of some twelve houses, pleasantly seated on a hill; before it three fertile isles, about it many of their cornfields, the place is very pleasant, and strong by nature, of this place the Prince is called Powhatan, and his people Powhatans. To this place the river is navigable: but higher within a mile, by reason of the rocks and Isles, there is not passage for a small boat, this they call The Falls. The people in all parts kindly **entreated** them, till being returned within twenty miles of James town, they gave just cause of **jealousy**: but had God not blessed the discoverers otherwise than those at the Fort, there had been an end of that plantation; for at the Fort, where they arrived the next day, they found 17 men hurt, and a boy slain by the savages, and had it not chanced a cross **barre** shot from the Ships struck down a bough from a tree amongst them, that caused them to retire, our men would have all been slain since they were all at work and their arms were stored away.

Hereupon the President was contented the Fort should be **palisaded**, the **ordnance** mounted, his men armed and exercised: for many were the assaults, and **ambushes** of the savages, and our men by their disorderly **straggling** were often hurt, when the savages by the nimbleness of their heels well escaped.

What happened next . . .

By late summer the colonists discovered that they had chosen an unhealthy location for Jamestown; men were becoming ill and dying as a result of living beside a diseased swamp. The problem was that the English had unknowingly brought typhoid (a disease marked by fever, diarrhea, headache, and intestinal inflammation caused by bacteria) and dysentery (severe diarrhea caused by infection) with them. Now, because of their own poor hygiene practices, the river had become an open sewer and a breeding ground for disease. In addition, many were suffering from salt poisoning. The force of the water coming down the river from the mountains was not enough to get past the tide rolling up from the Chesapeake Bay, so the settlers were drinking water that contained trapped sea salt.

Moment: Importance

Voices: Votes

Oration: An elaborate speech delivered in a formal manner

Contrive: Plan and build

Clapboard: A board with one edge thicker than the other used to cover the outer walls of houses

Relade: Reload

Overweening: Excessive

Exercise at arms: Training with weapons

Bough: A branch of a tree

Dilligence: Attentive to a task

Divers: Various

Entreated: Beg

Jealousy: Vigilance; excessive guarding of

Barre: Bar

Palisade: A fence of stakes for defense

Ordnance: Military supplies including weapons, ammunition, combat vehicles, etc.

Ambushes: Surprise attacks

Straggling: Scattering

By September 1608 three of the seven council members returned to England and three others died. Smith was the only councilor remaining in Virginia, so he became president of the colony by default (automatically). He was confronted with the impossible task of organizing unruly, inexperienced settlers into some sort of workforce. The ships had carried 105 men, but 48 of them were gentlemen who had never earned a living with their own hands. Only 24 were laborers. The settlers also realized they had not planted and harvested enough food—too many men had wasted their time searching for gold. Already 46 settlers had died of disease and lack of food. Smith had to contend with the well-organized Powhatans, who had again become suspicious of the Europeans. Although Smith was eager to negotiate peaceful relations, he was also willing to force the Powhatans to provide the settlers with grain. Reportedly Chief Powhatan agreed to trade meat and corn at the urging of his daughter Pocahontas (1595–1617). By most accounts, the Jamestown settlers would have perished had it not been for the assistance of Powhatan and Pocahontas.

Under Smith's leadership the inexperienced settlers built houses, erected a church, fortified Jamestown, and learned how to farm and fish. While Smith managed to keep the struggling colony from dissolving, however, he did so at the expense of his own popularity. He imposed strict rules and forced the colonists to obey his orders. As a result he caused much resentment and bitterness. In 1609 another group of settlers arrived from England. Along with them came several of Smith's old enemies, who plotted against him. In addition colonists had continuing problems with the Powhatans. Smith might have been able to weather these difficulties if he had not been severely wounded when a stray spark from a fire lit his gunpowder bag as he lay napping. The explosion and subsequent flames burned him so badly that his life was threatened. The following October he sailed back to England.

In January 1608 Jamestown burned to the ground. Only the arrival of supply ships and new settlers from England kept the colony from collapsing. That fall Smith was badly injured in a gunpowder accident, and he returned to England for medical help. Although he survived his wounds, he never returned to Jamestown. The colony quickly fell apart, and the winter of 1609–10 became known as the "starving time." The suffering was caused not only by a shortage of food but also by

The Pocahontas legend

One of the most popular American legends is the story about Pocahontas saving John Smith from being executed by her father, Powhatan. While the English settlers built the Jamestown settlement, Smith was put in charge of exploring the area. As he was drifting along the James River in his canoe he apparently came too close to one of Powhatan's treasure houses. Smith was taken prisoner by Powhatan's men and eventually forced to appear before the chief, who ordered his execution. Smith later described the scene in *The Generall Historie of Virginia*, and claimed that Pocahontas rescued him from certain death:

> At his [Smith's] entrance before the king, all the people gave a great shout. The queen of Appamatuck was appointed to bring him water to wash his hands, and another brought him a bunch of feathers, instead of a towel to dry them. Having feasted him after their best barbarous [uncivilized] manner they could, a long consultation was held but the conclusion was, two great stones were brought before Powhatan: then as many as could laid hands on him, dragged him to them, and thereon laid his head, and being ready with their clubs to beat out his brains, Pocahontas, the king's dearest daughter, when no entreaty [pleading] could prevail, got his head in her arms, and laid her own upon his to save him from death: whereat the emperor was contented he should live.
>
> . . .

Reprinted in: Colbert, David, ed. Eyewitness to America. *New York: Pantheon Books, 1997, pp. 17–18.*

Some scholars have questioned Smith's story because, in an earlier account of the same incident, he mentioned neither Pocahontas nor an execution. He said he was summoned before Powhatan, who questioned him about the presence of the English in Native American territory. After Smith gave his reply, the chief simply dismissed him and permitted him to return to Jamestown.

the settlers themselves. Many stole and sold their meager supplies, with the result that some men were fed while others died. Of the 490 settlers remaining in Virginia when Smith left, only 60 survived the winter. Soon the council in Virginia was in disorder, and in 1609 the London Company rewrote the charter, putting one man in charge. The royal council was also eliminated when the company took over the colony and reorganized to keep from going bankrupt. The former London Company was now The Treasurer and Company of Adventurers and Planters of the City of London for the First Colony in Virginia (usually called the Virginia Company).

In 1610 a new governor, Thomas West (Baron De La Warr; 1577-1618), arrived in Jamestown. The settlement was under a form of martial law (law administered by military forces), which had been initiated by Smith, and the colonists were being forced to work. Yet the survival of Virginia was still far from certain. In 1614 John Rolfe (1585–1622), one of the original settlers, took two important steps. First, he married Pocahontas, Powhatan's daughter, thus bringing about a truce between the Powhatans and the colonists. Second, Rolfe experimented with a West Indian species of tobacco and found that he could produce a crop of high enough quality to fetch good prices in England. Soon Virginia was in the midst of a tobacco boom, and the colony moved toward a plantation economy that thrived throughout the colonial period.

Yet further problems undermined these efforts. Once tobacco was found to be a profitable crop, laborers sent to work for the company were hired instead by local officials. This was probably because the officials wanted the workers for their own fields so they could increase their personal profits. By 1616 there were no profits for the original investors. Three years later the Virginia Company reorganized again, this time promising a less authoritarian (a concentration of power in a leader not responsible to the people) government and dividing the colony into four large settlements. At that time the company also authorized the formation of a general assembly, the House of Burgesses, to give people representation in governing the colony. This was the first elected representative body in America. Although a steady stream of settlers continued to flow into the colony, high death rates considerably reduced their numbers. Then a fatal blow came in 1622, when Powhatan's son Opechancanough, who no longer trusted the colonists, led the Powhatans in the massacre of 350 settlers—about one third of the community. On May 24, 1624, James I dissolved the bankrupt Virginia Company, and Virginia became the first royal colony in America.

Did you know . . .

- Gosnold objected to the site that was chosen for the Jamestown settlement, but he was overruled. He was one of several men who died of malaria in 1607.

- Smith gave the name New England to the northeast region of the United States. In 1614 he sailed to the area that is now Cape Cod, Massachusetts, calling it New England, and mapped part of the Atlantic coastline. Smith hoped to establish a colony in New England, and he wanted to go to Plymouth with the *Mayflower* settlers (see "The Pilgrims' Landing and First Winter"). None of these plans worked out however, and Smith never went back to America.

- The first African slaves in North America came ashore near Jamestown 1619. They were sold to a tobacco plantation owner by a Dutch trader in exchange for some supplies (see *Some Considerations on the Keeping of Negroes*).

- In 1994 the *Jamestown Rediscovery* archaeological project began excavating the ruins at the Jamestown site, and by 1998 twelve percent of the fort had been recovered. In 1996 archaeologists discovered the well-preserved skeleton of a white male who had been buried in a wooden coffin near the fort. After extensive investigation and testing, they concluded that the man was probably one of the "gentlemen" mentioned by Smith in his Jamestown account—the skeleton indicates that the man was not accustomed to manual labor. Scientists have further determined that the man, who is known as JR102C (a record number assigned by archaeologists), was nineteen to twenty-two years of age, stood around five feet five inches in height, and died of a massive, untreated gunshot wound to the leg.

- In the process of digging at the Jamestown site, archaeologists have confirmed that the colony served as a "dumping ground" for England. For instance, after the 1622 massacre the Master of the Ordnance (supervisor of military supplies) sent massive amounts of obsolete weapons and armor to Jamestown because they were unfit for "any moderne service" in England. Pieces of these weapons and armor, as well as everyday items like cooking utensils, pottery, bottles, and jars, are displayed at a nearby visitors center.

For more information

Barbour, Philip L., ed. *The Complete Works of Captain John Smith (1580–1631)*. 3 Volumes. Chapel Hill, N.C.: University of North Carolina Press, 1986.

Colbert, David, ed. *Eyewitness to America*. New York: Pantheon Books, 1997, pp. 16–17.

Haile, Edward Wright, ed. *Jamestown Narratives: Eyewitness Accounts of the Virginia Colony: The First Decade: 1607–1617*. Champlain, Va.: Round-house, 1998.

"Instructions for the Virginia Colony (1606)" in *Documents Relevant to the United States Before 1700*. http://www.geocities.com/Athens/Forum/9061/USA/colonial/bef1700.html Available September 30, 1999.

Jamestown Rediscovery. http://www.apva.org/ Available July 13, 1999.

Kelso, William M., Nicholas M. Luccketti, and Beverly A. Straube. *Jamestown Rediscovery IV*. Richmond, Va.: The Association for the Preservation of Virginia Antiquities, 1998.

Rountree, Helen Clark. *The Powhatan Indians of Virginia: Their Traditional Culture*. Norman, Okla.: University of Oklahoma Press, 1989.

William Bradford

"The Pilgrims' Landing and First Winter," an excerpt from Of Plymouth Plantation

Reprinted in *Eyewitness to America*
Published in 1997
Edited by David Colbert

In 1607, a year after the Virginia Company of London party embarked for Jamestown, the Virginia Company of Plymouth prepared for an expedition to Maine, which was the place that Bartholomew Gosnold (d.1607) had so glowingly praised. Gosnold's party had seen the region only in the summertime, however, and the Plymouth group were planning to stay permanently. They were completely unprepared for the long and bitterly cold Maine winter. Although most of the settlers managed to survive the harsh climate, one of the leaders died and another was called back to England. Finally the settlers dispersed and the English did not return to the area for another thirteen years.

The next attempt at colonization in New England came about as a result of the Puritan movement. Puritanism (a group that stressed strictness in matters of religion or conduct), in turn, was an outgrowth of Protestantism. The Protestant movement began in England in 1531, when King Henry VIII (1491–1547) decided to annul (make legally invalid or void) his marriage to Catherine of Aragon (1485–1536). (Protestantism was initiated in 1517 by German theologian

> "But that which was most sad, and lamentable, was, that in two or three months the half of their company died, especially in January and February, being the depth of winter, and wanting houses and other comforts;"

It was King Henry VIII's heavy emphasis on Roman Catholicism in the Church of England that led Puritans to seek a simpler religious life in the New World.

Reproduced by permission of The Library of Congress.

Martin Luther [1483–1546], who accused Roman Catholic Church leaders of corruption and misuse of power.) A staunch Roman Catholic, Henry wanted to marry again because Catherine had not borne him a son and he was determined to father a male heir to the throne. Yet Henry encountered strong resistance from the pope, who had the final authority to nullify marriages. Since Catherine was a Spanish princess and the Catholic Church depended upon Spain to fight Protestantism in Europe, the pope could not afford to alienate the Spanish by granting the annulment. Henry therefore broke with the Catholic Church and declared himself head of the Church of England, which he founded.

Henry's quarrel with Roman Catholicism was political, not religious. Although he closed monasteries (houses for monks, or men who took religious vows) and seized Catholic lands, he did not want to change the basic values of the church. Therefore he maintained most of the rituals, especially the elaborate ceremonies and fancy vestments (robes) worn by bishops and priests. Henry's daughter, Elizabeth I (1533–1603), also loved the grand processions and dramatic services, so she continued her father's policies. Her successor, James I (1566–1625), was similarly unwilling to make any changes. By this time many English Protestants were rebelling against the heavy emphasis on Catholicism in the Church of England. They wanted a simpler church, one that placed less emphasis on displays of wealth.

During the reign of James I many ministers and congregations refused to organize their worship services according to the requirements of the Church of England. Some critics, who became known as Puritans, felt that purification of the national church would solve the problems. At the same time a few dissenters (those who did not conform to the Church of England) were contending that the church was too corrupt to be saved and they wanted total separation. Since the king was head of both the church and the government, separation was considered a crime against the state. Nevertheless a congregation in Scrooby, England, declared themselves to be Nonconformists, or separatists. When the Scrooby leaders were persecuted in 1607 the congregation resolved to leave England and go to Leyden in the Netherlands (Holland), the most tolerant of the European states.

Life was pleasant in Leyden, and the Nonconformists were free to practice their religion. Nevertheless they were uneasy because their children were becoming more Dutch than English. Economic opportunities were also limited, and there were rumors that war would soon break out between Spain and the Netherlands. Many members of the group wanted to relocate in another country where they could speak the English language and bring up their children in a familiar Christian environment. They were determined not to return to England or move to New Netherland, the Dutch colony in America (see "Impressions of New Jersey and New York"). Calling themselves Pilgrims, they decided to settle instead at the northernmost end of the land granted to the Virginia Company.

William Bradford became the leader of the Pilgrim's venture to Plymouth and eventually the colony's governor. *Reproduced by permission of Corbis-Bettman.*

In 1619 the Pilgrims secured financing through Thomas Weston and Associates, an investment company, and the following year they left the Netherlands for America. Stopping first in England, they found that only one of their ships, the *Mayflower,* was seaworthy. The party consisted of one hundred and two men, women, and children, but they were not all Pilgrims. Several men called "merchant adventurers" represented the Weston company and did not share the Nonconformists' religious beliefs. Although no minister had joined the party, one of the members of the Leyden group, William Bradford (1590–1657), became a leader of the venture. On September 5, 1620, they set sail on the *Mayflower* for their destination in the New World.

Along the way the *Mayflower* encountered stormy weather, and the Pilgrims never arrived in Virginia territory. Instead they anchored the ship in Cape Cod harbor (off the coast of present-day Massachusetts), which was far north of their original destination. Since they were not on the land that had been legally granted to them, Bradford and forty other free adult males (those with voting rights) drafted and signed a

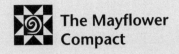

The Mayflower Compact

In the Name of God, Amen. We, whose names are underwritten, the loyal subjects of our dread Sovereign Lord King James, by the Grace of God of Great Britain, France, and Ireland King, Defender of the Faith, etc.

Having undertaken, for the Glory of God and Advancement of the Christian Faith and Honour of our King and Country, a Voyage to plant the First Colony in the Northern Parts of Virginia, do by these presents solemnly and mutually in the presence of God and one of another, Covenant and Combine ourselves together into a Civil Body Politic, for our better ordering and preservation and furtherance of the ends aforesaid; and by virtue hereof to enact, constitute and frame such just and equal Laws, Ordinances, Acts, Constitutions and Offices, from time to time, as shall be thought most meet and convenient for the general good of the Colony, unto which we promise all due submission and obedience. In witness whereof we have hereunder subscribed our names at Cape Cod, the 11th of November, in the year of the reign of our Sovereign Lord King James, of England, France and Ireland the eighteenth, and of Scotland the fifty-fourth, Anno Domino 1620.

Source: William Bradford. Of Plymouth Plantation, 1620–1647. Samuel Eliot Morison, ed. New York: Knopf, 1966, pp. 75–6.

new contract, the Mayflower Compact, in November 1620. The contract, which was based on Nonconformist church covenants, would allow the Pilgrims to establish a government with binding laws. However, they soon had to address the problem that they were only forty percent of the people aboard the ship. The rest, including men such as Miles Standish (1584–1656), were outsiders whom the Pilgrims called "strangers." The Mayflower Compact was intended to prevent conflict, provide for a government, and form a new religious society. It is considered the first democracy established by Europeans in North America.

While the *Mayflower* was anchored in Cape Cod harbor, Standish led an expedition inland. Leaving the ship in a small boat in November, they set out for the Hudson River, but bad weather forced them to return to the harbor at Cape Cod. Calling it Plymouth Harbor, they anchored near a rock that is now known as Plymouth Rock. The Pilgrims began settling their new colony on December 25, 1620, and elected John Carver (1576–1621) as their first governor. Although they faced a harsh winter in the Northeast, several factors worked in their favor. Unlike many ships that brought settlers to North America, the *Mayflower* remained at Plymouth and furnished housing until shelters had been built.

The colonists' first dwellings were small, one-room houses made of boards (not logs). The careful selection of a settlement site also gave them an advantage; rather than facing a "howling wilderness" they were able to nestle into a hillside that had once been inhabited by Native Americans. Fresh water was nearby, and they had access to corn Native Americans had put away for the winter.

Yet nearly half of the party died that first winter—the fate also of the earliest colonists at Jamestown (see "The Founding of Jamestown"). Although the Pilgrims and local Native Americans were aware of one another, they did not make contact during that difficult winter. The dying settlers maintained their distance, even though the Native Americans could have helped them. In turn, the Wampanoags, who had mixed experiences with Europeans, warily watched the newcomers. In the spring the surviving colonists were helped by Squanto (?–1622), a member of the neighboring Patuxet tribe; in his youth, he had been kidnapped and taken to England. During his captivity he had learned to speak English, so he was able to communicate with the settlers. Squanto helped the Pilgrims plant corn and other crops, and the next fall there was a plentiful harvest. The colonists invited the Native Americans to a celebration feast, which has become known as the first Thanksgiving in America (thanksgivings were common in England).

When Carver died in April 1621, Bradford was chosen to take his place as governor. He would be reelected thirty times between 1621 and 1656. During this period he repeatedly tried to leave the post, but he was such an effective leader that colonists always asked him to remain in office. Bradford was also the principal historian of the Plymouth Colony, and he began writing *Of Plymouth Plantation* in 1630. In the two-volume work he gave a detailed account of the migration of the Pilgrims to Plymouth and the subsequent hardships they faced in the New World. "The Pilgrims' Landing and First Winter," in which Bradford tells the story of the Pilgrims' first few months in their new colony, is an excerpt from *Of Plymouth Plantation*, Book I.

Things to Remember While Reading "The Pilgrims' Landing and First Winter":

- Bradford's narrative begins when the Pilgrims arrived at Cape Cod. They unloaded a boat (Bradford called it a ship) that had been stored, probably in pieces, on the *Mayflower*. They started putting it together ("mending" it) while Standish and others explored the mainland. When the ship was ready the Pilgrims set out for the Hudson River. After several mishaps amid a violent storm at sea, they returned to Cape Cod, where they finally started building their settlement in December.

- When winter set in over half of the Pilgrims died of disease and exhaustion. In the fourth paragraph Bradford described how "six or seven sound [healthy] persons" took care of the others, at the "hazard of their own health."

- Bradford wrote that during the winter Native Americans secretly watched the Pilgrims ("came skulking about them") and stole some of their tools. On March 16 one of the Native Americans, Samasett (also Samoset), entered the settlement. To the Pilgrims' surprise, he spoke English and he told them about Squanto, another Native American who also knew English and had even lived in England. Soon more Native Americans came to visit. Eventually the stolen tools were returned.

- Friendly visits and exchanges of gifts led to the signing of a treaty between the Pilgrims and the great Chief Massasoit. Bradford outlined the terms of the agreement, under which the two groups swore to protect one another and always to be at peace. He reported that, at the time he was writing his history, the peace had lasted for twenty-four years. Bradford concluded his account with a description of the plentiful harvest the Pilgrims gathered the following autumn.

"The Pilgrims' Landing and First Winter"

*Being thus arrived at Cape-Cod . . . they having brought a large ship with them out of England, stowed in quarters in the ship, they now got her out, and set their carpenters to work to trim her up, but being much bruised and shattered in the ship with foul weather, they saw she would be long in mending. Whereupon a few of them **tendered** themselves, to go by land and discover those nearest places, while the ship was in mending. . . . It was conceived there might be some danger in the attempt, yet seeing them **resolute** they were permitted to go, being 16 of them well armed under the conduct of Captain Standish. . . . After some hours sailing, it began to snow and rain, and about the middle of*

Tendered: Offered

Resolute: Bold, steady

Rudder: A flat piece of wood or metal attached to the stern (rear) of a ship so that the ship can be turned

Bade: Told

Herewith: By this means

Lusty: Full of strength

Sore: Severely

Colonial America: Primary Sources

*the afternoon, the wind increased, and the sea became very rough; and they broke their **rudder**, and it was as much as two men could do to steer her with a couple of oars. But their pilot **bade** them be of good cheer for he saw the harbor, but the storm increasing, and night drawing on, they bore what sail they could to get in, while they could see; but **herewith** they broke their mast in three pieces and their sail fell overboard, in a very high sea. . . .*

*But a **lusty** seaman which steered, bade those which rowed if they were men, about with her, or else they were all cast away; which they did with speed, so he bid them be of good cheer, and row justly for there was a fair sound before them, and he doubted not, but they should find one place or other, where they might ride in safety. And though it was very dark, and rained **sore**; yet in the end they got under the **lee** of a small island and remained there all that night in safety. . . .*

*But though this had been a day and night of much trouble, and danger unto them; yet God gave them a morning of comfort and refreshing (as usually he does to his children) for the next day was a fair sunshining day, and they found themselves to be on an island secure from the Indians; where they might dry their stuff, fix their pieces, and rest themselves, and gave God thanks for his mercies, in their **manifold deliverances**. And this being the last day of the week, they prepared there to keep the **Sabbath**; on Monday they **sounded** the harbor, and found it fit for shipping; and marched into the land, and found many cornfields, and little running brooks, a place (as they supposed) fit for **situation**, at least it was the best they could find, and the season, and their present necessity made them glad to accept of it. So they returned to their ship again with this news to the rest of their people, which did much comfort their hearts. . . .*

Afterwards [they] took better view of the place, and resolved where to pitch their dwelling; and the 25th day [December 25, 1620] began to erect the first house, for common use to receive them, and their goods. . . .

The Mayflower **not only carried the Pilgrims to Plymouth, but it also acted as shelter during their first few months in the New World.** *Reproduced by permission of The Library of Congress*

Lee: Side protected from the wind

Manifold deliverances: Various rescues

Sabbath: Sunday, observed among Christians as a day of rest and worship

Sounded: Measured the depth of

Situation: Living

*But that which was most sad, and **lamentable**, was, that in two or three months the half of their company died, especially in January and February, being the depth of winter, and wanting houses and other comforts; being infected with the **scurvy** and other diseases, which this long voyage and their **inaccommodate** condition had brought upon them; so as there died some times two or three of a day, in the forsaid time; that of one hundred and odd persons scarce fifty remained: and of these in the time of most distress there was but six or seven sound persons; who to their great commendations, be it spoken, spared no pains, night nor day, but with abundance of toil and hazard of their own health, fetched them wood, made them fires, dressed their meat, made their beads, washed their **loathsome** clothes, clothed and unclothed them. In a word did all the homely, and necessary offices for them, which dainty and queasy stomachs cannot endure to hear named and all this willingly and cheerfully, without any **grudging** in the least, showing herein their true love unto their friends and **brethren**. A rare example and worthy to be remembered, two of these seven were Mr. William Brewster, their Reverend Elder, and Miles Standish, their Captain and military commander, (unto whom myself, and many others were much **beholden** in our low, and sick condition). . . .*

*All this while the Indians came **skulking** about them, and would sometimes show themselves **aloof**, but when any approached near them, they would run away; and once they stole away their tools when they had been at work and were gone to diner. But about the 16th of March a certain Indian came boldly amongst them, and spoke to them in broken English which they could well understand, but marveled at it; at length they understood by **discourse** with him, that he was not of these parts, but belonged to the eastern parts where some English ships came to fish, with whom he was acquainted, and could name **sundry** of them by their names, amongst whom he had got his language. He became profitable to them in acquainting them with many things concerning the state of the country in the east parts where he lived . . . of the people here, of their names, number and strength, of their situation and distance from this place, and who was chief amongst them. His name was Samasett; he told them also of another Indian whose name was Squanto, a native of this place, who had been in England and could speak better English then himself. Being after some time of entertainment, and gifts dismissed, a while after he came again, and five more with him, and they brought again all the tools that were stolen away before, and made way for the coming of their great **Sachem**, called Massasoyt. Who about four or five days after came with the chief of his friends, and other attendance with the afore-*

Lamentable: Grievous

Scurvy: Disease marked by spongy gums loosening teeth, and bleeding into the skin

Inaccomodate: Uncomfortable

Loathsome: Disgusting

Grudging: Reluctance; resentment

Brethren: Referring to the members of a society, profession, or sect

Beholden: Indebted

Skulking: Moving about secretly

Aloof: Having no interest

Discourse: Conversation

Sundry: Numerous

Sachem: Native American chief

said Squanto. With whom after friendly entertainment, and some gifts given him, they made a peace with him (which has now continued this 24 years) in these terms:

1. That neither he nor any of his, should injure or do hurt, to any of their people.

2. That if any of his, did any hurt to any of theirs; he should send the offender, that they might punish him.

3. That if any thing were taken away from any of theirs, he should cause it to be restored; and they should do the like to his.

4. If any did unjustly war against him, they would aide him; if any did war against them, he should aide them.

5. He should send to his neighbors **confederates** to certify them of this [treaty], that they might not wrong them [the Pilgrims], but might be likewise comprised in the conditions of peace.

6. That when [Massasoyt's] men came to [the Pilgrims,] they should leave their bows and arrows behind them. . . .

They [the Pilgrims] began now to gather in the small harvest they had; and to fit up their houses and dwellings, against winter, being all well recovered in health and strength; and had all things in good plenty, for as some were thus employed in affairs abroad; others were exercised in fishing, about cod, and bass, other fish of which they took good store, of which every family had their portion; all the summer there was no want; and now began to come in store of fowl, as winter approached, of which this place did abound when they came first, (but afterward decreased by degrees), and besides water fowl, there was great store of wild turkeys, of which they took many, besides **venison** etc. Besides they had about a **peck** a meal a week to a person, or now since harvest, Indian corn to that proportion, which made many afterwards write so largely of their plenty here to their friends in England, which were not **fained**, but true reports.

Confederates: Ally; supporter

Venison: The flesh of deer used for food

Peck: Half a bushel or two gallons

Fained: False

What happened next . . .

After solving the initial problems of food and shelter, the Plymouth settlers realized they did not know how to run

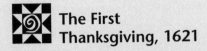

The First Thanksgiving, 1621

The Plymouth thanksgiving was described in a letter Edward Winslow, one of the colony's leaders, sent back to England:

> Our harvest being gotten in, our Governor sent four men on fowling [hunting birds], that so we might after a more special manner rejoice together, after we had gathered the fruit of our labours. The four in one day killed as much fowl as, with little help beside, served the Company [Plymouth inhabitants] almost a week. At which time, amongst other recreations, we exercised our arms [weapons], many of the Indians coming amongst us, and amongst the rest their greatest king, Massasoit with some 90 men, whom for three days we entertained and feasted. And they went out and killed five deer which they brought to the plantation [Plymouth] and bestowed on our Governor and upon the Captain and others.

Source: William Bradford. Of Plymouth Plantation, 1620–1647. Samuel Eliot Morison, ed. New York: New Modern Library, p. 90n.

businesses such as fur trading, which was thriving in other colonies. The colony ultimately proved to be a disappointment to its investors because Pilgrim leaders paid attention to immediate needs rather than long-term plans. For instance, despite extreme food shortages, they invited other Nonconformists to move to Plymouth from Leyden.

As the colony grew, the Pilgrims benefitted from their alliance with Massasoit (1580–1661), the Wampanoag leader who had helped them through the first winter. The result was peaceful trading relationships and an increased food supply in Plymouth. Nevertheless this harmony was disturbed when the colonists found themselves in the middle of battles between the Narragansetts and the Mohegans. Tensions continued to mount, and in the Pequot War (1637) the New England colonies formed an alliance with the Narragansetts to attack a Pequot fort at Mystic, Connecticut. Four hundred Pequots were killed while they were sleeping.

Native Americans were not the only unpredictable element at Plymouth. The colonists also had to contend with the merchant adventurers, many of whom committed crimes. In 1627 Bradford and seven other Pilgrims bought out the merchant adventurers and divided their property evenly among the colonists. As a result, the outcast merchants became part of Pilgrim society and were labeled "Old Comers." Although the Pilgrims had come to America to practice religious freedom, they did not extend the same rights to others. Therefore Plymouth, unlike other colonies in New England, did not become a haven for those who were fleeing persecution.

Plymouth did not have a formal government. In 1630 Bradford tried to forge relations with the more prosperous

Massachusetts Bay Colony, but he met resistance from Massachusetts residents. Plymouth finally adopted a formal constitution in 1636. The population grew steadily, reaching seven thousand by the time Plymouth finally became part of Massachusetts in 1691, thirty-four years after Bradford's death.

Did you know . . .

- Although historians have labeled the Plymouth Colony a democracy, there is little proof to support this claim. The people who signed the Mayflower Compact may have exercised power as a group, but they transferred all authority to the governor. When Bradford became governor in 1621, he served as principal judge and treasurer until 1637. He oversaw trade and agriculture, managed profits, and appointed allotments of land to settlers. Since he held executive (responsibility for enforcing laws) and legislative (responsibility for making laws) authority, only he could decide when freemen (former indentured servants who had earned their freedom) were allowed to take part in government. Bradford could also make decisions without the advice of others.

- The Plymouth settlers sent out their first ship loaded with goods—clapboards (boards with one edge thicker than the other used to cover the outer walls of houses) and beaver and otter skins—that were intended to provide a profit to their financial backers in England. The ship was seized by the French, however, and the colony soon became a disappointment to investors.

- Massasoit honored his treaty with the Plymouth colonists for forty years. During this time, the two groups exchanged many friendly visits. When the Wampanoag chief became ill, for instance, Plymouth leaders traveled to his home at Pokanoket to help cure their ally. On several occasions Massasoit or his fellow Wampanoags probably saved the colonists from slaughter by warning them of possible attacks by warring tribes.

For more information
Colbert, David. *Eyewitness to America.* New York: Pantheon Books, 1997, pp. 22–24.

Dubowski, Cathy East. *The Story of Squanto: First Friend of the Pilgrims.* Milwaukee: Gareth Stevens Publishers, 1997.

"The First Thanksgiving Proclamation (1676)" in *Documents Relevant to the United States Before 1700.* http://www.geocities.com/Athens/Forum/9061/USA/colonial/bef1700.html Available September 30, 1999.

Hays, Wilma Pitchford. *Rebel Pilgrim: A Biography of Governor William Bradford.* Philadelphia: Westminster Press, 1969.

"Massasoit." *Biographical Dictionary of Indians of the Americas,* Volume I. Newport Beach, Calif.: American Indian Publishers, 1991.

Middleton, Richard. *Colonial America: A History, 1585–1776.* Second edition. Malden, Mass.: Blackwell Publishers, 1996, pp. 75–80.

William Penn

The Propriety of Pennsylvania

**Reprinted in *In Their Own Words: The Colonizers*
Published in 1998
Edited by T. J. Stiles**

After the English colonized the mid-Atlantic coast and New England, they expanded westward with the founding of Pennsylvania. In 1681 King Charles II (1630–1685) gave a tract (large amount) of land, which he called "Pennsylvania" (Penn's Woods), to William Penn (1644–1718) to repay a debt he owed to Penn's father. Charles granted the land under a proprietary contract that gave Penn the right to establish and govern a colony with almost complete independence from England. Penn, a member of the Society of Friends, or Quakers, a religious sect that was greatly feared in England, decided to use the colony as a refuge for this religious group.

The Society of Friends had been started in the early 1650s by George Fox (1624–1691), an English cobbler (shoemaker) and shepherd. Fox believed he possessed the Inner Light, or Truth, which enabled him to communicate directly with God. He was convinced that everyone possessed an Inner Light. Fox and his followers became evangelicals (those who emphasize salvation by faith, the authority of the scripture, and the importance of preaching), calling on other Protestants to renounce the Church of England. Like the Puritans and

"Our people are mostly settled upon the upper rivers, which are pleasant and sweet, and generally bounded with good land."

William Penn receiving the charter of Pennsylvania from Charles II. *Reproduced by permission of the Mary Evans Picture Library.*

Nonconformists (those who did not conform to the Church of England), the Friends felt the national church relied too heavily on priests, rituals, and worship services. The Friends were given the nickname "Quakers" by critics who ridiculed their beliefs, but they eventually adopted the name themselves.

The Quakers were considered a threat to both church and state. Quakerism was soon outlawed and many Friends, including William Penn, spent time in jail. Penn and other wealthy members of the group searched for a place of refuge that would permit them to worship freely and make a decent living for their families. At first they considered West New Jersey in America, part of the holdings of Charles's brother James (1633–1701; later King James II), the Duke of York, where Quakers had already settled. Since Penn had been granted land in America, however, he decided to start a new colony where they would have great freedom to practice their religion. The British authorities also benefitted from the new colony because they got rid of the troublesome Quakers.

Penn began making plans for Pennsylvania. In April 1681 he sent his cousin, William Markham, to America to form a governing council. When he arrived, Markham met with Native Americans and Europeans who lived in the territory to inform them of Penn's authority over the land. The following October, Penn dispatched a group of commissioners to choose a site for a port city, which would be called Philadelphia (a Greek word for "brotherly love"). Since Penn could not fund the entire venture himself, he organized the Free Society of Traders, a group of wealthy Quaker investors. Each investor purchased ten thousand acres and held a seat on the governing council. Between 1682 and 1683 they sent fifty ships to America. Penn's next step was to advertise Pennsylvania among Quakers in England, Wales, Holland, and Germany, hoping to attract new settlers. He also welcomed non-Quakers. When Penn went to Pennsylvania to take his post as governor in 1682, farms had been established, the city was being built, and new settlers were arriving from Ireland and Wales. The population had already reached four thousand. Penn then bought the three neighboring counties in Delaware from the Duke of York in order to expand his colony.

William Penn wrote *The Propriety of Pennsylvania* as an advertisement encouraging Europeans to settle in his new colony.

Perhaps the most important features of the Pennsylvania plan were the frame of government and charter of liberties, which guaranteed equality and fairness for its people. Penn envisioned a generous, free society in which taxes were low, no limit was placed on land holdings, and Native Americans were treated equally with Europeans. Moreover, he promoted complete religious tolerance, and he gave freedman (citizen) status to any male who owned fifty acres of farmland or paid taxes. The colony would be administered by the governor and the general council; these governing bodies proposed and passed laws. All citizens, including servants, would have certain rights and privileges, and there would be no established church.

Soon after arriving in Pennsylvania in 1682, Penn wrote *The Propriety of Pennsylvania* as an advertisement for his new colony. The document also revealed his fascination with Native American culture.

Things to Remember While Reading *The Propriety of Pennsylvania:*

- Penn was a social reformer and advocate of religious freedom, but he also realized his venture in Pennsylvania would succeed only if he turned a profit. To make money he had to attract settlers to his new colony. Therefore in sections I and IV he promoted life in Pennsylvania by praising the richness of the land, the healthy air, the convenience of river transportation, and easy access to ocean trade.

- Notice that Penn gave an extensive description of Native Americans in the area. So that they would not seem strange to his readers he compared them with familiar groups—Italians, Jews, Africans. Penn had respect for Native Americans, and he was critical of the negative influence of Europeans on native culture. In section XIX he observed, "Since the European came into these parts, they [Native Americans] are grown great lovers of strong liquors, rum especially, and for it exchange the richest of their skins and furs." He was referring to the European practice of getting Native Americans drunk in order to obtain the best deals on trading transactions. The colonists also used the same method with so-called "whisky treaties," whereby they tricked Native Americans into giving away vast amounts of land. Penn was equally critical of attempts to convert Native Americans to Christianity. In section XXV he wrote, "The worst is that they [Native Americans] are worse for the Christians, who have propagated [increased] their vices, and yielded them tradition for ill, and not for good things. . . ."

- Penn insisted on buying land from Native Americans, rather than simply seizing it or using the whiskey treaty trick. In 1682 the Native Americans and Quakers signed a treaty at a council meeting described by Penn in section [X]XIII. They agreed to "live in love as long as the sun gave light," thus forming one of the longest-lasting peace treaties between Native Americans and European settlers.

- In section XXVI Penn stated that the Native Americans were "of the Jewish race" and "of the stock of the Ten [lost] Tribes"—a common theory in the seventeenth century. He was referring to the "lost tribes of Israel." According to the Bible, ten Israelite tribes were taken to Assyria after the

Assyrians conquered Israel in 722 B.C. No one knows what happened to the tribes, although numerous theories have placed them in Arabia, India, Ethiopia, and the Americas. Early Christian leaders claimed Native North Americans were the lost tribes.

- In section XXVII Penn noted that "The first planters in these parts were Dutch, and soon after them the Swedes and Finns. . . ." The Dutch founded the nearby colony of New Netherland in 1624; it was taken over by the English in 1664 and renamed New York. The Swedes and Finns started New Sweden (present-day Delaware and New Jersey) in 1634; it was occupied by the Dutch in 1655. (See "Impressions of New Jersey and New York.")

The Propriety of Pennsylvania

For the Province, the general condition of it take as followeth:

*I. The country itself in its soil, air, water, seasons, and produce both natural and artificial is not to be **despised**. The land containeth diverse sorts of earth. . . . God in his wisdom having ordered it so, that the advantages of the country are divided, the backlands being generally three to one richer than those that lie by navigable waters. . . .*

VI. Of living creatures: fish, fowl, and beasts of the woods, here are diverse sorts, some for food and profit, and some for profit only. . . . The creatures for profit only by skin or fur, and that are natural to these parts, are the wild cat, panther, otter, wolf, fox, fisher, minx, muskrat; and of the water, the whale for oil, of which we have good store; and two companies of whalers, whose boats are built, will soon begin their work, which hath the appearance of a considerable improvement. To say nothing of our reasonable hopes of good cod in the bay. . . .

*XI. The Natives I shall consider in their persons, language, manners, religion, and government, with my sense of their original. For their persons, they are generally tall, straight, well-built, and of singular **proportion**; they **treat** strong and clever, and most walk*

Despised: Looked down upon

Proportion: Size

Treat: Behave

with a **lofty** chin. Of complexion, black, but by **design,** as the gypsies in England: They grease themselves with bear's fat clarified, and using no defense against sun or weather, their skins must needs be **swarthy.**

Their eye is little and black, not unlike a straight-looked Jew; the thick lip and flat nose, so frequent with the East Indians and Blacks, are not common to them; for I have seen as comely European-like faces among them of both, as on your side of the sea; and truly an Italian complexion hath not much more of the white, and the noses of several of them have as much of the Roman.

XII. Their language is lofty, yet narrow, but like the Hebrew; in signification full, like short-hand in writing; one word serveth in the place of three, and the rest are supplied by the understanding of the hearer. . . . I have made it my business to understand it, that I might not want an interpreter on any occasion. And I must say, that I know not a language spoken in Europe that hath words of more sweetness and greatness, in accent and emphasis, than theirs. . . .

VXI. Their diet is maize, or Indian corn, diverse ways prepared: sometimes roasted in the ashes, sometimes beaten and boiled with water, which they call Homine. They also make cakes, not unpleasant to eat. They likewise eat several sorts of beans and peas that are good nourishment. . . .

XIX . . . in **liberality** they excell; nothing is too good for their friend. Give them a fine gun, coat, or any other thing, it may pass twenty hands, before it sticks. Light of heart, strong affections, but soon spent; the most merry creatures that live, feast and dance perpetually. . . . .

Some kings have sold, others presented me with several **parcels** of land; the pay or presents I made them were not **hoarded** by the particular owners, but the neighboring kings and their clans being present when the goods were brought out, the parties chiefly concerned consulted, what and to whom they should be give them? To every king then, . . . is a proportion sent. . . . Then that king subdivideth it in like manner among his dependents, they hardly leaving themselves an equal share with one of their subjects; and be it on such occasions, at festivals, or at their common meals, the kings distribute, and to themselves last . . . [the kings divide their lands before keeping any for themselves].

Since the European came into these parts, they [Native Americans] are grown [have become] great lovers of strong liquors, rum

Lofty: Noble

Design: To indicate with a distinctive mark, sign, or name

Swarthy: Of a dark color, complexion, or cast

Liberality: Generousity

Parcels: Portions of land

Hoarded: Collected greedily

especially, and for it exchange the richest of their skins and furs. If they are **heated** with liquors, they are restless till they have enough to sleep. That is their cry, Some more, and I will go to sleep; but when drunk, one of the most **wretchedest** spectacles in the world.

XX. In sickness, [they are] impatient to be cured, and for it give anything, especially for their children, to whom they are extremely natural [i.e., to whom they show natural affection]. They drink at those times a Teran or **decoction** of some roots in spring water; and if they eat any flesh, it must be of the female of any creature. If they die, they bury them with their apparel, be they men or women, and the nearest kin fling in something precious with them, as a token of their love. Their mourning is blacking of their face, which they continue for a year. . . .

XXII. Their government is by kings, which they call Sachema, and those by succession, but always of the mother's side. For instance, the children of him that is now king, will not succeed, but his brother by the mother, or the children of his sister, whose sons (and after them the children of her daughters) will reign; for no woman inherits. The reason they **render** for this way of **descent** is that their issue may not be **spurious**. . . .

XIII. Every king hath his council, and that consists of all the old and wise men of his nation. . . . 'Tis admirable to consider, how powerful the kings are, and yet how they move by the breath of their people. I have had occasion to be in council with them upon treaties for land, and to adjust the terms of trade.

Their order is thus: The king sits in the middle of an **half moon**, and hath his council, the old and wise on each hand; behind them, or at a little distance, sit the younger fry [youngsters], in the same figure. Having consulted and resolved their business, the king ordered one of them to speak to me; he stood up, came to me, and in the name of his king saluted me, then took me by the hand, and told me that he was ordered by his king to speak to me, and that now it was not he, but the king that spoke, because what he should say was the king's mind. He first prayed me to excuse them that they had not complied with me the last time; he feared, there might be some fault in the interpreter, being neither Indian nor English. Besides, it was the Indian custom to **deliberate**, and take up much time in council, before they resolve; and that if the young people or owners of the land had been as ready as he, I had not met with so much delay.

Having thus introduced the matter, he fell to the bounds of the land they had agreed to dispose of, and the price (which [land] now

Heated: Drunk

Wretchedest: Extremely

Decoction: An extract obtained by boiling

Render: To agree on and report

Descent: Lineage

Spurious: Of illegitimate birth

Half moon: Half circle

Deliberate: Consider or discuss a matter carefully

William Penn concluding a treaty with the Delaware Indians.

is little and dear, that which would have bought twenty miles, not buying now two). During this time that this person spoke, not a man of them was observed to whisper or smile; the old, grave, the young, reverent in their **deportment**; they do speak little, but fervently, and with elegancy. I have never seen more natural **sagacity**, . . .

When the purchase was agreed, great promises passed between us of kindness and good neighborhood, and that the Indians and English must live in love, as long as the sun gave light. Which done, another made a speech to the Indians, in the name of all the Sachamakers or kings, first to tell them what was done; next, to charge and command them, to love the Christians, and particularly to live in peace with me, and the people under my government; that many governors had been in the river, but that no governor had come himself to live and stay here before; and having now such a one that had treated them well, they should never do him or his any wrong. At every sentence of which they shouted, and said Amen, in their way. . . .

Deportment: The manner in which one conducts oneself

Sagacity: The quality of being keen in sense of perception

*XXV. We have agreed, that in all differences between us, six of each side shall end the matter. Don't abuse them, but let them have justice, and you will win them. The worst is that they are the worse for the Christians, who have **propagated** their vices, and yielded them tradition for ill, and not for good things. . . .*

*XXVI. For their **original**, I am ready to believe them of the Jewish race, I mean, of the stock of the Ten [lost] Tribes. . . .*

*XXVII. The first planters in these parts were Dutch, and soon after them the Swedes and Finns. The Dutch applied themselves to **traffic**, the Swedes and Finns to **husbandry**. There were some disputes between them [for] some years, the Dutch looking upon them as intruders upon their purchase and possession, which was finally ended in the surrender made by. . . . the Swedes' governor, to Peter Stuyvesant, governor for the States of Holland, **Anno** 1655.*

*XXVIII. The Dutch inhabit mostly those parts of the province that lie upon or near to the bay, and the Swedes the **freshes** of the river Delaware. There is no need of giving any description of them, who are better known there than here; but they are a plain, strong, industrious people, yet have made no great progress in culture or propagation of fruit trees, as if they desired rather to have enough, than plenty or traffic. But I presume the Indians made them the more careless, by furnishing them with the means of profit, to wit, skins and furs, for rum and such strong liquors.*

They kindly received me, as well as the English, who were few, before the people concerned with me came among them. I must commend their respect to authority, and kind behavior to the English. . . .

*XXXI. Our people are mostly settled upon the upper rivers, which are pleasant and sweet, and generally bounded with good land. The planted part of the province and territories is cast into six counties: Philadelphia, Buckingham, Chester, New Castle, Kent, and Sussex, maintaining about four thousand souls. The General Assemblies have been held, and with such **concord** and dispatch that they sat but three weeks, and at least seventy laws were passed without one **dissent** in any material thing. But of this more hereafter, being yet raw and new in our **gear**.*

*However, I cannot forget their singular respect to me in this infancy of things, who by their own private expenses so early considered mine for the public, as to present me with an **impost** upon cer-*

Propagation: To cause to spread out and affect a greater number or greater area

Original: Origins

Traffic: Trade

Husbandry: The cultivation or production of plants and animals; agriculture

Anno: In the year

Freshes: Newest

Concord: A state of agreement; harmony

Dissent: Difference of opinion

Gear: Adjustment

Impost: Tax

*tain goods **imported** and **exported**; which after my acknowledgments of their affection, I did as freely remit to the province and traders to it. And for the well government of the said counties, courts of justice are established in every county, with proper officers, as justices, sheriffs, clerks, constables, etc., which courts are held every two months. But to prevent lawsuits, there are three peace-makers chosen by every county court, in the nature of common **arbitrators**, to hear and end differences **betwixt** man and man; and spring and fall there is an orphan's court in each county, to inspect and regulate the affairs of orphans and widows.*

*XXXII. Philadelphia, the expectation of those that are concerned in this province, is at last laid out to the great content of those here. . . . It is advanced within less than a year to about **four score** houses and cottages, such as they are, where merchants and handicrafts are following their **vocations** as fast as they can, while the countrymen are close at their farms. . . .*

What happened next . . .

Penn lived in Pennsylvania for only two years. During that time conflict broke out among various religious groups in the colony, disturbing the spirit of harmony and tolerance. Political squabbles also arose between poor landowners and the more privileged members of the Free Society of Traders. In 1684 Penn returned to England to fight against the persecution of Quakers and to settle a dispute over the southern boundary of his colony, which bordered Maryland. In the meantime King William III (1650–1702) and Queen Mary II (1662–1694) had ascended the throne, so Penn no longer had a personal relationship with the monarchy. Since he was absent from Pennsylvania, he lost his authority there as well. In 1692 the Crown (royal government) withdrew Penn's proprietorship (ownership), but restored it two years later.

Penn finally went back to Pennsylvania in 1699 only to face growing opposition from settlers who wanted the English government to take over the colony. Staying for another two years, he helped draft the Charter of Privileges (1701),

Imported: Brought in from a foreign country for trade or sale

Exported: Sent to another country for trade or sale

Arbitrators: People chosen to settle a dispute

Betwixt: Between

Four score: Eighty

Vocations: Professions

Colonial America: Primary Sources

legal reforms that increased the power of the elected assembly. But affairs in England called Penn home later that year, and he never again saw Pennsylvania. Upon his death in 1718 the proprietorship was passed to his son Thomas.

Pennsylvania continued to thrive in spite its problems. The Quaker philosophy of religious and ethnic tolerance became increasingly popular in Europe. During the eighteenth century Pennsylvania was the fastest-growing colony in America, and Philadelphia was the most important urban center.

Did you know . . .

- Maryland was the first English proprietary colony in America. George Calvert (1580–1632), first Baron (Lord) Baltimore, received a grant of land in northern Virginia, which he named Mary's Land for Queen Henrietta Maria. After Calvert died in 1643, the grant was transferred to his son Cecilius (1605–1675), second Baron Baltimore. The Calverts undoubtedly wanted to make money on their new venture. As Roman Catholics they also hoped to provide a place in America where members of their faith could enjoy religious and political freedom.

- When the Quakers arrived in Pennsylvania they encountered a variety of religious groups that were already established in the area—among them Swedish Lutheran, Dutch Reformed, German Lutheran, Anglican, Anabaptist, and Presbyterian. In 1685 Penn optimistically commented on the diversity of the population: "The People are a Collection of divers [various] Nations in Europe: As, French, Dutch, Germans, Swedes, Danes, Finns, Scotch, Irish and English; and of the last equal to all the rest." As Penn learned later, this mixture of religious beliefs was a natural source of conflict.

- Although Pennsylvania was a success, the colony yielded very little profit for Penn. When renters and landowners did not pay their bills, Penn ultimately was responsible for their debts. He was also swindled by one of his agents. Crushed by the financial burden, he went to debtor's prison in 1707. Five years later he began negotiating with the Crown for the sale of Pennsylvania, but during these discussions he suffered a series of disabling strokes.

- Pennsylvania had a growing population of Africans, both slave and free. Although Quakers became increasingly uncomfortable with slavery from the 1750s onward and even participated in the early abolition (antislavery) movement, they owned slaves until the eve of the American Revolution (see *Some Considerations on the Keeping of Negroes*).

For more information

Bailyn, Bernard. *Voyagers to the West: A Passage in the Peopling of America on the Eve of the Revolution.* New York: Vintage, 1986.

Foster, Genevieve. *The World of William Penn.* New York: Scribner's, 1973.

Middleton, Richard. *Colonial America: A History, 1585–1776,* Second edition. Malden, Mass.: Blackwell Publishers, 1996, pp. 161–68, 199–202.

"Penn's Plan for a Union" in *Documents Relevant to the United States Before 1700.* http://www.geocities.com/Athens/Forum/9061/USA/colonial/bef1700.html Available September 30, 1999.

Quakers in Brief: an overview of the Quaker movement from 1650 to 1990. http://www.cryst.bbk.ac.uk/~ubcg09q/dmr/intro.htm Available September 30, 1999.

Stiles, T. J., ed. *In Their Own Words: The Colonizers.* New York: Berkeley Publishing, 1998, pp. 305–09.

Wildes, Harry Emerson. *William Penn.* New York: Macmillan, 1974.

Per (Peter) Kalm

"Impressions of New Jersey and New York"

Reprinted in *Major Problems in American Colonial History*
Published in 1993
Edited by Karen Ordahl Kupperman

W hile the English were establishing colonies along the Atlantic coast and in New England, the Dutch (people from the Netherlands) had been settling New Netherland, the region that is now New York State. In search of a Northwest Passage (a natural water route between the Atlantic and Pacific oceans), the Dutch sent English navigator Henry Hudson (?–1611) to the same region that John Cabot (c.1450–c.1499) had explored for the English. In 1609 Hudson led an expedition to New York Bay and up the river that now bears his name. Instead of finding the Northwest Passage, Hudson and his men discovered an equally profitable resource: native peoples who had an abundance of animal skins and furs. Thus the Dutch, in competition with the French, started a thriving fur trade with Native Americans. Over the next decade trade was conducted by independent trappers who roamed the wilderness, lived among the Native Americans in the winter, and then sold their furs to Dutch merchants in the spring. Trading procedures became more commercialized in 1621 with the formation of the Dutch West India Company, which was also granted a charter (contract) for the colony of New Netherland.

"The country, especially that along the coasts in the English colonies, is inhabited by Europeans, who in some places are already so numerous that few parts of Europe are more populous."

A trading post on Kent Island like the one the Dutch West India Company established in New Netherland.

Reproduced by permission of Archive Photos, Inc.

At first the company set up trading posts, which also served as forts (military headquarters) that protected the trade routes. The posts at Fort Orange (present-day Albany, New York) and on "the Manhates" (Manhattan Island) soon grew into small settlements surrounded by farms. Beavers were the most important fur-bearing animals, and since they were less plentiful around Manhattan, Albany became the center of Dutch trade. During the annual spring fur-trading season, merchants swarmed to the trading post to await the arrival of traders bringing pelts (the skin of an animal). Albany was a booming town, and even local settlers bought and sold furs—they needed an income for the winter, when the trading post was virtually deserted.

Actual colonization of New Netherland began in 1624 when the Dutch West India Company paid thirty Walloon (people from southern and southeastern Belgium and adjacent parts of France) families to settle in the New World (a European term for North and South America). They settled on farms around Manhattan and Fort Orange and in the Connecticut River valley, where the company had another fort. The settlement on Manhattan, which was named New Amsterdam in 1626, became the center of Dutch control of New Netherland. Within forty years the population of New Amsterdam had reached nearly two thousand. Fort Orange remained a struggling outpost until the 1630s, when the Dutch West India Company authorized one of its directors, Kiliaen Van Rensselaer (1595–1644), to bring new settlers from the Netherlands. Called a patroon (proprietor), Van Rensselaer founded Rensselaerswyck, a patroonship (vast estate) that surrounded Albany and extended along both sides of the Hudson River. In the 1640s and 1650s the Dutch established villages that became the present-day New York cities of Schenectady and Kingston. They also expanded onto Long Island and into New Jersey (the Dutch town of Pavonia is now Jersey City), which were also part of New Netherland. Finally, the Dutch took over Swedish settlements on the Delaware River near present-day New Castle, Delaware.

By the early 1660s New Netherland was having serious economic and political problems. The main reason was that the director general (governor) and his council were appointed by the Dutch West India Company primarily to oversee the fur trade. Governing was therefore only a secondary role. Their main responsibility was to rent company lands to farmers and chartered (establish) towns to settlers. They also established contacts with Native American fur traders, which presented a difficult challenge. Almost immediately the company was involved in a conflict between the Mohicans (an Algonquin tribe) and the Mohawks (one of the Five Nations of the Iroquois) over control of trade. At first the Dutch remained neutral, but they finally aligned themselves with the Mohicans in 1642. An even greater issue was farmland; at first, New Netherland officials acquired land through treaties with the Native Americans. But peaceful relations broke down when, from 1643 to 1645, the Dutch killed more than a thousand Native Americans over alleged treaty violations.

Another explosive situation was created by the diversity of Europeans settlers in the area. Half of the inhabitants of New Netherland and adjoining New Sweden (captured by the Dutch in 1655) were Germans, Swedish, Finns, Norwegians,

Kiliaen van Rensselaer brought new settlers from the Netherlands to encourage the growth of the settlements that would later become New York and New Jersey. *Reproduced by permission of The Library of Congress.*

French, English, Jews, and Africans. With the exception of African slaves, all had been attracted to the area by the promise of religious freedom. Yet the Dutch were Calvinists (those who believe in the strong emphasis on the sovereignty of God, the depravity of mankind, and the doctrine of predestination) and wanted the Dutch Reformed Church to be the official state religion. The New Netherland government had no better success in controlling its own Dutch settlers, who could bypass the council and take grievances directly to the Dutch West India Company. Another problem was that the company was losing money. In 1629 ownership of land had been opened to patroons like Van Rensselaer, and ten years later merchants with no connection to the company were allowed to participate in the fur trade.

The Dutch West India Company attempted to control the situation by appointing Peter Stuyvesant (1610–1672), an arrogant Dutch military leader, as governor of New Netherland. Stuyvesant took his post in 1647, and during the next seventeen years he caused considerable unrest by imposing heavy taxes and passing laws that prohibited religious freedom. For instance, Stuyvesant issued an ordinance that outlawed meetings and gatherings of people who were not members of the Dutch Reformed Church. This made it nearly impossible for other religious groups to assemble and worship. When the directors at the Dutch West India Company headquarters in Amsterdam asked Stuyvesant to be more lenient, their plea landed on deaf ears. The ordinance preventing worship remained in place throughout the Dutch regime in New Netherland.

Stuyvesant also made positive progress, such as improving relations with nearby English settlements and promoting commerce. Nevertheless in 1649 the irate citizens of New Amsterdam forced him to declare the city a municipality (self-governing political unit). Stuyvesant's mismanagement and harsh rule eventually led to the downfall of New Netherland. In 1664, after the English victory over the Netherlands in the Second Anglo-Dutch War, England asserted its rights to

New Netherland (which was part of the territory claimed by Cabot in 1497). The Dutch quickly surrendered during a peaceful invasion, and King Charles II (1630–1685) awarded the colony to his brother James, Duke of York (1633–1701; later King James II). New Netherland was renamed New York, and New Amsterdam became New York City.

The English guaranteed that the inhabitants of the former New Netherland, whatever their nationality or religion, could remain in the colony. However, this open-minded policy only resulted in the continuation of political and religious strife in New York. For instance, conflict over land titles started when the English split the southern part of the colony into East Jersey and West Jersey. In 1681 the Quaker founders of Pennsylvania (see *The Propriety of Pennsylvania*) bought East Jersey, unleashing conflict that resulted in the creation of the independent proprietary colony of New Jersey in 1738. Eight years later long-standing religious animosities (ill-will or resentment) came to a head when Jacob Leisler (1640–1691), a German merchant and militia officer, tried to prevent Roman Catholic domination of the royal government of New York. Although Leisler managed to maintain Protestant control, he was executed for treason and his rebellion only intensified religious differences.

In the late 1600s the British attempted to unite New York, New Jersey, and New England under the rule of royal governor Edmund Andros (1637–1714), but colonists turned against him. Nevertheless, Andros succeeded in negotiating the Covenant Chain (1677). An alliance between the English and the Iroquois, the chain proved to be effective against the French—who had always been a threat to both the Dutch and the English—during the French and Indian Wars (1689–1763). Spanning into the latter half of the eighteenth century, the wars hindered settlement of the western part of the colony. However, the more populous areas of New York and New Jersey continued to attract various ethnic and religious groups during that time.

Despite being a multicultural society that was headed by the English, however, New York was still dominated by the

During the seventeen years that Peter Stuyvesant served as governor of New Netherland he imposed heavy taxes and limited religious freedom.
Reproduced by permission of The Library of Congress.

Dutch. They held most of the property and wealth, and real change in power did not take place until the early 1750s, when the Dutch and English intermingled to form a new aristocracy (small privileged class) and political power structure. It was at that time that the language and social customs of the English began to replace Dutch culture. A vivid picture of life in New York and New Jersey during this transition period was provided by Swedish traveler Per (Peter) Kalm in *Travels into North America, Containing Its Natural History and a Circumstantial Account of Its Plantations and Agriculture* . . . (translated into English and published in 1770). Kalm also gave a brief history of the colony.

Things to Remember While Reading "Impressions of New Jersey and New York":

- In the paragraph on "Indians" Kalm remarked on the absence of Native Americans from land they had previously inhabited in the New York-New Jersey region. He went on to note that "The Indians have sold the land to the Europeans, and have retired further inland." The words "sold" and "retired" suggest that Native Americans—in this case the Algonquians—had voluntarily turned their lands over to European settlers. As a matter of fact, Algonquian peoples were either killed or forced out by Europeans during the seventeenth century.

- Kalm described the Jews he visited in New York. The first recorded Jews in North America—the Ashkenazim (European Jews) and Sephardim (Spanish Jews)—had arrived in New Amsterdam a century earlier, in 1654 and 1655. Between 1690 and 1710 Jews of Anglo-German heritage migrated to New York City; in 1730 they built the first synagogue (Jewish house of worship) in North America.

- Near the end of Impressions of "New Jersey and New York," Kalm tried to account for the inhabitants of Albany, New York, whom he found to be extremely selfish and greedy. Since they were so different from other people in New York, Kalm concluded that in the early days the Dutch, in desperation, had sent a "pack of vagabonds" to clear the remote frontier around Fort Orange (Albany). The Dutch West India Company indeed had difficulty attracting settlers to this part of the colony. In the 1630s, after the failure of the patroon system, the company offered property to colonists who could pay their own passage to America and would invest in the New Netherland venture. Each of these settlers was required, however, to bring along a family of at least five members. Kalm was probably referring to this policy when he wrote that "a few honest families were persuaded to go with them, in order to keep them in bounds."

"Impressions of New Jersey and New York"

Trenton [New Jersey] is a long narrow town, situated at some distance from the Delaware River, on a sandy plain; it belongs to New Jersey, and they reckon it thirty miles from Philadelphia. . . . [F]rom Trenton to New Brunswick, the travellers go in wagons which set out every day for that place. Several of the inhabitants however **subsist** *on the transportation of all sorts of goods, which are sent every day in great quantities, either from Philadelphia to New York, or from there to the former place. Between Philadelphia and Trenton all goods are transported by water, but between Trenton and New Brunswick they are carried by land, and both these means of transportation belong to people of this town. . . .*

We continued our journey in the morning; the country through which we passed was for the greatest part level, though sometimes there were some long hills; some parts were covered with trees, but by far the greater part of the country was without woods; on the other hand I never saw any place in America, the city excepted, so well peopled. An old man, who lived in the neighborhood and accompanied us a short distance, assured me however that he could well remember the time when between Trenton and New Brunswick there were not above three farms, and he reckoned it was about fifty and some odd years ago. During the greater part of the day we saw very extensive cultivated fields on both sides of the road, and we observed that the country generally had a noticeable **declivity** *towards the south. Near almost every farm was a spacious orchard full of peaches and apple trees, and in some of them the fruit had fallen from the trees in such quantities as to cover nearly the whole surface of the ground. Part of it they left to rot, since they could not take care of it all or consume it.*

Subsist: Live

Declivity: Slopping down

"men of eighteen different languages"

In 1643 the Dutch freed the French Jesuit priest Isaac Jogues (1607–1646) from captivity among the Iroquois. On the way back to Quebec Jogues passed through New Amsterdam. In a letter to Dutch patroon David de Vries (1593–?1655), Jogues gave his impressions of the multi-ethnic society he found in New Amsterdam.

On the island of Manhattes [Manhattan], and in its [surrounding area], there may well be four or five hundred men of different sects [religious groups] and nations. The Director General [Governor Peter Stuyvesant] told me that there were men of eighteen different languages; they are scattered here and there on the river, above and below, as the beauty and convenience of the spot has invited each to settle. Some mechanics, however, who ply [work diligently] their trade are ranged under the fort; all the others are exposed to the incursions [invasions] of the natives [Native Americans], who in the year 1643, when I was there, actually killed some two score [forty] Hollanders, and burnt many houses and barns full of wheat. . . .

No religion is publicly exercised but the Calvinist [Dutch Reformed; a Protestant religious group], and orders are to admit none but Calvinists, but this is not observed. For besides the Calvinists there are in the colony Catholics, English Puritans, Lutherans, Anabaptists, here called Mennonites, etc. When anyone comes to settle in the country, they lend him horses, cows, etc.; they give him provisions, all which he returns as soon as he is at ease [comfortable]; and as to the land, after ten years he pays to the West India Company the tenth of the produce which he reaps.

Reprinted in: Stiles, T. J., ed. In Their Own Words: The Colonizers. New York: Berkeley Publishing, 1998, pp. 205–07.

Concise: Expressing much in a few words

Breadth: Measurement from side to side

Threshing: Separation of seed from a harvested plant

Garret: A room or unfinished part of a house just under the roof

Wherever we passed by we were welcome to go into the fine orchards and gather our hats and pockets full of the choicest fruit, without the owner so much as looking at us. Cherry trees were planted near the farms, on the roads, etc.

The barns had a peculiar kind of construction in this locality, of which I shall give a **concise** *description. The main building was very large almost the size of a small church; the roof was high, covered with wooden shingles, sloping on both sides, but not steep. The walls which supported it were not much higher than a full grown man; but on the other hand the* **breadth** *of the building was all the greater. In the middle was the* **threshing** *floor and above it, or in the loft or* **garret***, they put the unthreshed grain, the straw, or anything else,* according to the season. On one side were stables for the horses, and on the other for the cows. The young stock had also their particular stables or stalls, and in both ends of the building were large doors, so that one could drive in with a cart and horses through one of them, and go out at the other. Here under one roof therefore were the thrashing floor, the barn, the stables, the hay loft, the coach house, etc. This kind of building is used chiefly by the Dutch and Germans, for it is to be observed that the country between Trenton and New York is not inhabited by many Englishmen, but mostly by Germans or Dutch, the latter of which are especially numerous.

Indians. *Before I proceed I must mention one thing about the Indians or old Americans; for this account may find readers, who, like many people of my acquaintance, have the opinion that North America is almost wholly inhabited by savage or* **heathen** *nations; and they may be astonished that I do not mention them more frequently in my account. Others may perhaps imagine that when I state in my journal that the country is widely cultivated, that in several places houses of stone or wood are built, round which are grain fields, gardens and orchards, that I am speaking of the property of the Indians. To undeceive them I shall here give the following explanation. The country, especially that along the coasts in the English colonies, is inhabited by Europeans, who in some places are already so numerous that few parts of Europe are more* **populous**. *The Indians have sold the land to the Europeans, and have* **retired** *further inland. In most parts you may travel twenty Swedish miles, or about a hundred and twenty English miles, from the coast, before you reach the first habitation of the Indians. And it is very possible for a person to have been at Philadelphia and other towns on the seashore for half a year without so much as seeing an Indian. . . .*

About noon we arrived at New Brunswick, *(situated about thirty miles from Trenton and sixty from Philadelphia), a pretty little town in the province of New Jersey, in a valley on the west side of the river Raritan. On account of its low location, it cannot be seen (coming from Pennsylvania) before you get to the top of the hill, which is quite close to it. The town extends north and south along the river. The German inhabitants have two churches, one of stone and the other of wood. The English church is likewise of the latter material, but the Presbyterians are building one of stone. The Town Hall makes a good appearance. Some of the other houses are built of brick, but most of them are made either wholly of wood, or of brick and wood. The wooden buildings are not made of strong timber, but merely of boards or*

Heathen: An uncivilized or irreligious person

Populous: Thickly settled

Retired: Departed

*planks, which are within joined by **laths**. Houses built of both wood and brick have only the wall towards the street made of the latter, all the other sides being boards. This peculiar kind of **ostentation** would easily lead a traveller who passes through the town in haste to believe that most of the houses are built of brick. The houses are covered with shingles. Before each door is a **veranda** to which you ascend by steps from the street; it resembles a small balcony, and has benches on both sides on which the people sit in the evening to enjoy the fresh air and to watch the passers-by. The town has only one street lengthways, and at its northern **extremity** there is a cross street: both of these are of a considerable length.*

*The river Raritan passes close by the town, and is deep enough for large sailing vessels. Its breadth near the town is about the distance of a common gun shot. The tide comes up several miles beyond the town, which contributes not a little to the ease and convenience of securing vessels which dock along the bridge. The river has generally very high and steep banks on both sides, but near the town there are no such banks, because it is situated in a low valley. One of the streets is almost entirely inhabited by Dutchmen who came **hither** from Albany, and for that reason it is called Albany Street. These Dutch people keep company only with themselves, and seldom or never go amongst the other inhabitants, living as it were quite separate from them. . . .*

[New York]

The Jews. *Besides the different **sects** of Christians, many Jews have settled in New York, who possess great privileges. They have a **synagogue**, own their **dwelling-houses**, possess large **country-seats** and are allowed to keep shops in town. They have likewise several ships, which they load and send out with their own goods. In fine, they enjoy all the privileges common to the other inhabitants of this town and province. . . .*

During my residence in New York, both at this time and for the next two years, I was frequently in company with Jews. I was informed among other things that these people never boiled any meat for themselves on Saturday, but that they always did it the day before, and that in winter they kept a fire during the whole Saturday. They commonly eat no pork; yet I have been told by several trustworthy men that many of them (especially the young Jews) when travelling, did not hesitate the least about eating this or any other meat that was put before them, even though they were in company with Christians. I was in their synagogue last evening for the first time, and to-

Laths: Thin narrow strips of wood nailed to rafters as a groundwork for tiles or plaster

Ostentation: Excessive display

Veranda: Roofed open gallery or porch attached to the exterior of a building.

Extremity: Farthest point

Hither: Toward here

Sects: Religious groups

Synagogue: House of worship for the Jewish congregation

Dwelling-house: A shelter (as a house) in which people live

Country-seats: Houses or estates in the country

day at noon I visited it again, and each time I was put in a special seat which was set apart for strangers or Christians. A young **rabbi** read the divine service, which was partly in Hebrew and partly in the **Rabbinical** dialect. Both men and women were dressed entirely in the English fashion; the former had their hats on, and did not once take them off during the service. The **galleries**, I observed, were reserved for the ladies, while the men sat below. During prayers the men spread a white cloth over their heads, which perhaps is to represent **sackcloth**. But I observed that the wealthier sort of people had a much richer cloth than the poorer ones. Many of the men had Hebrew books, in which they sang and read alternately. The rabbi stood in the middle of the synagogue and read with his face turned towards the east; he spoke however so fast as to make it almost impossible for any one to understand what he said. . . .

The first colonists in New York were Dutchmen. When the town and its territories were taken by the English and left to them by the next peace in exchange for **Surinam**, the old inhabitants were allowed either to remain at New York, and enjoy all the privileges and **immunities** which they were possessed of before, or to leave the place with all their goods. Most of them chose the former; and therefore the inhabitants both of the town and of the province belonging to it are still for the greatest part Dutch, who still, and especially the old people, speak their mother **tongue**.

They were beginning however by degrees to change their manners and opinions, chiefly indeed in the town and in its neighborhood; for most of the young people now speak principally English, go only to the English church, and would even take it amiss if they were called Dutchmen and not Englishmen. . . .

The Dutch Settlers. But the lack of people in this province may likewise be accounted for in a different manner. As the Dutch, who first cultivated this section, obtained the liberty of staying here by the treaty with England, and of enjoying all their privileges and advantages without the least limitation, each of them took a very large piece of ground for himself, and many of the more powerful heads of families made themselves the possessors and masters of a country of as great territory as would be sufficient to form one of our moderately-sized, and even one of our large, **parishes**. Most of them being very rich, their envy of the English led them not to sell them any land, but at an excessive rate, a practice which is still punctually observed among their descendants. The English therefore, as well as people of other nations, have but little encouragement to settle here. On the

Rabbi: Official leader of a Jewish congregation

Rabbinical: Of or relating to rabbis or their writings

Galleries: Outdoor balconies

Sackcloth: A coarse cloth of goat or camel's hair or of flax, hemp, or cotton

Surinam: Suriname, a country in South America; once controlled by the Dutch

Immunities: Freedoms or exemptions

Tongue: A spoken language

Parishes: Local church communities composed of the members of a Protestant Church

other hand, they have sufficient opportunity in the other provinces to purchase land at a more moderated price, and with more security to themselves. It is not to be wondered then, that so many parts of New York are still uncultivated, and that it has entirely the appearance of a frontier-land. This instance may teach us how much a small mistake in a government can hamper the settling of a country. . . .

Trade. . . . Albany carries on a considerable commerce with New York, chiefly in furs, boards, wheat, flour, peas, several kinds of timber, etc. There is not a place in all the British colonies, the Hudson's Bay settlements excepted, where such quantities of furs and skins are bought of the Indians as at Albany. Most of the merchants in this town send a clerk or agent to Oswego, an English trading town on Lake Ontario, to which the Indians come with their furs. I intend to give a more minute account of this place in my Journal for the year 1750. The merchants from Albany spend the whole summer at Oswego, and trade with many tribes of Indians who come with their goods. Many people have assured me that the Indians are frequently cheated in disposing of their goods, especially when they are drunk, and that sometimes they do not get one half or even one tenth of the value of their goods. I have been a witness to several transactions of this kind. The merchants of Albany glory in these tricks, and are highly pleased when they have given a poor Indian, a greater portion of brandy than he can stand, and when they can, after that, get all his goods for mere **trifles.** *The Indians often find when they are sober again, that they have for once drunk as much as they are able of a liquor which they value beyond anything else in the whole world, and they are quite insensible to their loss if they again get a* **draught** *of this* **nectar.** *Besides this trade at Oswego, a number of Indians come to Albany from several places especially from Canada; but from this latter place, they hardly bring anything but beaver skins. . . .*

The Dutch in Albany. The inhabitants of Albany and its **environs** *are almost all Dutchmen. They speak Dutch, have Dutch preachers, and the divine service is performed in that language. Their manners are likewise quite Dutch: their dress is however like that of the English. It is well known that the first Europeans who settled in the province of New York were Dutchmen. During the time that they were the masters of this province, they seized New Sweden of which they were jealous. However, the pleasure of possessing this conquered land and their own was but of short duration, for towards the end of 1664 Sir Robert Carr, by order of King Charles the second, went to New York, then New Amsterdam, and took it. Soon after Colonel Nicolls went to*

Trifles: Something of little value

Draught: Drink

Nectar: Something delicious to drink

Environs: Surroundings

Colonial America: Primary Sources

Albany, which then bore the name of Fort Orange, and upon taking it, named it Albany, from the Duke of York's Scotch title. The Dutch inhabitants were allowed either to continue where they were, and under the protection of the English to enjoy all their former privileges, or to leave the country. The greater part of them chose to stay and from them the Dutchmen are descended who now live in the province of New York, and who possess the greatest and best estates in that province.

The **avarice**, selfishness and **immeasurable** love of money of the inhabitants of Albany are very well know throughout all North America, by the French and even by the Dutch, in the lower part of New York province. I was here obliged to pay for everything twice, thrice and four times as much as in any part of North America which I have passed through. If I wanted their assistance, I was obliged to pay them very well for it, and when I wanted to purchase anything or be helped in some case or other, I could at once see what kind of blood ran in their veins, for they either fixed **exorbitant** prices for their services or were very reluctant to assist me. Such was this people in general. However, there were some among them who equalled any in North America or anywhere else, in politeness, equity, goodness, and readiness to serve and to oblige; but their number fell far short of that of the former. If I may be allowed to declare my **conjectures**, the origin of the inhabitants of Albany and its neighborhood seems to me to be as follows. While the Dutch possessed this country, and intended to people it, the government sent a pack of **vagabonds** of which they intended to clear their native country, and sent them along with a number of other settlers to this province. The vagabonds were sent far from the other colonists, upon the borders towards the Indians and other enemies, and a few honest families were persuaded to go with them, in order to keep them in bounds. I cannot in any other way account for the difference between the inhabitants of Albany and the other descendants of so respectable a nation as the Dutch, who are settled in the lower part of New York province. The latter are civil, obliging, just in prices, and sincere; and though they are not **ceremonious**, yet they are well meaning and honest and their promises may be relied on. . . .

Dutch Food. The whole region about the Hudson River above Albany is inhabited by the Dutch: this is true of Saratoga as well as other places. During my stay with them I had an opportunity of observing their way of living, so far as food is concerned, and wherein they differ from other Europeans. Their breakfast here in the country

Avarice: Greediness

Immeasurable: Limitless

Exorbitant: Excessive

Conjectures: A conclusion based on a summation or guesswork

Vagabonds: People moving from place to place without a fixed home

Ceremonious: Conventional acts of politeness or etiquette

*was as follows: they drank tea in the customary way by putting brown sugar into the cup of tea. With the tea they ate bread and butter and radishes; they would take a bite of the bread and butter and would cut off a piece of the radish as they ate. They spread the butter upon the bread and it was each one's duty to do this for himself. They sometimes had small round cheeses (not especially fine tasting) on the table, which they cut into thin slices and spread upon the buttered bread. At noon they had a regular meal and I observed nothing unusual about it. In the evening they made a porridge of corn, poured it as customary into a dish, made a large hole in the center into which they poured fresh milk, but more often **buttermilk**. They ate it taking half a spoonful of porridge and half of milk. As they ordinarily took more milk than porridge, the milk in the dish was soon consumed. Then more milk was poured in. This was their supper nearly every evening. After that they would eat some meat left over from the noonday meal, or bread and butter with cheese. If any of the porridge remained from the evening, it was boiled with buttermilk in the morning so that it became almost like a **gruel**. In order to make the buttermilk more tasty, they added either syrup or sugar, after it had been poured into the dish. Then they stirred it so that all of it should be equally sweet. Pudding or pie, the Englishman's perpetual dish, one seldom saw among the Dutch, neither here nor in Albany. But they were indeed fond of meat. . . .*

Buttermilk: The liquid left after butter has been churned from milk or cream

Gruel: A thin porridge

What happened next . . .

During the late 1750s, the final decade of the colonial period, New York made its first steps toward independence from England. As the fur trade declined, settlers in the Hudson River valley had turned their attention to growing wheat. Fishing and shipping became the other principal industries. New York City was now a thriving commercial and cultural center, and its first institution for higher learning, King's College (now Columbia University), had opened in 1754. Fifteen years before the American Revolution (1775–83), New York opposed repressive English commercial laws. As smugglers deliberately violated the Navigation Acts (a series of laws, enacted 1660–73, that protected English shipping and trade in America), New

York colonists were taking a stand against policies that prevented the establishment of an American-based economy.

Did you know . . .

- The Dutch West India Company imported Africans to New Netherland as slave laborers. African men loaded cargo from ships into warehouses and worked as field hands on farms. Women performed domestic chores as well as gardening and light farm tasks. Almost all of the Dutch settlements used slaves, who were taken from various parts of Africa. In 1664, when the English took over New Netherland, around three hundred slaves and seventy-five free blacks were living in New Amsterdam. A census taken in 1698 showed that 2,170 Africans, mostly slaves, were living in the entire colony.

- Stuyvesant tried to expel Jews who arrived in New Netherland in 1654. Resisting his order, they appealed to fellow Jews who were major investors in the Dutch West India Company. The investors successfully persuaded company directors to override Stuyvesant's prejudices and allow the new settlers to stay in the colony.

- In 1660 New Amsterdam had thirteen hundred inhabitants and more than three hundred dwellings. Yet the town was a dreadful place: the fort was nearly in shambles, raw sewage filled the streets, and hogs roamed freely—thus spreading the sewage into yards and walkways. Stuyvesant and the council tried to clean up the town by fining residents who did not confine their animals (the required method was to put rings in the hogs' noses) and prohibiting the building of outhouses beside public highways.

- Although the fur trade continued after the English took over New Netherland, fur-bearing animals were nearly all killed off at the turn of the eighteenth century. Native Americans then either had to trap in other areas or buy furs from more distant tribes whose lands still had a plentiful supply of animals. By 1700 Albany merchants were engaging in illegal fur trade with the French in Montreal.

For more information

Burrows, Edwin G., and Mike Wallace. *Gotham: A History of New York City to 1898*. New York: Oxford University Press, 1999, pp. 3–244.

"Charter of the Dutch West India Company (1621)" in *Documents Relevant to the United States Before 1700*. http://www.geocities.com/Athens/Forum/9061/USA/colonial/bef1700.html Available September 30, 1999.

De Leeuw, Adéle. *Peter Stuyvesant*. Champaign, Ill.: Garrard Publishing Company, 1970.

Goodfriend, Joyce. *Before the Melting Pot: Society and Culture in Colonial New York City*. Princeton, N.J.: Princeton University Press, 1992.

Henry Hudson and the Half Moon. http://www.ulster.net/~hrmm/halfmoon/halfmoon.htm Available September 30, 1999.

Kupperman, Karen Ordahl, ed. *Major Problems in American Colonial History*. Lexington, Mass.: D. C. Heath, 1993, pp. 277–82.

The Life and Times of Henry Hudson, explorer and adventurer. http://www.georgian.net/rally/hudson/ Available September 30, 1999.

Middleton, Richard. *Colonial America: A History, 1585–1776*. Second edition. Malden, Mass.: Blackwell Publishers, 1996, pp. 114–120, 127–135.

Social Issues 2

Documents in this chapter trace significant social issues confronted by American colonists in the seventeenth and eighteenth centuries. Conflict with Native Americans was an ongoing crisis as settlers tried to acquire more land, and tensions frequently escalated into full-scale war. *A Relacion of the Indyan Warre* is an account by Rhode Island colonist **John Easton** of the events leading up to King Philip's War, one of the most devastating confrontations of the colonial period. Problems with Native Americans also led to conflicts among the colonists themselves. For example, a letter written by **Elizabeth Bacon**, who defended the rebellion her husband Nathaniel led against the royal government of Virginia. Nathaniel Bacon charged that frontier farmers were not being adequately protected against Native American raids. However, Bacon's views were not shared by all Virginians: Colonist **William Sherwood** charged Bacon himself with lawlessness and arrogance.

One of the most infamous events in early American history was the Salem witchcraft trials. A transcript of a trial written by **Cotton Mather** and **Ezekiel Cheever** shows that the woman who was willing to admit she was a "witch" was set free, while the one who refused to plead guilty was executed.

Excerpts from **Samuel Sewall**'s diary give glimpses into the closed world of the Puritan elite, which lead to the trials. *A Brief Narrative of the Case and Tryal of John Peter Zenger* highlights another famous court proceeding, the trial of New York newspaper publisher John Peter Zenger, who was accused of seditious libel. The not-guilty verdict rendered by the jury set a precedent for freedom of the press in America.

By the late 1600s the majority of immigrants in North America were English indentured servants. Although they worked in all of the colonies, the majority labored on plantations in the South. Living conditions for servants were extremely harsh, and the practices of plantation owners came under increased scrutiny, especially in England. In his history of Virginia, planter **Robert Beverley** vigorously defended the system, calling it both lawful and humane. Excerpts from Beverley's book, *The History and Present State of Virginia,* present Virginia laws that regulated the treatment of servants and slaves. At the time Beverley issued his defense, plantation owners were increasingly relying on African slaves instead of white indentured servants as a source of labor. Slaves had lived in the colonies since the 1620s, but by the early 1700s the slave trade had become a vital part of the colonial economy in both the North and South. Religious leaders had privately opposed the owning of slaves, but Quaker preacher **John Woolman** was the first to wage a public campaign. Woolman took a stand against slavery in his essay titled *Some Considerations on the Keeping of Negroes.* It is considered the first widely published abolitionist statement in America.

Religion was also a source of conflict in all the colonies, but the most pronounced differences occurred in New England where Puritan leaders controlled every aspect of community life. One of the best-known incidents took place when Plymouth colonists broke up a May Day celebration in the nearby town of Merry Mount. A portion of the colorful account of the event written by **Thomas Morton**, a vocal critic of the Puritans, who had organized the festivities. Puritan officials constantly had problems with dissidents in their own ranks. Among the most outspoken was Anne Marbury Hutchinson, who was banished from Massachusetts Bay because she challenged the authority of Puritan ministers. **Excerpt From the Trial of Anne Hutchinson** presents Hutchinson asserting her right to hold religious meetings.

John Easton

A Relacion of the Indyan Warre

Reprinted in *In Their Own Words: The Colonizers*
Published in 1998
Edited by T. J. Stiles

By the mid-1600s, less than half a century after the English had opened the way for full-scale European settlement, serious crises were emerging in the American colonies. At first tensions were direct results of a steadily increasing population: massive influxes of settlers required more land, additional dwellings and other accommodations, greater food supplies, expanded trade and transportation networks, and more laborers. The immediate victims were Native Americans, who suffered mistreatment at the hands of colonists grabbing land and natural resources. Among the colonists themselves, religious differences escalated into confrontations, land squabbles caused rebellions, and class divisions bred unrest.

A major issue was the way the colonies were governed. This problem had emerged in the first few years of the settlement period and quickly gained momentum in the seventeenth century. By the late 1600s all thirteen colonies had come under the control of the English. Governing bodies therefore consisted either of proprietors (individuals granted ownership of a colony and full rights of establishing a government and distributing land) hired by wealthy investors or

"So the English were afraid and Philip was afraid and both increased in arms; but for forty years' time reports and jealousies of war had been very frequent, that we did not think that now a war was breaking forth."

councils controlled by the monarchy (king or queen) and aristocracy (elite social class) in England. Many of the investors and aristocrats remained in England, while others took positions of power in colonial governments. Trade, treaties, and taxation were legislated for the benefit of England. The colonial population, however, was highly diverse, consisting of a complex mixture of ethnic, religious, and social groups (see *The Propriety of Pennsylvania* and "Impressions of New Jersey and New York"). During the eighteenth century a uniquely "American spirit" was taking shape. Colonists were not only questioning English rule but also rebelling against various forms of authority. Demanding the rights and freedoms—religious, political, economic, and individual—symbolized by the New World (European term for North and South America), Americans were setting the stage for revolution.

The first American rebels were the Native Americans. As previous documents have shown, Native Americans initially welcomed the European settlers, with whom they willingly shared their land and resources. Slowly they came to realize that the foreign invaders, by clearing vast territories for towns and farms, were violating native traditions. Native Americans believed that a Great Spirit had created a plentiful and harmonious world in which human beings are no more important than other creatures. Therefore they placed great emphasis on giving proper respect to nature. Native Americans managed their land so that it would accommodate all living creatures, taking only what they needed. For instance, to show their respect for nature they thanked a tree for dying and providing them with wood for a fire. They thanked an animal they had killed for giving up its flesh to feed them and its skin to clothe them. Native Americans were shocked to discover that the Europeans viewed humans as the dominant creatures in nature and thus felt free to change the world for their own advantage.

Native Americans were equally troubled about being forced to convert to Christianity and accept European customs. During the early colonial period they regarded the Christian God as simply another name for the Great Spirit. They saw no real need to change their own religious practices. Then, after being nearly annihilated (killed) by smallpox and other European diseases, they accepted the European view that believing in the Christian God was the only way they could save themselves. Moreover, they were dependent on European-made goods—weapons, cooking utensils, and tools—they received in exchange for jewelry, furs, and other trade items. Consequently they had no choice other than to cooperate with the Europeans.

After several decades of European domination, however, Native Americans throughout North America began raising concerns about the disappearance of their land and traditional culture. In fact, native resistance is a central theme in the history of colonial America. For instance, the Pueblo revolutionary Popé (d. 1692) led the first organized Native North American rebellion against Europeans when he drove the Spanish out of New Mexico (see "New Mexico Indians Eager for Conversion"). Although Spaniards eventually returned to the Southwest, the Pueblos are credited with halting Spanish expansion into territories that comprised the original thirteen colonies.

Native groups living near heavily colonized areas along the Atlantic coast staged similar efforts at resistance, but with less success. In spite of numerous treaties with colonists and powerful tribal alliances such as the Powhatans, the Five Nations, and the Hurons, Native Americans had difficulty holding onto their lands and traditions. Repeatedly they resorted to uniting with one European power against another in order to keep political power. From the earliest days of European settlement, Native Americans and colonists were continually engaged in minor skirmishes and prolonged battles. As time went on, these conflicts escalated into full-fledged wars, which usually ended in disaster for Native Americans. One of the most famous wars took place in New England, between the Puritans and the Wamapanoags.

In the Puritan colonies of Plymouth and Massachusetts Bay, one of the primary goals was to promote Christianity among Native Americans. The Puritans were, in effect, a Protestant equivalent of the Spanish friars (a member of a religious order combining life as a monk and outside religious activity) in the Southwest (see "New Mexico Indians Eager for Conversion") and French missionaries in Canada (see "Jolliet

Kateri Takakwitha a Native American women who voluntarily converted to Christianity. Unlike Takakwitha, many Native Americans felt as if they were force to convert to Christianity in order maintain a trading relationship with the Europeans.
Reproduced by permission of UPI/Bettmann.

John Eliot preaching to the Massachusetts Native Americans. Eliot's efforts to convert Native Americans was encouraged by Puritan officials.
Reproduced by The Library of Congress. Drawing by J. A. Oertel.

and Marquette Travel the Mississippi"). In the Plymouth Colony, Puritan officials enthusiastically promoted the activities of clergymen such as John Eliot (1604–1690), who established more than fourteen Native American "praying villages" for the Wampanoags, an Algonquian-speaking people. In these villages the Wampanoags were taught English customs and underwent religious instruction, often with Native American tutors. Eliot even compiled an Algonquian translation of the Bible for converts who could not read English. Eventually the Wampanoags resented efforts to Europeanize them. They became uncomfortable with the fact that they were offending the Great Spirit by converting to Christianity as well as needlessly slaughtering animals for the fur trade. In particular the heavy emphasis on furs disrupted their traditional culture and economy by fostering wars with neighboring tribes over trapping grounds. By 1675 Wampanoag leaders were ready to push the Puritans off their land and reclaim their own religion and culture.

At the forefront of this rebellion was Metacom (also Metacomet; c.1639–1676), a sachem (chief) the colonists knew as King Philip. Metacom was one of five children of Chief Massasoit (1580–1661), who had helped the Plymouth colonists (see "The Pilgrims' Landing and First Winter"). Massasoit died in 1661 and a year later Metacom, then in his mid-twenties, assumed leadership of the Wampanoags. He dedicated himself to maintaining the Wampanoag Confederacy, which consisted of many villages and families. As English population and power continued to grow, the confederacy began to splinter. This was due in part to the influence of colonial authorities and missionaries. Metacom's land formed a border zone between Plymouth Colony, Rhode Island, and the Massachusetts Bay Colony capital in Boston, each of which wanted to claim the territory. In order to hold onto his political influence, the sachem sold tracts of land to various colonists. Resulting conflicts over the borders of these lands, however, were rarely settled to his satisfaction. Colonial courts seemed biased and insensitive to the Native Americans' concerns. The tribes were also angered by colonists' efforts to influence Native American politics.

The conflict over land reached a crisis in 1667. In violation of an agreement with Metacom, the Plymouth Colony authorized the purchase of land inside Wampanoag borders for the town of Swansea. Tribal war parties, possibly led by Metacom, began to gather around Swansea in an effort to intimidate the colonists. In 1671 Plymouth officials demanded a meeting with the chief. When he arrived they forced him at gunpoint to surrender his warriors' firearms and to sign a treaty. This treaty placed the Wampanoags under Plymouth rule and challenged previous land sales to other colonies. Metacom complained to the Massachusetts Bay Colony, but he received no support. Instead, both Plymouth and Massachusetts Bay, which had formed the United Colonies several years earlier, forced him to sign the new treaty.

Around this time Metacom started planning the uprising that came to be known as King Philip's War. Although he received the backing of Wampanoag leaders, Metacom knew his tribe was too small to fight the English alone. Therefore, he sought support from other Native American groups. He managed to win over the Nipmucks, who were also bitter toward the colonists. He had difficulty, however, in forming an alliance with the Narragansetts, the most powerful tribe in the region and enemies of the Wampanoags. Metacom was now in a difficult position; he had not gained enough support to launch an uprising, so he had to play a waiting game whereby he tried to prevent his angry warriors from raiding colonial villages. Rumors of Metacom's plans reached colonial authorities in 1674. Soon afterward the body of John Sassamon, a Christianized Native American, was found in a pond. It turned out that Sassamon had told the English about Metacom's plan. The colonists tried and then hanged three Wampanoags for committing the murder. On the scaffold (platform where criminals are hanged) one of the three men supposedly confessed that Metacom had ordered the killing of Sassamon.

Metacom saw no other alternative than to declare war on the Puritans. Colonial officials commanded Metacom to disarm his warriors, but he remained defiant. To head off a bloody conflict a group of Rhode Island colonists arranged to meet Metacom at Trip's Ferry in Rhode Island. One of the members of the delegation was John Easton, who wrote an account of the meeting, in which he described the positions of both the Wampanoags and the Puritans. This document gives modern readers an insight into the frustration and distrust that led each side to believe that outright war was the only way to resolve their differences.

Things to Remember While Reading
A Relacion of the Indyan Warre:

- After reviewing the events that led up to the confrontation, in the fifth paragraph Easton began a description of the colonists' meeting with Metacom. Notice that they were initially "friendly together," and each side stated a desire to avoid a war. Easton wrote that the colonists were convinced the Wampanoags would accept arbitration, that is, they "might choose an Indian king, and the English might choose the governor of New York" as representatives who would resolve differences.

- Then Easton outlined the misunderstanding that led to the eventual failure of the negotiations. Since the colonists thought the Wampanoags had agreed to future arbitration, they assumed the meeting was postponed until a later date. Therefore they prepared to leave because they saw no need for any further discussion ("it was not convenient for us right now"). But when "Philip charged it to be dishonesty in us to put off the hearing of the complaints," the colonists agreed to listen to him.

- Metacom—referred to as Philip throughout the document—presented the Englishmen with numerous grievances. He reminded them that his father, Massasoit, had helped them when they came to New England—He "was as a great man and the English as a little child." Not only did Massasoit protect the colonists from other tribes, he also gave them corn, taught them how to plant, and "gave them a hundred times more land than now the king had for his own people." In spite of this gracious treatment, the Wampanoags were dealt with unfairly by the English. If "twenty of [the Wampanoags'] honest Indians testified that an Englishman had done them wrong, it was as nothing," Philip said, "but if one of their worst Indians testified against any Indian or their king when it pleased the English, that was sufficient." Philip went on to charge that the colonists cheated the Native Americans out of land, both by ignoring treaties and taking advantage of their addiction to alcohol and getting them drunk. In fact, he said later, "the English were so eager to sell the Indian liquors that most of the Indians spent all [their money] in drunkeness." Another problem was that the Englishmen would not fence their cattle and horses, and the animals destroyed the Wampanoags' corn.

- Easton concluded by noting that the English had already been aware of these "grand grievances," but they had hoped to resolve their differences peaceably. Before leaving, the colonists warned the Wampanoags to "lay down their arms, for the English were too strong for them." They responded that "the English should do to them as they did when they were too strong for the English." Although the colonists "departed without any discourtesies, Josiah Winslow, the Plymouth governor soon notified them that he "intended in arms to conform [subdue] Philip." Within a week the "war thus begun."

A Relacion of the Indyan Warre

*In the winter in the year 1674, an Indian was found dead; and by a **coroner['s] inquest** of Plymouth colony judged murdered. . . . The dead Indian was called Sassamon, and a Christian that could read and write. . . .*

*The report came that the three Indians had confessed and accused Philip so as to [have] employ[ed] them, and that the English would hang Philip. So the Indians were afraid, and reported that the English had flattered them (or by threats) to **belie** Philip that they might kill him to have his land. . . . So Philip kept his men in arms.*

*Plymouth governor [Josias Winslow] required him to disband his men, and informed him his jealousy was false. Philip answered he would do no harm, and thanked the governor for his information. The three Indians were hung, [but] to the last denied the fact; but one broke the **halter**, as it was reported then, desire[d] to be saved, and so was a little while then. [He] confessed they three had done the fact, and then he was hanged; and it was reported Sassamon, before his death, had informed [the English] of the Indian plot, and that if the Indians knew it they would kill him, and that the **heathen** might destroy the English for their wickedness as God had permitted the heathen to destroy the Israelites of old.*

*So the English were afraid and Philip was afraid and both increased in arms; but for forty years' time reports and jealousies of war had been very frequent, that we did not think that now a war was breaking forth. But about a week before it did we had cause to think it would; then to **endeavor** to prevent it, we sent a man to Philip that if he would come to [Trip's] ferry we would come over to speak with him. About four miles we had to come thither. . . .*

*He called his council and agreed to come to us; [he] came himself, unarmed, and about forty of his men, armed. Then five of us went over. Three were **magistrates**. We sat very friendly together. We told him our business was to endeavor that they might not reserve [intend] or do wrong. They said that that was well; they had done no wrong; the English had wronged them. We said we knew the English said the Indians wronged them, and the Indians said the English wronged them, but our desire was the quarrel might rightly be decided in the best way, and not as dogs decide their quarrels.*

Coroner's inquest: An investigation of any death thought to be other than natural causes performed by a public officer

Belie: To give a false impression of

Halter: A rope with a noose used for execution by hanging

Heathen: An uncivilized or irreligious person

Endeavor: To strive to achieve or reach

Magistrate: An official entrusted with the administration of laws

*The Indians owned that fighting was the worst way; then they **propounded** how right might take place; we said by **arbitration**. They said all English agreed against them; and so by arbitration they had had much wrong, many square miles of land so taken from them, for the English would have English arbitrators. . . . We said they might choose an Indian king, and the English might choose the governor of New York, that neither had cause to say either were parties in the difference. They said they had not heard of that way, and said we honestly spoke; so we were persuaded [that] if that way had been **tendered** they would have accepted.*

*We did endeavor not to hear their complaints, [and] said it was not convenient for us now. . . . But Philip charged it to be dishonesty in us to put off the hearing of the complaints; therefore we consented to hear them. They said they had been the first in doing good to the English, and the English the first in doing wrong; [he] said when the English first came, their king's [Philip's] father [Massasoit] was as a great man and the English as a little child. He **constrained** other Indians from wronging the English, and gave them corn, and showed them how to plant, and was free to do them any good and had let them have a hundred times more land than now the king had for his own people. . . .*

*And another **grievance** was if twenty of their honest Indians testified that an Englishman had done them wrong, it was as nothing; but if one of their worst Indians testified against any Indian or their king when it pleased the English, that was sufficient. Another grievance was, when their kings sold land, the English would say it was more than they agreed to, and a writing must be proof against all them, and some of their kings had done wrong to sell so much. He left his people none; and some being given to drunkeness, the English made them drunk, and then cheated them in bargains. But now their kings were forewarned not to part with land for nothing in comparison to the value thereof. . . .*

Native American leader, Metacom, also known as King Philip, who lead an unsuccessful attempt to oust settlers from New England known as King Philip's War.

Propounded: Offered for discussion or consideration

Arbitration: The hearing and determination of a case in controversy by a third party

Tendered: Offered

Constrained: Restrained

Grievance: Complaint

Another grievance: the English cattle and horses still increased that when they [the Indians] removed thirty miles from where English had anything to do, they could not keep their corn from being spoiled. They never being used to fence, and thought when the English bought land of them that they would have kept their cattle upon their own land. Another grievance: the English were so eager to sell the Indians liquors that most of the Indians spent all in drunkeness. . . .

We knew before these were their grand complaints, but then we only endeavored to persuade that all complaints might be righted without war. . . . We endeavored that, however, they should lay down their arms, for the English were too strong for them. They said the English should do to them as they did when they were too strong for the English.

*So we departed without any **discourtesies**; and suddenly had [a] letter from Plymouth['s] governor, [that] they intended in arms to conform [subdue] Philip . . . and in a week's time after we had been with the Indians the war thus begun.*

Discourtesies: Rude acts

What happened next . . .

In July 1675 Metacom's men again assembled outside Swansea and King Philip's War was shortly underway. The uprising was apparently touched off more by the rage of Metacom's people than by any plan. When a colonial army tried to besiege Metacom near his home on Mount Hope, he escaped with his warriors and their families. Then, joining forces with Nipmuck allies, he attacked and burned villages west and south of Boston. Native American groups in the Connecticut River valley also rose in revolt when anxious colonists overreacted to the violence. Finally, in late December, the Narragansetts joined the uprising after English forces attacked their village. During the following winter, joint tribal raiding parties burned several colonial towns, sending English refugees streaming into Boston.

In the meantime, while Metacom was seeking new alliances in the Hudson River valley, Mohawk warriors and New York colonists attacked his party. All but forty of his men

"land is everlasting"

In 1742 Cannassatego, an Iroquois chief, made the following speech to Pennsylvania colonists while negotiating a new land and trade treaty. Note that he apologized for not bringing a bigger gift. The chief pointed out that colonists had reduced his people to poverty and thus he could not afford any more skins.

We know our lands are now become more valuable: the white people think we do not know their value; but we are sensible that the land is everlasting, and the few goods we receive for it are soon worn out and gone. For the future we will sell no lands but when Brother Onas [one of the Pennsylvania proprietors] is in the country; and we will know beforehand the quantity of the goods we are to receive. Besides, we are not well used with respect to the lands still unsold by us. Your people daily settle on these lands, and spoil our hunting. . . .

It is customary with us to make a present of skins whenever we renew our treaties. We are ashamed to offer our brethren [brothers (the colonists)] so few; but your horses and cows have eat the grass our deer used to feed on. This has made them scarce, and will, we hope, plead in excuse for our not bringing a larger quantity: if we could have spared more we would have given more; but we are really poor; and desire you'll not consider the quantity, but, few as they are, accept them in testimony of our regard.

Reprinted in: Gunn, Giles, ed. Early American Writing. *New York: Penguin Books, 1994, pp. 407–08.*

were killed, and his prestige was shattered. The Mohawks continued their attacks from the west and, joined by other Native American tribes and colonists, finally defeated Metacom. As the uprising lost momentum, some of the sachem's former supporters organized a squad and began tracking Metacom down. His wife and son were captured and apparently sold in the West Indies as slaves. Finally, on August 12, Metacom's dwindling band was surrounded, and he was shot by a Native American serving with the colonial forces. Metacom's head was cut off and hacked into quarters. The pieces were sent to the colonial capitals, where they were placed on public display for more than twenty years.

Metacom's defeat had disastrous consequences for the New England tribes. The Wampanoags and their allies were helpless against the colonists, who numbered seventy thousand and had a large supply of food and ammunition. The war had totally destroyed the Wampanoags' habitat, so they were not prepared for the upcoming winter. Colonial authorities pursued surviving tribes and either killed them or sold them into slavery. Any remaining native peoples were forced into isolated settlements. Within a brief period of time the Native American way of life had completely disappeared from New England.

Did you know . . .

- King Philip's War not only weakened the power of the Native Americans in New England but also had a devastating impact on the English colonies. Before the year-long conflict was over, twelve towns were destroyed and half of the remaining seventy-eight were seriously damaged. The colonies accumulated huge debts, which produced lasting economic hardship. About ten percent of the adult males in New England had been killed—making it the most costly war in American history (measured by the proportion of casualties to total population).

- The praying villages were additional casualties of King Philip's War. Although the majority of Christianized Native Americans were loyal to the colonists, Puritan officials herded them onto Deer Island near Boston, Massachusetts. At the end of the war only four villages remained, and any hope of achieving racial harmony was all but doomed.

- Wampanoag legend holds that Metacom's warriors stole his severed head and secretly buried it near Mount Hope. Some Wampanoags claim that Metacom's spirit still speaks to them.

For more information

Cwiklik, Robert. *King Philip and the War with the Colonists.* Englewood Cliffs, N.J.: Silver Burdett Publishers, 1989.

Josephy, Alvin M. "The Betrayal of King Philip," in *The Patriot Chiefs: A Chronicle of Native American Resistance.* New York: Viking, 1969, pp. 31–62.

Middleton, Richard. *Colonial America: A History, 1585–1776.* Second edition. Malden, Mass.: Blackwell Publishers, 1996, pp. 157–59.

Sewall, Marcia. *Thunder from the Sky.* New York: Antheneum Books for Young Readers, 1995.

Stiles, T. J., ed. *In Their Own Words: The Colonizers.* New York: Berkeley Publishing, 1998, pp. 231–33.

Elizabeth Bacon

A Letter From Elizabeth Bacon

William Sherwood

"A Narrative of Bacon's Rebellion"

**Reprinted in *Major Problems in American Colonial History*
Published in 1993
Edited by Elizabeth Ordahl Kupperman**

During the seventeenth century trouble began brewing along the frontiers of most colonies, as European settlers expanded onto Native American land. In New England tensions between settlers and Native Americans resulted in the Pequot War (1637). Similar conflicts had been taking place in Virginia since the 1640s, but the situation was complicated by serious problems within the colony. These problems could be traced back to the founding of Jamestown (1607), the first settlement and capital of Virginia (see "The Founding of Jamestown").

The original leaders of Jamestown were English gentlemen (members of the nobility) of high social, economic, and educational standing. Within twenty years, however, this group had either gone back to England or died without leaving descendants to take their place. By the 1630s more rugged, self-made families had risen to positions of authority in Virginia. But, like the earlier leaders, they too failed to pass their power on to the next generation. In the latter half of the seventeenth century a third aristocracy (social and government elite) emerged. Sons of influential English merchants and government officials began to settle in the colony in the mid-seventeenth century.

> "...The Indians taking advantage of these civil commotions, have committed many horrid murders..."

William Berkeley, royal governor of Virginia, initiated the Franchise Act which enabled him to place the colony's wealth in the hands of a few well-off property owners. *Reproduced by permission of Archive Photos, Inc.*

This new wave of settlers were sent by the king, who wanted to gain more control of Virginia. They were aristocrats whose families owned property or had made investments in the colony. Virginia had originally been owned by the Virginia Company (a group of investors based in London, England), but the colony had been under the control of the British government since 1624, when the Virginia Company declared bankruptcy (went out of business because of lack of funds). Although Virginia was not yet under a royal charter (direct rule of the English king), various monarchs had been trying to take advantage of the huge tobacco profits that could be made in Virginia. (Tobacco was the principal crop in Virginia. A broad-leaf plant grown in warm climates, tobacco was processed and then sold in Europe, where it was in great demand for smoking in pipes.) Planters had become quite prosperous and owned large tracts of land that produced high tax revenues for England. Within ten years the king's plan had succeeded, and a new elite that was favorable to the king dominated Virginia politics.

In 1670 William Berkeley (1606–1677), the royal governor (the highest colonial official, appointed by the king), initiated the Franchise Act. This law gave voting rights only to landowners and people who owned houses. It also enabled Berkeley to appoint a royal council that would move to place the colony's wealth in the hands of a few well-to-do property owners. (The royal council was a committee appointed by the governor—with the approval of the king—that helped administer the colony.) He named this group the Green Spring faction after his Virginia plantation. Before Berkeley took office ten years earlier, the Virginia assembly (House of Burgesses; the first representative government in America) and the royal council had formed a unified government. Now there was a deep division between social classes. Council members, who came from ruling families, were the governor's inner circle and exercised central authority. On the other side of the divide stood the majority of colonists who were not part of the elite class. In an effort to maintain local representation, leaders from settlements throughout Virginia took seats in the House of Burgesses. These actions alarmed the Green Spring faction, who protested that the socially inferior assemblymen were unfit for governing.

In the meantime, more unrest was brewing. By the mid-1600s a high percentage of the Virginia population was composed of male indentured servants (immigrants who signed a contract to work for a specific length of time) or former servants. (See "Servants and Slaves in Virginia.") Most of them had no families—male servants outnumbered female servants by four or six to one—so they did not contribute to the social stability of the colony. In addition they led difficult lives. They were worked extremely hard by masters who were driven by the quest for wealth in a thriving tobacco industry (the death rate among servants was reportedly over forty percent). Servants' lives generally did not change for the better if they survived to gain freedom from their indenture contracts. They could rarely afford to buy farms, even though land was inexpensive, because they did not save enough money for surveyor's fees, livestock, and equipment. As a result, only six percent of ex-servants became successful planters who employed their own workers. The majority were tenant farmers (farmers who rented land), overseers (supervisors), or laborers (traveling workers). Many lived on the frontier, and they had no representation in Virginia society because they did not have the right to vote. Most lived an aimless, rootless existence, spending their time drinking and having wild parties. Colonists looked down on these people as socially inferior and a source of trouble, even danger, in the colony.

Despite these problems, the colony continued to grow (the population was 30,000 in 1670), and soon the borders of the settlement were reaching Native American territory. The rough, unruly frontier settlers did not get along with the native peoples, whom they often accused of stealing from their farms. One of the first serious conflicts occurred in 1675, when members of the Doeg tribe killed an overseer. The Virginia government responded by forming a militia (citizens' army) led by George Mason and John Brent. When the militia attacked two Native American cabins, they did not realize that Susquehannocks were inside instead of Doegs. After killing fourteen Susquehannocks, the militia continued their advance. Five Susquehannock chiefs immediately protested that recently murdered colonists had been killed by a Seneca war party, not by Susquehannocks. The Virginians refused to believe them, claiming Susquehannocks had recently been seen in the area, wearing the clothes of murdered settlers. The Virginians then executed the chiefs (put them to death). In retaliation, the Native Americans launched more attacks. To avoid an outright war, Berkeley told Virginians not to cross the borders of the colony.

This measure was completely ineffective because the boundaries of Native American territory had been lost when colonists began moving west onto native land. The fighting simply escalated, and many frontier colonists, including women and children, were killed by raiding warrior parties. At this point Berkeley tried to end the conflict by declining to launch another attack. Many Virginians protested, accusing him of trying to protect the fur trade with Native Americans. They contended that the fur trade was important to Berkeley because it ensured his support among local wealthy merchants. Berkeley himself had another motive for keeping peace with Native Americans, as he wanted to convert the native peoples to Christianity so that land could eventually be obtained in an orderly manner. The complicated situation only served to distance Berkeley even more from settlers, especially in Charles and Henrico counties. Frontiersmen in these outlying areas continued fighting to protect their property. Since they could get no leadership from Berkeley, they turned instead to Nathaniel Bacon (1647–1676).

Bacon was an unusual figure on the Virginia frontier. He was born into the English aristocracy and attended Cambridge University and Gray's Inn (a law school). After graduating he traveled throughout Europe. In 1673 he married Elizabeth Duke, daughter of Edward Duke. They traveled to Virginia and settled at Curl's Neck in Henrico County, on the James River near the border of Native American territory. Because of Bacon's connections, he quickly gained influence in the colony. His uncle was a member of the royal council, which made it easy for the younger Bacon also to gain a seat on the council. A rebel, Bacon set out to change the system as soon as he took office. He aligned himself with the common people and tried to solve their problems. He charged Berkeley with taking the side of

Native American groups against Virginia farmers in conflicts that were becoming more frequent. Bacon then organized a group of frontiersmen, with reinforcements from the Ocaneechee tribe, to go against the Susquehannocks in defiance of Berkeley. The newly formed militia immediately tracked down a group of Susquehannocks and defeated them. Berkeley was furious with Bacon and declared him a traitor (one who betrays his government).

By now Berkeley realized his government was in trouble. Therefore, in May 1676 he ordered new elections and issued a declaration. Defending his own actions as governor, he suggested several measures to resolve the crisis. The assembly met in Jamestown on June 5 to act on Berkeley's proposals, which included three important features. First, he planned to pardon Bacon and give him a commission to raise a militia against Native Americans. Second, Berkeley wanted to draft a measure that permitted Virginians to trade only with "friendly Indians." Finally, he planned to abolish the Franchise Act of 1670, thus restoring the vote to all freemen (former indentured servants who had gained their freedom), not just landowners.

The Virginia legislators approved all of these proposals. Nevertheless, Bacon was dissatisfied because they planned to draw militia members from the entire colony, whereas Bacon wanted to use men from the border territories. He felt they would be more willing to fight and had a greater stake in the conflict because they had farms in the area. Bacon also demanded that the militia be formed immediately instead of waiting for three months until taxes had been raised to fund the operation. On June 23, 1676, Bacon led four hundred armed men up the steps of the Jamestown assembly hall, effectively starting Bacon's rebellion. Immediately there was a confrontation between the legislators and the militia, and Bacon threatened violence. After forcing the assembly to exempt (free or release from liability) him and his men from arrest for causing a disturbance, Bacon and the demonstrators eventually left the assembly hall. Berkeley was humiliated because the legisla-

Colonist Nathaniel Bacon accused William Berkeley of siding with Native Americans instead of the Virginia settlers.
Reproduced by permission of Archive Photos, Inc.

ture had given in to Bacon's demands, so he declared Bacon a traitor once again. Berkeley also called up the colonial militia.

When Bacon and his men returned on July 30, they easily overcame the colonial militia and drove Berkeley out of Jamestown to his plantation on the eastern coast. This time Bacon carried with him a manifesto (statement) titled "in the Name of the People of Virginia," which accused Berkeley of committing numerous injustices. With Berkeley absent, Bacon now had control of Jamestown. The governor sneaked back into Jamestown, however, while Bacon was leading his men out into the country to attack the Pawmunkeys, another Native American tribe. On September 18 Bacon launched a final assault on Jamestown, burning the settlement to the ground. By now lawlessness reigned, and Berkeley escaped once again as looters (robbers) ransacked his plantation at Green Spring.

Bacon's Rebellion: Two opposing views

Although Bacon claimed he had unanimous support for his actions, many Virginians denounced him. Among the most vocal critics of Bacon were colonists who lived on plantations along the coast, away from the frontier regions. They accused Bacon and his men of being troublemakers who were deliberately violating the law and provoking Native Americans so they could seize more land. The planters issued their own protests to Berkeley, demanding protection from Bacon and his ruthless band of lawbreakers. The crisis threatened to shake the foundations of Virginia government, as colonists were not only trying to fend off the Native Americans but were also pitted against one another in a struggle for power.

Eyewitness accounts provide modern readers with a vivid picture of the chaotic events surrounding Bacon's Rebellion. One account is a letter that Elizabeth Bacon, wife of Nathaniel Bacon, wrote to her sister in 1676 at the height of the rebellion. In the letter Elizabeth portrayed Nathaniel as a hero who had the full support of all the colonists. A completely different view was expressed by colonist William Sherwood in a detailed narrative of the conflict, also written in 1676. Defending the actions of Berkeley, Sherwood depicted Bacon as a "perverse man" and his militia as "rabble."

Things to Remember While Reading A Letter From Elizabeth Bacon:

- Elizabeth and Nathaniel Bacon immediately settled on the frontier when they arrived in Virginia. Therefore Elizabeth had never known the comfort and security of life in Jamestown, which by 1676 had become relatively secure from Native American attacks. Frontier settlers were exposed to the daily threat of Native American raids. Frontier life was especially dangerous for colonial women and children. They were frequently left alone while men worked in the fields or traveled to distant towns to conduct business and buy supplies. Consequently large numbers of colonial women and children were killed or kidnapped by Native Americans (see *A Narrative of the Captivity and Restauration of Mrs. Mary Rowlandson*) along the American frontier.

- Problems began when settlers claimed vast tracts of unsettled land, then let their livestock graze in native pastures and cornfields. Contending colonists were violating treaties, Native Americans raided frontier farms, taking cattle and hogs and destroying crops. As the confrontation escalated, many colonists and Native Americans were killed. Neither side would relent, however, each saying they had to defend their treaty rights.

- Notice the tone of panic in Elizabeth Bacon's letter; she was clearly fearful of being killed. Note, too, that she expressed absolute support for her husband's efforts to help the frontier farmers, an expected sentiment from a loyal wife. Yet she also echoed the outrage of colonists who genuinely felt they had been betrayed by Berkeley's government. Her letter depicts the deep divisions between classes in Virginia. In spite of crops being destroyed and settlers being murdered each day, she wrote, Berkeley had done nothing. In fact, she accused Berkeley of siding with the Native Americans and warning them about Bacon's attack plans: "but the Governour were so much the Indians' friend and our enemy, that he sent the Indians word that Mr. Bacon was out against them, that they might save themselves." Bacon was also bitter toward colonists who supported Berkeley because he had given them political favors: "there was not anybody against him [Bacon] but the Governour and a few of his great men, which have got their Estates by the Governour." And she ridiculed Berkeley for sending his wife (his "Lady") to England to plead the governor's case with the king.

A Letter From Elizabeth Bacon

Dear Sister,

*I pray God keep the worst Enemy I have from ever being in such a sad condition as I have been in . . . occasioned by the troublesome Indians, who have killed one of our **Overseers** at an **outward** plantation which we had, and we have lost a great stock of cattle, which we had upon it, and a good crop that we should have made there, such plantation Nobody **durst** come **nigh**, which is a very great loss to us.*

*If you had been here, it would have grieved your heart to hear the pitiful complaints of the people, The Indians killing the people daily the [Governor, William Berkeley] not taking any notice of it for to **hinder** them, but let them daily do all the mischief they can: I am sure if the Indians were not cowards, they might have destroyed all the upper plantations, and killed all the people upon them; the Governour so much their friend, that he would not suffer anybody to hurt one of the Indians; and the poor people came to your brother [in-law] to desire him to help against the Indians, and he being very much concerned for the loss of his Overseer, and for the loss of so many men and women and children's lives every day, he was willing to do them all the good he could; so he begged of the Governour for a **commission** in several letters to him, that he might go out against them, but he would not grant one, so daily more mischief done by them, so your brother not able to endure any longer, he went out without a commission. The Governour being very angry with him put out high things against him, and told me that he would most certainly hang him as soon as he returned, which he would certainly have done; but what for fear of the Governour's hanging him, and what for fear of the Indians killing him brought me to this sad condition, but blessed be God he came in very well, with the loss of a very few men; never was known such a fight in*

Overseers: Supervisors

Outward: Distant

Durst: Dare

Nigh: Near; nearly

Hinder: Stop

Commission: Appointment that authorizes power to form a militia

A confrontation between Nathaniel Bacon (right) and Virginia governor William Berkeley at Jamestown in 1676. Bacon eventually led a rebellion against Berkeley. *Reproduced by permission of The Granger Collection Ltd.*

*Virginia with so few men's loss. The fight did continue nigh a night and a day without any **intermission.** They did destroy a great many of the Indians, thanks be to God, and might have killed a great many more, but the Governour were so much the Indians' friend and our enemy, that he sent the Indians word that Mr. Bacon was out against them, that they might save themselves. After Mr. Bacon was come in he was forced to keep a guard of soldiers about his house, for the Governour would certainly have had his life taken away privately, if he would have*

Intermission: Short breaks in activity

*had opportunity; but the country does so really love him, that they would not leave him alone anywhere; there was not anybody against him but the Governour and a few of his great men, which have got their Estates by the Governour; surely if your brother's crime had been so great, all the country would not have been for him, you never knew any better beloved than he is. I do **verily** believe that rather than he should come to any hurt by the Governour or anybody else they would most of them willingly lose their lives. The Governour has sent his Lady [wife] into England with great complaints to the King against Mr. Bacon, but when Mr. Bacon's and all the people's complaints be also heard, I hope it may be very well. Since your brother came in he hath sought to the Governour for commission, but none would be granted him, so that the Indians have had a very good time, to do more mischief. They have murdered and destroyed a great many whole families since, and the men resolving not to go under any but your brother, most of the country did rise in Arms [take up weapons], and went down to the Governour, and would not stir till he had given a commission to your brother which he has now done. He is made General of the Virginia War, and now I live in great fear, that he should lose his life amongst them. They are come very nigh our Plantation where we live.*

Verily: Truly

Things to Remember While Reading "A Narrative of Bacon's Rebellion by William Sherwood":

- Colonist William Sherwood gave a different perspective on Bacon's Rebellion. He accused Bacon and his men of being troublemakers who deliberately violated the law. Even worse, he saw Bacon as nothing more than a power-hungry tyrant who had no real interest in defending frontier farmers. In fact, Sherwood sarcastically commented that "their General Mr. Bacon" neglected his duty; once Bacon received his military commission he did not leave town as the assembly had expected. Instead, he and his men remained in Jamestown "drinking and domineering" for four days. During this time the frontier was left undefended and eight colonists were killed—some of them relatives of Bacon's own men.

- Sherwood expressed the position of "the most moderate people" (perhaps upper-class colonists) who were appalled by the unruly behavior of frontiersmen. Note that he was distressed by the actions of "Land lopers" who, in defiance of the law, took thousands of acres of land and then did nothing with it. He showed sympathy for Native Americans who were beaten and abused by uncivilized settlers, in spite of Berkeley's direct orders against such treatment. He said this was "one of the great causes of the Indians' breach of peace."

- Keep in mind that English authorities wanted to convert Native Americans to Christianity. Therefore Sherwood may have been more concerned about "the great scandal upon the Christian Religion" than by any injustices done to Native Americans. Such behavior, he wrote, "makes so few Indian converts."

"A Narrative of Bacon's Rebellion by William Sherwood"

. . .[E]very one **endeavours** to get great **tracts** of Land, and many turn Land **lopers**, some take up 2000 acres, some 3000 Acres, others ten thousand Acres, nay many men have taken up thirty thousand Acres of Land, and never cultivated any part of it, only set up a hog house to save the Laps, thereby preventing others **seating**, so that too many rather than to be **Tenants**, seat upon the remote barren Land, whereby **contentions** arise between them and the Indians, yet people are not content, but **encroach** upon them, taking up the very Towns or Land they are seated upon, turning their Cattle and hogs on them, and if by **Vermin** or otherwise any be lost, then they exclaim against the Indians, beat & abuse them (notwithstanding the Governour's endeavour to the contrary) And this by the most moderate people is looked upon, as one of the great causes of the Indians' **breach of peace,** for it is the opinion of too many there, (and especially of their General Mr. Bacon) that faith is not to be kept with **heathens,** this brings great scandal upon the Christian Religion, and makes few Indians converts. . . .

Endeavors: Attempts; strives

Tracts: Large areas of land

Lopers: Trespassers

Seating: Settling

Tenants: One who temporarily occupies property of owned by another

Contentions: Disputes; controversies

Encroach: Advance beyond proper or legal limits

Vermin: Various small destructive or obnoxious animals

Breach of peace: Breaking of a treaty

Heathens: Uncivilized or irreligious people

.... *but now Mr. Bacon having a* **Commission,** *shows himself in his colours [shows his true nature], and hangs out his flag of* **defiance** *(that is) Imprisoning several loyal Gentlemen and his* **rabble** *used* **reproachful** *words of the Governour. . . . These threatenings and* **compulsions** *being upon them, the* **Assembly** *granted whatever he demanded, so that it was imagined he & his soldiers would march out of Town, yet they continued drinking and* **domineering,** *the frontier Counties being left with very little force [military defense], and the next day came the sad news that the Indians had that morning killed Eight people within thirty Miles of town, in the families of some of them that were with Mr. Bacon, yet they hastened not away, but the next day having forced an* **Act of Indemnity,** *and the Assembly being at the Burgesses' request dissolved, Mr. Bacon after four days' stay, marched out of Town. Thus Mr. Bacon having his Commission, men, Arms &* **provision** *gave out he would go against the Indians, but that (as it now plainly appeareth) was the last of his thoughts . . .*

During Mr. Bacon's thus **Lording it,** *and seizing the estates of such as he terms* **Traitors to the Commonality** *in which & in* **revelling** *& drinking most of his forces were employed, The Indians taking advantage of these civil commotions, have committed many horrid murders, in most part of the Country, which is altogether unable to resist them, their Arms & Ammunition being seized by Mr. Bacon's rabble for fear they should be employed against him, and daily murders were committed not only in the frontier Counties, but in the* **inward** *Counties. . . .*

What happened next . . .

Bacon's Rebellion might have lasted longer if Bacon himself had not become ill and died the following October. After his death, the insurrection (rebellion) was put down by Berkeley, who executed twenty-three of Bacon's men—in spite of a royal order pardoning all participants except Bacon. Berkeley finally gave up his position as governor to Herbert Jeffreys, who appointed a commission to investigate the uprising. The commission members mostly blamed Bacon and his ability to influence the leaderless frontiersmen.

Commission: Appointment that authorizes power to form a militia

Defiance: Challenging authority

Rabble: Disorderly or disorganized crowd of people

Reproachful: Expressing blame

Compulsions: Impulses to act

Assembly: Legislature; House of Burgesses

Domineering: Overbearing

Act of Indemnity: An official act of the legislature, guaranteeing freedom from being held liable

Provision: Military supplies

Lording it: Using power irresponsibly

Traitors to the Commonality: Betrayers of the common people

Revelling: Having wild parties

Inward: Interior

Colonial America: Primary Sources

Did you know . . .

- Historians have long debated the impact of Bacon's Rebellion on colonial American life. In the nineteenth century many thought the insurrection was a bid for American independence from England, and that Bacon was nearly equal in importance to George Washington, a revered leader in the American Revolution (1775–83; a conflict in which American colonists gained independence from British rule). Other scholars point out, however, that Bacon had no clear philosophy of liberation, and he was not fighting the English. They also suggest that the rebellion was mainly personal revenge on the part of Bacon against Berkeley. Therefore, because Bacon considered his own motives a priority over the interests of the colony, he is considered less of a hero. Some historians have even linked Bacon's Rebellion to the full-scale use of slavery in America. They note that after the insurrection, plantation owners decided African slaves were easier to control than indentured servants.

For more information

"Bacon's Declaration in the Name of the People (30 July 1676)" in *Documents Relevant to the United States Before 1700*. http://www.geocities.com/Athens/Forum/9061/USA/colonial/bef1700.html Available September 30, 1999.

Bacon's Rebellion. http://www.infoplease.com/ce5/CE00404.5.html Available September 30, 1999.

Harrah, Madge. *My Brother, My Enemy*. New York: Simon & Schuster Books for Young Readers, 1997.

Kupperman, Karen Ordahl, ed. *Major Problems in American Colonial History*. Lexington, Mass.: D. C. Heath, 1993, pp. 202–05.

Middleton, Richard. *Colonial America: A History, 1585–1776*. Second Edition. Malden, Mass: Blackwell Publishers, 1996, pp. 149–54.

Webb, Stephen Saunders. *1676: The End of American Independence*. New York: Knopf, 1984.

Cotton Mather and Ezekiel Cheever

Mather-Cheever Account of the Salem Witch Trials

Reprinted in *Eyewitness to America*
Published in 1997
Edited by David Colbert

Samuel Sewall

Diary Entries of Samuel Sewall

Reprinted in *Early American Writing*
Published in 1994
Edited by Giles Gunn

During the colonial period most people had little understanding of their natural environment, so they looked to supernatural forces (spirits) for solutions to their problems. To Native Americans, Africans, and some Europeans, magic and religion were inseparable. They believed that people with special powers (called priests, shamans, and witches by various groups) could control good and evil spirits with prayer and rituals. Shamans, priests, and witches used special objects called charms—bags of herbs, magical stones, crucifixes—to ward off evil spirits. One of their rituals was fortune-telling, which involved predicting future events by "reading" a pattern of tea leaves, the shape of a raw egg dropped into a bowl, or the arrangement of special pebbles thrown onto the ground.

Shamans, priests, and witches also used their powers to ward off diseases. Before the introduction of modern medicine people dreaded sickness or accidents. It was believed illness and death came from spiritual as well as natural causes. Thus they called upon healers, or "white" (good) witches, who combined charms with medicinal roots, barks, and herbs to produce cures. But numerous other practices were equally effec-

"It was noted that in her, as in others like her, that if the afflicted went to approach her, they were flung down to the ground."

tive. If a cow was going dry (producing less and less milk), for instance, a European might pour milk over a red-hot iron poker while repeating the names of the Trinity (the Father, Son, and Holy Spirit). Freckles might be removed by washing one's face with cobwebs.

Good spirits were relied upon to favorably influence events. Priests infused the spirits of animals into young Native American warriors to protect them in battle. Africans conjured up the spirits of gods who guided them in their religious ceremonies. On the other hand, evil spirits were greatly feared. Europeans believed that a "black" witch could control the thoughts and actions of others for evil purposes. In fact, most believers in magic perceived the word *witch* as meaning an evil sorcerer (a person who uses power gained from the assistance or control of evil spirits) or sorceress.

Native Americans were strong believers in magic, and believed that their enemies used magic against them. Africans believed that the spirits of evil witches left them while they were asleep and entered the bodies of animals. The bewitched animals then fled to a meeting with other witches and consumed a human soul, thus killing the person belonging to that soul.

Europeans tended to single out a particular person, usually an old woman, who made a covenant (contract) with the Devil to torment good people. They believed that witches flew through the air to engage in sexual orgies (a sexual encounter involving many people) with the Devil. Moreover, it was thought that a witch (again usually a woman) signed a pact with the Devil in order to get revenge on a neighbor or an enemy. For example, a witch was empowered to cause the death of a child, produce crop failures, or prevent cream from being turned into butter. Witches could also enter the bodies of animals as "familiars" (demons or evil spirits believed to act as intimate servants) and prowl around undetected.

It was believed that witches could be detected. One way was to make a witch's cake from grain mixed with a substance from a bewitched victims's body, such as urine, and bake it in ashes. The cake would then be fed to a familiar, which would reveal the name of the witch who had cast the spell. Another way to identify a witch was to find out whether the suspect poked pins into a rag doll or a clay model of a victim to work her magic. People suspected of practicing witchcraft would be given the chance to confess their sins and renounce (give up) their covenant with the Devil. Only by opening themselves to God, they could rejoin the community.

The glaring exception was the witchcraft hysteria that erupted in Salem Village in the Massachusetts Colony. During the winter of 1691–92, a group of young girls met in secret to read their fortunes. Most of them worked as servants in the area, but one was Elizabeth Parris, the daughter of the local Puritan minister. (Puritans were part of a religious group that believed in strict moral and spiritual codes.) She knew that Puritans strictly forbade magic. Nevertheless she participated in the ritual, which involved dropping a raw egg white into a bowl and then "reading" the future from its shape. As the girls watched in horror, the egg white took the form of a coffin (a sign of death). Elizabeth instantly felt like someone was pinching and suffocating her, then she began to hallucinate (false or distorted perceptions of objects or events). The other girls were seized by the same sensations, and doctors were called to examine them. Finding no physical problems, the doctors suggested the symptoms had been caused by witchcraft.

In an effort to track down the witch who had cast a spell on the girls, a concerned neighbor asked the Parrises' Caribbean slave, Tituba, to bake a witch cake. But the cake did not reveal the culprit. Finally the girls confessed that they had been bewitched by Tituba and two old women in the village. By April the girls were identifying others as witches, including a former minister, and soon accusations were flying around the colony. When the hysteria finally died down, 156 suspected witches were in prison. Thus began one of the most infamous events in American history. The trials violated many proper legal procedures. For instance, the judges were not trained lawyers, and suspects were not allowed to have attorneys. The court also accepted "spectral evidence"—that is, an accuser's claim that a specter (spirit) resembling the "witch" had committed evil deeds. Since the Puritans believed such a specter could be seen only by the victim, other witnesses could not prove whether accusations were true or false.

In June 1692 Puritan leaders decided to appoint a special court to try the suspected witches. By this time witch hysteria had been sweeping Europe for more than 250 years and in New England for several decades. In 1684 Increase Mather

(1639–1723), a Puritan clergyman and well-known intellectual, had published *Remarkable Providences*. The book was a collection of "proofs of witchcraft," which Mather had found in the work of other writers. Mather and his son Cotton actively promoted the Salem witch trials. In 1689 Cotton Mather published *Memorable Providences Relating to Witchcraft and Possession*, which stirred up antiwitch mania. Four years later he wrote *Wonders of the Invisible World*, in which he defended the trials as the only way to rid the colony of the influence of the Devil.

Cotton Mather and Ezekiel Cheever, a clerk of the court, wrote an account of the Salem trials. The following excerpt shows a typical exchange, in this case between a magistrate (judge; here unnamed) and two accused witches, Susannah Martin and Mary Lacey.

Increase Mather, a leading intellectual and one of the most prolific writers of New England Puritanism was active in promoting the Salem witch trials.
Reproduced by permission of Archive Photos, Inc.

Things to Remember While Reading Mather-Cheever Account of the Salem Trials:

- Mather and Cheever supposedly provided a "report" on the Salem trials, yet Mather in particular was later faulted for fueling the witch-hunt mania. The account of the interrogation of Martin and Lacey is an example of how Mather and Cheever presented events from a biased point of view.

- Susannah Martin was a sixty-seven-year-old widow who freely spoke her mind and denied all charges against her. Note that Mather and Cheever had already concluded Martin was a witch. They saw spectral (ghostly) evidence in her behavior: "The cast of Martin's eye struck people to the ground, whether they saw that cast or not." In other words, she had put a spell on the witnesses by giving them the "evil eye." Believers in the supernatural thought a witch was capable of inflicting harm with a single glance. In the interview with the magistrate Martin engaged in extensive word play, evading his questions and leaving his statements open to interpretation. Their exchange is a good example of the Puritan belief that witches could make evil spirits invade the body of a human being. For instance, the magistrate referred to "their Master" (the Devil), "Black Art" (witchcraft), and Martin's "Appearance" (the form she took as a witch). Martin was found guilty and later hanged.

- Mather and Cheever also observed spectral evidence in Mary Lacey's actions. They wrote that she cast a spell on the maid, Mary Warren, and she "struck down with her eyes." Notice the contrast between Lacey's cooperative responses and Martin's unwillingness to admit any guilt. Lacey, who had been a witch for "Not above a week," readily confessed that she had committed all kinds of acts associated with witches—talking with the Devil (who appeared in the shape of a horse), "afflicting" other people with a spell, even riding on a stick or pole "above the trees." For her cooperation Lacey was found not guilty and spared from execution.

Mather-Cheever Account of the Salem Trials

Martin pleaded Not Guilty to the **indictment** *of witchcraft brought in against her.*

The evidence of many persons very sensibly and grievously bewitched was produced. They all complained of the prisoner as the person whom they believed at the cause of their miseries. And now, as well as in the other trials, there was an extraordinary **endeavor** *by witchcraft, with cruel and frequent fits, to* **hinder** *the poor sufferers from giving their complaints. The cast of Martin's eye struck people to the ground, whether they saw that cast or not.*

These were among the passages between the **Magistrates** *and the Accused:*

MAGISTRATE: "Pray, what ails these people?"

MARTIN: "I don't know."

MAGISTRATE: "But what do you think **ails** *them?"*

MARTIN: "I don't desire to spend my judgement upon it.

Indictment: Charge with a crime

Endeavor: Attempt; strive

Hinder: To obstruct or delay

Magistrates: An official entrusted with the administration of the laws

Ails: Feel ill

MAGISTRATE: "Don't you think they are bewitched?"

MARTIN: "No, I do not think they are."

MAGISTRATE: "Tell us your thoughts about them then."

MARTIN: "No, my thoughts are my own, when they are in; but when they are out they are another's. Their Master—"

MAGISTRATE: "Their Master? Who do you think is their Master?"

MARTIN: "If they be dealing in the Black Art, then you may know as well as I."

MAGISTRATE: "Well, what have you done towards this?"

MARTIN: "Nothing at all."

MAGISTRATE: "Why, 'tis you or your Appearance."

MARTIN: "I cannot help it."

MAGISTRATE: "Is it not your Master? How comes your Appearance to hurt these?

MARTIN: "How do I know? He that appeared in the shape of Samuel, a glorified Saint, may appear in anyone's shape."

It was noted that in her, as in others like her, that if the **afflicted** went to approach her, they were flung down to the ground. And, when she was asked the reason of it, she said, "I cannot tell. It may be the Devil bears me more **malice** than another."

. . . Mary Lacey was brought in, and Mary Warren [went] in a violent fit.

MAGISTRATE: "You are here accused for practising witchcraft upon Goo Ballard; which way do you do it?"

LACEY: "I cannot tell. Where is my mother that made me a witch, and I knew it not?"

MAGISTRATE: "Can you look upon that maid, Mary Warren, and not hurt her? Look upon her in a friendly way."

She trying so to do, struck her down with her eyes.

MAGISTRATE: "Do you acknowledge now you are a witch?"

LACEY: "Yes."

MAGISTRATE: "How long have you been a witch?"

LACEY: "Not above a week."

MAGISTRATE: "Did the Devil appear to you?"

LACEY: "Yes."

Afflict: To distress so severely as to cause persistent suffering or anguish

Malice: Desire to cause pain, injury, or distress to another

Colonial America: Primary Sources

"A Brand Pluck'd out of the Burning"

In 1692 Puritan minister Cotton Mather (1663–1728) wrote an essay titled "A Brand Pluck'd out of the Burning," in which he described the possession of a young woman named Mercy Short. After taking her into his home Mather observed one of her fits and conversations with evil spirits:

> Reader, If thou hadst a Desire to have seen a Picture of Hell, it was visible in the doleful [sad] Circumstances of Mercy Short! Here was one lying in Outer Darkness, haunted by the Divel [Devil] and his Angels, deprived of all common Comforts, tortured with most cruciating [excruciating; extremely painful] Fires. Wounded with a thousand Pains all over, and cured immediately, that the Pains of those Wounds might bee repeated.
>
> Her Discourses [conversations] to Them [evil spirits] were some of the most Surprising Things imaginable, and incredibly beyond what might have been expected, from one of her small Education or Experience. In the Times of her Tortures, Little came from her, besides direful [desperate] Shrieks, which were indeed so frightful, as to make many people Quitt [leave] the Room. Only now and then any Expressions of marvellous Constancy [steadiness] would bee heard from her; [for instance] "Tho' you kill mee, I'll never do what you would have mee.—Do what you will, yett with the Help of Christ, I'l never touch your Book.—Do, Burn mee then, if you will; Better Burn here, then [than] Burn in

Cotton Mather was a prominent participant in the Salem witch trials.

Hell." But when her Torturer went off, Then t'was that her senses being still detained in a Captivity to the Spectres [spirits], as the only object of them. Wee were Ear-witnesses to Disputacions [disputations; arguments] that amazed us. Indeed Wee could not hear what They said unto her; nor could shee herself hear them ordinarily without causing them to say over again: But Wee could Hear Her Answers, and from her Answers Wee could usually gather the Tenour [tenor; meaning] of Their Assaults.

Reprinted in: Burr, George Lincoln, ed. Narratives of the Witchcraft Cases 1648–1706. *New York: Barnes & Noble, 1946.*

MAGISTRATE: "In what shape?"

LACEY: "In the shape of a horse."

MAGISTRATE: "What did he say to you?"

LACEY: *"He bid me not to be afraid of any thing, and he would bring me out; but he has proved a liar from the beginning."*

MAGISTRATE: *"Did he bid you worship him?"*

LACEY: *"Yes, he bid me also to afflict persons."*

MAGISTRATE: *"Who did the Devil bid you afflict?"*

LACEY: *"Timothy Swan. Richard Carrier comes often a-nights and has me to afflict persons."*

MAGISTRATE: *"Did you at any time ride upon a stick or pole?"*

LACEY: *"Yes."*

MAGISTRATE: *"How high?"*

LACEY: *"Sometimes above the trees."*

Another participant in the Salem trials was Samuel Sewall (1652–1730), a prominent Boston businessman and judge, who was appointed to the panel of magistrates. He is best known today for his remarkable diary, which provides a vivid account of life in colonial New England, including the Salem trials. In the following entries from the diary, dated August and September 1692, Sewall commented on the executions of several people.

Things to Remember While Reading Diary Entries of Samuel Sewall:

- Keep in mind that the witch trials were conducted by the elite Puritan ruling class, who were convinced that they were following the will of God. Sewall was a member of that group, as were Mather and Cheever, whom he mentioned in his diary. In fact, Mather and others met at Sewall's home to discuss "publishing some Trials of the Witches." Sewall's diary gives insight into the Puritans' actions—and perhaps their desperation—during the trials. For instance, on August 25 they held a fast (a day of going without food) to seek God's help in ending a drought (a

An accused witch being led to execution. *Painting by Thomas Satterwhite Noble. Reproduced by permission of AP/Wide World Photos.*

prolonged period without rainfall) and other adverse events, which they possibly associated with witchcraft.

- The Puritans were determined to obtain confessions from suspected witches, but they were also anxious to justify their decisions. For instance, interrogators piled stones on Giles Corey for two days until he died because he would not admit to the charges against him. Sewall apparently needed to defend this act because he noted that Corey himself had crushed someone to death eighteen years earlier. As proof against Corey he cites the report that Corey's "spectre" (spirit) appeared to Anne Putnam the night before the execution and told her he had killed the man. Sewall took comfort in Mather's view that "they [several convicted witches] all died by a righteous sentence." Sewall noted that some people thought Mr. Burrough (one of the executed men) was innocent, but he dismissed them as merely "unthinking persons." In the brief but dramatic description of the reprieve (postponement of punishment) of Dorcas Hoar, Sewall indicated that the Puritans would call off an execution if a person confessed. Note, too, that Sewall mentioned Richard Carrier, whom Mary Lacey (in the Mather-Cheever document above) singled out as one who told her to "afflict persons."

Diary Entries of Samuel Sewall

*April 11, 1692. Went to Salem, where, in the meeting-house, the persons accused of witchcraft were examined; was a very great assembly; 'twas awful to see how the **afflicted** persons were agitated. Mr. Noyes pray'd at the beginning, and Mr. Higginson concluded.*

*August 19, 1692. This day George Burrough, John Willard, John Proctor, Martha Carrier and George Jacobs were **executed** at Salem, a very great number of spectators being present. Mr. Cotton Mather was there, Mr. Sims, Hale, Noyes, Chiever, &c. All of them said they were innocent, Carrier and all. Mr. Mather says they all died by a righteous sentence. Mr. Burrough by his speech, prayer, **protestation** of his innocence, did much move unthinking persons, which occasions their speaking hardly concerning his being executed.*

*August 25. **Fast** at the old [First] Church, respecting the witchcraft, **drought**, &c.*

Monday, September 19, 1692. About noon, at Salem, Giles Corey was press'd to death for standing mute; much pains was used with him two days, one after another, by the Court and Capt. Gardner of Nantucket who had been of his acquaintance: but all in vain.

Afflicted: To distress so severely as to cause persistent suffering or anguish

Executed: To put to death in compliance with a legal sentence

Protestation: A solemn declaration

Fast: Going without eating food

Drought: A long period with no rain

Colonial America: Primary Sources

"the blame and shame of it"

Samuel Sewall regretted his participation as a judge in the Salem witch trials of 1692–93. On January 14, 1697—a special day of atonement set aside by the Massachusetts legislature—Sewall stood and faced the congregation in the Old South Church at Boston. The Reverend Samuel Willard then read aloud this statement Sewall had written:

> *Samuel Sewall, sensible of the reiterated [repeated] strokes of God upon himself and his family; and being sensible, that as to the guilt contracted, upon the opening of the late Commission of Oyer and Terminator [the court that conducted the witchcraft trials] at Salem (to which the order for this day relates), he is, upon many accounts, more concerned than any* *that he knows of, desires to take the blame and shame of it, asking pardon of men, and especially desiring prayers that God, who has an unlimited authority, would pardon that sin and all his other sins; personal and relative: And according to his infinite benignity [kindness], and sovereignty [supreme power], not visit the sin of him, or of any other, upon himself or any of his, nor upon the land: But that He [God] would powerfully defend him against all temptations to sin, for the future; and vouchsafe [to grant as a special favor] him the efficacious [having the power to produce a desired effect], saving conduct of his word and spirit.*

Reprinted in: Gunn, Giles, ed. Early American Writing. New York: Penguin Books, 1994, pp. 246–47.

---

*September 20. Now I hear from Salem that about 18 years ago, he [Giles Corey] was suspected to have stamp'd and press'd a man to death, but was cleared. 'Twas not remembered till Anne Putnam was told of it by said Corey's **spectre** the sabbath-day night before execution.*

*September 21. A petition is sent to town in behalf of Dorcas Hoar, who now confesses: accordingly an order is sent to the sheriff to **forbear** her execution, notwithstanding her being in the **warrant** to die tomorrow. This is the first condemned person who has confess'd.*

*Thursday, September 22, 1692. William Stoughton, **Esqr.**, John Hathorne, Esqr., Mr. Cotton Mather, and Capt. John Higginson, with my Brother . . . were at our house, speaking about publishing some Trials of the Witches.*

Spectre: Spirit; ghost

Forbear: To hold back or abstain

Warrant: Judicial order

Esqr.: Esquire; used as a title of courtesy

What happened next . . .

The Salem witch trials resulted in hundreds of accusations, more than one hundred guilty verdicts, and the executions of twenty persons, mostly women. Nineteen people were hanged for refusing to give confessions, four died in prison, and as Sewall noted, one man was crushed to death with stones during questioning. Within a year Puritan ministers were expressing grave doubts about the trials. Foremost among them was Increase Mather, who wrote *Cases of Conscience Concerning Evil Spirits* (1693), in which he attacked the use of spectral evidence. Cotton Mather also changed his mind, eventually supporting his father's view that the witch hunts had been unjustified. By 1697 Massachusetts officials concluded that the trials had been a terrible mistake. The governor pardoned all condemned prisoners, and the legislature designated January 14 as a special day of atonement (expression of regret and request for forgiveness). Sewall, too, had begun to regret the role he played in the tragedy, and he wrote an admission of error and guilt. On January 14 he stood in front of the congregation in the Old South Church at Boston as the Reverend Samuel Willard read the statement aloud.

Did you know . . .

- Historians suggest that the Salem witch hysteria was unleashed because the Puritans were afraid their way of life was coming to an end. In the late 1680s the Massachusetts Bay Colony lost its charter (a grant or guarantee of rights, franchises, or privileges from the sovereign power of a state or country), which had allowed the Puritans to wield absolute power through self-government. The new charter of 1691 brought the colony under the control of the English Crown (royal government). It required Puritans to share votes and public offices with Anglicans (members of the Church of England). Since Puritans genuinely believed that good and evil spirits fought for human souls, they thought witches were moving among them and causing evil events such as loss of the charter.

- Scholars have analyzed the Salem community for patterns of witchcraft accusations. They found that the majority of accusers came from rural Salem Village, and a third of the accusations originated from members of the Putnam family. Suspected witches were generally prosperous older women who were unmarried and childless and lived in Salem Town, the commercial center of the area. Many of the young girls who made accusations had lost a parent in Native American raids and worked as servants around Salem.

- Sewall mentioned the names of many men who were executed. Among them was John Proctor, who is a main character in *The Crucible*, a drama about the Salem witch trials by modern playwright Arthur Miller (1915–). Miller based other characters on actual people involved in the trials, including Tituba and Elizabeth Parris.

- Superstitions about evil spirits did not disappear in the American colonies after the miscarriage of justice at Salem. Accusations of witchcraft continued to surface until the early eighteenth century.

- Astrology was the most popular method of predicting the future among Europeans in the American colonies. Astrology is based on the belief that the Earth is a microcosm (miniature replica) of the heavens and that the motions of the stars affect all aspects of human life. Individual horoscopes were cast to determine the ideal time to get married, plant crops, embark on sea voyages, conceive children, or administer medical cures. Christian mystics (believers in the supernatural), who considered humans to be part of the spiritual world, used astrology as part of their religious systems. One of these groups was the Rosicrucians, a hermit community led by Johannes Kelpius, who migrated from Germany in 1694. They occupied caves along the Wissahickon Creek outside of Philadelphia, Pennsylvania, and regularly relied on astrology to order their lives.

For more information

Colbert, David, ed. *Eyewitness to America.* New York: Pantheon Books, 1997, pp. 39–41.

Demos, John P. *Entertaining Satan: Witchcraft and the Culture of Early New England.* New York: Oxford University Press, 1982.

Gunn, Giles, ed. *Early American Writing.* New York: Penguin Books, 1994, pp. 246–47.

Kent, Deborah. *Salem Massachusetts*. New York: Dillon Press, 1996.

Kupperman, Karen Ordahl, ed. *Major Problems in American Colonial History*. Lexington, Mass.: D. C. Heath, 1993, pp. 169–74.

Rice, Earle. *The Salem Witch Trials*. San Diego, Calif.: Lucent Books, 1997.

Salem Witchcraft Hysteria. http://www.nationalgeographic.com/features/97/salem/ Available September 30, 1999.

Susanna North Martin. http://www.rootsweb.com/~nwg/sm.html Available September 30, 1999.

A Brief Narrative of the Case and Tryal of John Peter Zenger

Reprinted in *Eyewitness to America*
Published in 1997
Edited by David Colbert

Freedom of the press is the liberty to publish information, regardless of content, without the approval or control of government agencies. It is considered one of the most important rights in a democratic society. During the colonial period, however, there was no freedom of the press. Throughout Europe publication of information was tightly monitored in order to suppress public criticism of religious leaders and monarchs (heads of kingdoms or empires). According to English law, which was also the law of the American colonies, criticism of the government in any form was considered to be a crime called seditious libel (inciting rebellion against government through unjust or untrue statements). Even if the information was deemed to be true, it could be found libelous. Judges usually decided whether or not printed material was seditious.

Freedom of the press was not a new concept in the seventeenth and eighteenth centuries. The issue came to light soon after the invention of the printing press in the late 1400s. Official censorship of published materials began in 1501 when Pope Alexander VI (1431–1503; the pope is the head of the Roman Catholic Church) required printers to submit all their

". . . .Men who injure and oppress the people under their administration provoke them to cry out and complain; and then make that very complaint the foundation for new oppressions and prosecutions."

work to the church for approval before publication. The pope took this step in order to prevent heresy (violation of church law), which was punishable by fine and excommunication (banishment from the church).

In England the struggle for freedom of the press began in the early 1500s when unauthorized publications offended the monarchy. In 1534 a royal proclamation (order issued by the king) declared that all printed materials had to be licensed before being published. During the 1660s prominent English intellectuals such as the poet John Milton (1608–1674) and the philosopher John Locke (1632–1704) argued for greater freedom of the press. Although censorship (examining printed materials) laws were abolished in 1695, tight restrictions on the press were continued through seditious libel laws.

In the early 1700s English critics John Trenchard and Thomas Gordon attacked the seditious libel laws and defended freedom of speech in a series of publications called *Cato's Letters.* An avid reader of *Cato's Letters* in the American colonies was James Alexander (1691–1756), the attorney general for New Jersey and New York (until 1738 these colonies shared the same government). Alexander was a political rival of William Cosby, the royal governor of New York. (A royal governor was appointed by the king of England.) In 1733 Alexander was joined by a group of lawyers, merchants, and other citizens to publish the *New-York Weekly Journal.* They intended the newspaper to be a political forum for colonists who opposed Cosby's administration. Alexander and his friends claimed that, in 1733, the governor had misused his power by dismissing Lewis Morris (1671–1746) as chief justice (principal judge of the colonial court) and replacing him with James De Lancey (1703–1760), a long-time Cosby ally.

The backers of the *Journal* hired German-born printer John Peter Zenger (1697–1746) to be the publisher of the newspaper. The first issue appeared on November 5, 1733. Since Zenger had not fully mastered the English language, he did not contribute any major articles. Most of the pieces, which accused Cosby of governing without the will of the people, were written by Alexander. Yet Zenger was responsible for every word that was printed because he was the publisher.

After the *Journal* had been running for nearly a year, the New York council, the group of men appointed to assist the royal governor in ruling the colony, decided to punish Zenger. They ordered the burning of four especially offensive issues of the newspaper and arrested Zenger. Showing a clear prejudice against the printer, the government set his bail (payment for freedom from imprisonment before a trial) at four hundred pounds (a sum of British money), plus two hundred pounds in bail insurance (money put aside in case bail money could not be raised). He could not raise the funds, so he remained in jail. For several days he was held in isolation, then he spent almost ten months behind bars. During this time Anna Zenger published the newspaper each week by smuggling her husband's instructions out of the jail.

As publisher of the *New-York Weekly Journal* John Peter Zenger (standing in the witness box) was responsible for the allegedly libelous statements printed in the paper. *Reproduced by permission of the Corbis Corporation (Bellevue).*

Alexander and his colleague William Smith volunteered to represent Zenger in court. Zenger was put on trial for criminal libel in April 1735. Alexander and Smith immediately challenged the appointment of De Lancey, who was obviously loyal to Cosby, as the judge in the trial. The Cosby administration then disbarred (expelled from the legal profession) Alexander and Smith and delayed the case until the following August. Cosby also removed Alexander from his position on the governor's council. At that point Alexander and Smith turned to Andrew Hamilton (1676–1741), speaker of the Pennsylvania Assembly and the most prominent lawyer in the American colonies. When the trial resumed in August, Hamilton created a stir in the courtroom because no one knew he would be representing Zenger—he had been preparing for the trial in secret. Presenting the case for the New York government was Richard Bradley, the attorney general (chief legal officer). De Lancey was still the presiding judge.

Things to Remember While Reading
A Brief Narrative of the Case and Tryal of John Peter Zenger:

- The following excerpts from *A Brief Narrative of the Case and Tryal of John Peter Zenger* present the major arguments in the trial. The speakers are New York attorney general Richard Bradley, who argued the government's case against Zenger. Andrew Hamilton presented Zenger's defense, and James De Lancey (Mr. Chief Justice) was the judge.

A Brief Narrative of the Case and Tryal of John Peter Zenger

In opening arguments Bradley presented the government's case, saying that Zenger was guilty of making false or injurious statements about Cosby and his administration. According to Bradley, Hamilton admitted that Zenger had published statements that fit the definition of libel. In fact, he said, "if such papers are not libels,. . . there can be no such thing as libel." Hamilton responded to Bradley by claiming that although Zenger had indeed published statements that were offensive to Cosby, he had simply printed the truth. Hamilton also pointed out that Bradley had not accused Zenger of printing any false statements.

*ATTORNEY GENERAL BRADLEY: . . . The case before the Court is, whether Mr. Zenger is guilty of **libelling** his Excellency the Governor of New-York, and indeed the whole Administration of the Government. Mr. Hamilton has confessed the printing and publishing, and I think nothing is plainer, than that the words in the information [newspapers; evidence against Zenger] are scandalous, and tend to **sedition**, and to **disquiet** the minds of the people of this **province**. And if such papers are not libels, I think it may be said, there can be no such thing as a libel.*

*MR. HAMILTON: May it please your Honour [Chief Justice]; I cannot agree with Mr. Attorney. For tho' I freely acknowledge, that there are such things as libels, yet I must insist at the same time, that what my client is charged with, is not a libel; and I observed just now, that Mr. Attorney in defining a libel, made use of the words scandalous, **seditious**, and tend to disquiet the people; but . . . he omitted the word "false.". . .*

De Lancey then stepped in, telling Hamilton that libel is never justified, whether it is true or not. But Hamilton would not give up.

Libelling: To make statements that are published without just cause and tend to expose another to public contempt

Sedition: Incitement of resistance against lawful authority

Disquiet: Disturb

Province: Colony

Seditious: Disposed to arouse or take part in resisting lawful authority

MR. CHIEF JUSTICE: You cannot be admitted, Mr. Hamilton, to give the truth of a libel in evidence. A libel is not to be justified; for it is nevertheless a libel that it is true.

MR. HAMILTON: I am sorry the Court has so soon resolved upon that piece of law; I expected first to have been heard to that point. I have not in all my reading met with an authority that says, we cannot be admitted to give the truth in evidence. . . .

MR. CHIEF JUSTICE: The law is clear, That you cannot justify a libel. . . .

Finally Hamilton ignored De Lancey and turned to the jury. In a dramatic speech he told the jurors that the law required them, not the judge, to decide the case. He reminded them that as residents of the court jurisdiction ("neighbour-hood") where the alleged crime took place, they had the best knowledge of the facts. He went on to say he had no fear that they would decide against his client because they were "honest and lawful men." Hamilton freely admitted that Zenger

Alexander Hamilton (standing far right) during his defense of John Peter Zenger. Hamilton won the case and established freedom of the press in the colonies. *Reproduced by permission of The Library of Congress.*

had printed libelous statements, but he knew the jurors would agree that truth was the real issue. Hamilton warned the jurors not to let the trial become a "Star-Chamber" (a secret court that violates the rights of an innocent person). The accusation of libel, he said, is a way for men in power to silence. He concluded by appealing to the jury to take a stand against oppression and defend the right to speak and write the truth.

MR. HAMILTON: I thank your Honour. Then, gentlemen of the jury, it is to you we must now appeal, . . . [you have been chosen from] the neighborhood where the fact [supposed libel] is alleged to be committed; and the reason of your being taken out of the neighborhood is, because you are supposed to have the best knowledge of the fact that is to be tried. And were you to find a **verdict** *against my client, you must take upon you to say, the papers referred to in the information, and which we acknowledge we printed and published, are false, scandalous, and seditious; but of this I can have no* **apprehension.** *You are citizens of New-York; you are really what the law supposes you to be, honest and lawful men; and, according to my* **brief,** *the facts which we offer to prove were not committed in a corner; they are notoriously known to be true; and therefore in your justice lies our safety. And as we are denied the liberty of giving evidence, to prove the truth of what we have published, I will beg leave to lay it down as a standing rule in such cases, that the suppressing of evidence ought always to be taken for the strongest evidence; and I hope it will have that weight with you. . . .*

It is true in times past it was a crime to speak truth, and in that terrible **Court of Star-Chamber,** *many worthy and brave men suffered for so doing; and yet even in that court, and in those bad times, a great and good man dared to say, what I hope will not be taken* **amiss** *of me to say in this place, to wit, the practice of informations for libels is a sword in the hands of a wicked King, and an* **arrant** *coward to cut down and destroy the innocent; the one cannot, because of his* **high station,** *and the other dares not, because of his want of courage, revenge himself in another manner.*

ATTORNEY GENERAL BRADLEY: Pray Mr. Hamilton, have a care what you say, don't go too far neither, I don't like those liberties.

MR. HAMILTON: I hope to be pardon'd, Sir, for my **zeal** *upon this occasion: It is an old and wise caution, that when our neighbour's house is on fire, we ought to take care of our own. For tho', blessed be God, I live in a government where liberty is well understood, and freely enjoy'd; yet experience has shown us all (I'm sure it has to me) that a bad* **precedent** *in one government, is soon set up for an authority in another; and*

Verdict: The decision reached by a jury at the conclusion of a trail

Apprehension: Fear

Brief: A concise statement of a client's case made out for the instruction of Counsel in a trial at law

Court of Star-Chamber: A court set up by English kings to punish political opponents (1400s–1641); a term for unfair judicial proceedings

Amiss: Misunderstood

Arrant: Extreme

High station: Upperclass; high social position

Zeal: Enthusiastic

Precedent: An act or instance that can be used as an example in dealing with similar situations

therefore I cannot but think it mine, and every honest man's duty, that (while we pay all due obedience to men in authority) we ought at the same time to be upon our guard against power, wherever we apprehend that it may affect ourselves or our fellow-subjects. . . .

*. . . . Men who injure and **oppress** the people under their administration provoke them to cry out and complain; and then make that very complaint the foundation for new oppressions and prosecutions. I wish I could say there were no instances of this kind. But to conclude; the question before the court and you, gentlemen of the jury, is not of small nor private concern, it is not the cause of a poor printer, nor of New-York alone, which you are now trying; No! It may in its consequence, affect every freeman that lives under a British government on the main [continent] of America. It is the best cause. It is the cause of liberty; and I make no doubt but your upright conduct, this day, will not only entitle you to the love and esteem of your fellow-citizens; but every man, who prefers freedom to a life of slavery, will bless and honour you, as men who have baffled the attempt of **tyranny**; and by an impartial and uncorrupt verdict, have laid a noble foundation for securing to ourselves, our **posterity**, and our neighbours, that to which nature and the laws of our country have given us a right—the liberty—both of exposing and opposing **arbitrary** power (in these parts of the world, at least) by speaking and writing truth. . . .*

When the time came to reach a verdict, De Lancey instructed the jury to ignore Hamilton's argument because it was not based on the law. In fact, he said he ("the court") was better qualified than the jurors to decide "a matter of law." Ignoring De Lancey's instructions, the jury determined that Zenger's articles were based on fact and declared him not guilty.

MR. CHIEF JUSTICE: Gentlemen of the jury. The great pains Mr. Hamilton has taken, to show how little regard juries are to pay to the opinion of the judges; and his insisting so much upon the conduct of some judges in trials of this kind; is done, no doubt, with a design that you should take but very little notice of what I may say upon this occasion. I shall therefore only observe to you that, as the facts or words in the information are confessed: the only thing that can come in question before you is, whether the words, as set forth in the information, make a libel. And that is a matter of law, no doubt, and which you may leave to the court. . . .

The Jury withdrew, and in a small time returned, and being asked by the clerk, whether they were agreed of their verdict, and whether

Oppress: Persecute in an unjust manner

Tyranny: Oppressive power

Posterity: All future generations

Arbitrary: Depending on individual discretion and not fixed by law

Foreman: The spokesman for a jury

Huzzas: Expressions or shouts of acclaim often used to express joy

*John Peter Zenger was guilty of printing and publishing libels in the information mentioned? They answered by Thomas Bunt, their **Foreman**, Not Guilty. Upon which there were three **Huzzas** in the hall which was crowded with people, and the next day I was discharged from my imprisonment.*

What happened next . . .

The Zenger trial verdict established truth as a defense against libel charges. It is considered the first significant victory for freedom of the press in America. The following year Hamilton wrote an account of the trial, which was published as *A Brief Narrative of the Case and Tryal of John Peter Zenger* (1736). His report was later issued in several editions and generated considerable interest in the American colonies and in Britain. In 1737 Zenger was appointed public printer for New York, and the next year he was awarded the same position in New Jersey. Although he had risen in his profession, he and his family continued to live in near poverty. Zenger died in 1746, leaving behind a wife and six children. Anna Zenger published the *Journal* until December 1748. John Zenger, one of the printer's sons from an earlier marriage, then managed the newspaper until it ceased publication in 1751.

Did you know . . .

- After Zenger was arrested, court officials refused to carry out the Council's order to burn the four "libelous" issues of the *New-York Journal*. Finally the sheriff's African slave set fire to the newspapers.

- The Zenger trial had a far-reaching impact on opposition to English control of the American colonies. Historians note that although the case did not change the law, it influenced the writing of the United States Constitution (1787). In 1789 the framers (composers) added ten amendments (changes or additions), called the Bill of Rights, that would guarantee individual liberties under the Federal government. Freedom of the press is one of the rights protected by the First Amendment, which states: "Congress shall make no law respecting an establishment of religion, or prohibiting the free exercise thereof; or abridging the freedom of speech or of the press; or the right of people peaceably to assemble; and to petition the government for redress [corrections] of grievances [problems]."

- At one point in the trial Hamilton warned the jurors not to let De Lancey turn the hearings into a "Court of Star-Chamber." Set up by English kings in the 1400s to punish political enemies, the Court of Star-Chamber was abolished in 1641. "Star chamber" then became a term for unfair judicial proceedings. An example of a star chamber was the Salem witch trials (see Mather-Cheever Account of the Salem Witch Trials). In the Salem trials the accused "witches" were not allowed to have attorneys and there was no jury. The panel of judges permitted the use of spectral evidence ("proofs" of evil spirits), which had no legal basis. The Salem judges had absolute power. They brought charges, called witnesses, heard testimony, determined guilt, ordered sentences, and carried out the executions of nineteen innocent people.

For more information

Colbert, David. *Eyewitness to America.* New York: Pantheon Books, 1997, pp. 41–44.

Krensky, Stephen. *The Printer's Apprentice.* New York: Bantam Doubleday Dell Books for Young Readers, 1996.

Putnam, William Lowell. *John Peter Zenger and the Fundamental Freedom.* Jefferson, N.C.: McFarland and Co., 1997.

Robert Beverley

"Servants and Slaves in Virginia," an excerpt from **The History and Present State of Virginia**

Reprinted in *Major Problems in American Colonial History*
Published in 1993
Edited by Karen Ordahl Kupperman

One of the first colonies to experience a widespread need for workers was Virginia. By 1612, after five years of extreme hardship, the Jamestown settlers realized they could not get rich from gold and silver (see "The Founding of Jamestown"). They realized that if they wanted to remain in North America they would have to rely on local natural resources (materials supplied by nature, such as minerals and plant life). They also had to turn a profit for the Virginia Company, a group of private investors who financed the venture.

In order to meet these goals they needed to grow products that could be traded for English-made goods. The early colonists therefore began searching for a staple (main) crop they could produce with their own labor and use as the basis of their economy. In 1614 John Rolfe (1585–1622), one of the original Jamestown settlers, experimented with a West Indian type of tobacco and found that he could grow a crop of high enough quality to fetch good prices in England. (Tobacco is a broad-leaf plant that is grown in warm climates. In the seventeenth century it was harvested, dried, and shredded primarily for smoking in pipes. Native Americans had long been using

> "I can't forbear affirming, that the work of their Servants, and Slaves, is no other than what every common Freeman do's."

John Rolfe cultivating
tobacco in Jamestown. Rolfe
was largely responsible for
the development of
Virginia's tobacco industry,
which eventually led to the
wide-spread use of slavery.
*Reproduced by permission of
Corbis-Bettmann.*

tobacco in this manner.) Tobacco was in great demand in Europe, and within a few years Virginia was in the midst of a tobacco boom that soon expanded into neighboring Maryland.

The flourishing economy caused another problem: a severe labor shortage. Workers were needed to plant, harvest, and process the tobacco grown on huge plantations in Virginia and Maryland. Soon a similar need for workers existed in the rich farmlands of Pennsylvania and in developing industries in

New England and the mid-Atlantic colonies (New York, New Jersey, Pennsylvania, and Delaware). Taking advantage of a crisis caused by low wages and overpopulation in England, employers used various strategies to encourage immigrants (people who settle in a foreign country) to take jobs in the colonies. Laborers came by the thousands to work for farmers, planters, bakers, blacksmiths, bricklayers, butchers, chair makers, coopers, masons, plasterers, potters, tailors, weavers, and wheelwrights (people who build and repair wheels).

By the early 1700s laborers comprised the majority of new arrivals in America, and most of them were indentured servants (immigrants who signed a contract to work for a certain length of time; also called bound laborers). For instance, three-quarters of English arrivals in the Chesapeake region (Virginia and Maryland, which border the Chesapeake Bay) came as bound laborers. According to some estimates, one-half to two-thirds of all Europeans who traveled to the colonies were committed to some form of labor contract. As many as fifty thousand convicts served out sentences of seven to fourteen years as indentured servants.

Until the early 1700s most indentured servants were English men and women, who signed a contract to work for an employer for four to seven years. Pennsylvania farmers and Maryland and Virginia plantation owners relied on indentured servants to plant and harvest their crops. Historians suggest the indenture system may have been created specifically to fill labor needs in America, since there was no similar arrangement in England. Indentured servitude may have been a combination of the traditional English practices of apprenticeship (learning a trade while working without pay for a master craftsman) and short-term agricultural employment. The indenture system was advantageous to both the laborer and the employer (also called the master). During the contract period the servant received several benefits, including free passage to America, shelter, food, clothing, and no hard labor on Sunday. Upon completion of a contract, the servant was typically given a suit of clothing or a dress, a few barrels of corn, and as much as sixty acres of land. Many were also awarded extra items called "freedom dues," which were determined according to gender. A man might receive a horse, a gun, or tools, and a woman would be given a cow or a spinning wheel.

In return the employer not only was assured a work force but he could also increase his land holdings. For each servant he brought to the colony he was granted a tract (wide area) of land, which was known as a headright. Perhaps most important for the employer, an indentured servant was an affordable investment. Tobacco planters, for example, needed a large number of workers to increase production on their plantations. One possible source of labor was African slaves, who had been imported from the Caribbean since 1619, but they were too expensive (a slave could cost three times as much as an indentured servant). Planters at first tried to use Native Americans as workers, but the experiment ended in disaster. Native Americans either resisted forced labor or they died of European diseases while in captivity.

Indentured servitude was attractive to immigrants because they had a chance to improve their lives in America. But the road to success was not easy, and they encountered many difficulties. Servants could be subjected to harsh conditions and physical abuse. Tobacco planters were mainly concerned with making a profit, so they required both men and women servants to work long hours at exhausting tasks. Since a master had the right to sell a contract, a servant could be obligated to a different master for the rest of the term. An employer could also extend a contract if a servant ran away or became pregnant. In spite of strict laws, servants were frequently beaten, given an inadequate diet, and provided virtually no medical care. High death rates in some areas meant that many indentured servants—forty percent in Maryland and Virginia—died before they could complete their contracts.

During the height of the tobacco boom, in the 1650s, nearly fifty percent of freed servants started farms on the rapidly expanding Virginia frontier. Some took as long as twelve years to become independent farmers, but they managed to realize their dreams of a better life in the New World (European term for North America and South America) Many also achieved a higher social status because they joined a small group of landowners who had the right to vote and exercise other privileges of citizenship. Nevertheless an equal number of freed servants could not afford to start farms or improve their social condition. Unable to save money during servitude, they could not pay surveyors' fees, register their land, and buy

"I have nothing to Comfort me"

In 1623 Richard Frethorne, an indentured servant in Virginia, wrote a letter to his parents in England about his miserable experience. The following excerpt details his lack of proper food and clothing. (The Virginia legislature later passed law requiring masters to furnish servants adequate food, clothing, shelter, medical care, and other protections.)

. . . . I have nothing to Comfort me, nor is there nothing to be gotten here but sickness, and death, except that one had money to lay out in some things for profit; But I have nothing at all, no not a shirt to my backe, but two Rags nor no Clothes, but one poor suit, nor but one pair of shoes, but one pair of stockings, but one Cap, but two [collar] bands, my Cloak is stolen by one of my own fellows. . . . I am not half a quarter so strong as I was in England, and all is for want of victuals [food], for I do protest unto you, that I have eaten more in a day at home than I have allowed here for a Week. You have given more than my day's allowance to a beggar at the door. . . .

Reprinted in: Kupperman, Karen Ordahl, ed. *Major Problems in American Colonial History.* Lexington, Mass.: D. C. Heath, 1993, pp. 93–94.

equipment. (Surveyors measure the land.) Most therefore had to continue working as servants. By the mid-1700s even fewer servants could improve their circumstances because less land was available.

Another problem was that males far outnumbered females—in some areas there were six men for each woman. The reason for this was that employers preferred male servants who could do heavy work such as clearing the land, cultivating the soil, and building houses and barns. Women were usually household servants, so they were a luxury that could be afforded only by the wealthiest employers. The imbalance between men and women meant that few servants married and had families, especially in the Chesapeake region (Virginia and Maryland). Women sometimes benefitted from this situation, however, since they had a choice of men and therefore had better prospects of getting married. Yet family life was deeply affected by the high death rate—more than two-thirds of all marriages lasted fewer than ten years. Remarriage became quite common, over time producing a new kind of family with half-brothers and half-sisters and step-parents and stepchildren. At the same time, twenty percent of servants' children were orphaned by age twelve and many lived with only one parent. As a result, special courts were established to oversee the care of children without parents, placing them with guardians or in orphanages (group homes).

At the turn of the eighteenth century slaves began outnumbering indentured servants on southern plantations. By this time slaves cost only slightly more than indentured servants, and they could be purchased for life rather for a certain number of years. This change happened because of resourceful marketing; Caribbean slave traders had successfully promoted the benefits of slave labor for producing such staple crops as tobacco in the Chesapeake and rice in Carolina. Although slavery was the main form of labor used in the South, it did not cause the elimination of the indentured servant practice. Planters relied on both white indentured servants and African slaves, who usually worked together. Robert Beverley (1673–1722), a Virginia planter, described this situation in "Servants and Slaves in Virginia," which is part of his book *The History and Present State of Virginia.*

Things to Remember While Reading "Servants and Slaves in Virginia":

- Beverley was a prominent Virginia plantation owner and government official. Perceiving the need for an accurate history of the colony, he published *The History and Present State of Virginia* in 1705—nearly a century after the founding of Virginia. The book was such a success that it was reprinted several times, attracting many immigrants to the colony. Keep in mind that Beverley intended "Servants and Slaves in Virginia" as a kind of "advertisement" to recruit indentured servants. Therefore he made an effort to place the duties, laws, and treatment of slaves and servants in a positive light.

- Beverley was careful to note that "Sufficient Distinction" was made between white female servants and black female slaves. White women were "rarely or never put to work in the Ground." That is, they did not perform such tasks as cultivating the soil or planting crops. To discourage mistreatment of women servants, the law required that a planter pay the highest taxes on white women he used for work in the fields, whereas he would pay no taxes on those who did other work such as household tasks. A woman slave, however, commonly worked in the fields, and the planter paid the same amount of tax on a woman slave whether she worked outside or indoors.

- Beverley was troubled by the fact that in England "Service of this Country" (servitude in America) was rumored to be "strangely cruel, and severe." He was determined to set the record straight, claiming that servants and slaves did not have to work any harder than a freedman (freed servant) or an overseer (supervisor). In fact, he wrote, that slaves in Virginia probably were forced to work less than farmhands and laborers in England.

- Beverley listed twelve Virginia laws that protected servants and required their masters to treat them "as tenderly as possible." In general, the laws gave servants court protection from mistreatment and contract violation, rights to personal property, guarantee of freedom dues, disability rights, and a grant of land.

"Servants and Slaves in Virginia"

Their Servants, they distinguish by the Names of Slaves for Life, and Servants for a time.

*Slaves are the Negroes, and their **Posterity**, following the condition of the Mother, according to the **Maxim**, **partus sequitur ventrem** They are call'd Slaves, in respect of the time of their Servitude, because it is for Life.*

*Servants, are those which serve only for a few years, according to the time of their **Indenture**, or the **Custom of the Country**. The Custom of the Country takes place upon such as have no Indentures. The Law in this case is, that if such Servants be under Nineteen years of Age, they must be brought into Court, to have their Age **adjudged**; and from the Age they are judg'd to be of, they must serve until they*

Posterity: Descendants

Maxim: Wise saying

Partus sequitur ventrem: Latin for status proceeds from the womb; that is if the mother is a slave her child will be a slave

Indenture: Contract

Custom of the country: Laws of the colony

Adjudged: To decide or rule upon as a judge

Four and twenty: Twenty-four

A Virginia planter and his clerk overseeing slaves pack dried tobacco leaves for shipment to England.
Reproduced by permission of The Granger Collection.

Imployed: Employed

Tilling: Cultivating

Manuring: Fertilizing with animal manure

Overseers: Supervisors

Freemen: Servants released from service

Planters: Owners of plantations

reach **four and twenty:** But if they be adjudged upwards of Nineteen, they are then only to be Servants for the term of five Years.

The Male-Servants, and Slaves of both Sexes, are **imployed** together in **Tilling** and **Manuring** the Ground, in Sowing and Planting Tobacco, Corn. . . . Some Distinction indeed is made between them in their Cloaths, and Food; but the Work of both, is no other than what the **Overseers**, the **Freemen**, and the **Planters** themselves do.

Sufficient Distinction is also made between the Female-Servants, and Slaves; for a White Woman is rarely or never put to work in the Ground [in the field], if she be good for any thing else: And to Discourage all Planters from using any Women so, their Law imposes the heaviest Taxes upon Female-Servants working in the Ground, while it suffers all other white Women to be absolutely exempted: Whereas on the other hand, it is a common thing to work a Woman Slave out of Doors; nor does the Law make any distinction in her Taxes, whether her Work be Abroad [in other places], or at Home.

Colonial America: Primary Sources

Because I have heard how strangely cruel, and severe, the Service of this Country [servitude in America] is represented in some parts of England; I can't **forbear** affirming, that the work of their Servants, and Slaves, is no other than what every common Freeman **do's.** Neither is any Servant requir'd to do more in a Day, than his Overseer. And I can assure you with a great deal of Truth, that generally their Slaves are not worked near so hard, nor so many Hours in a Day, as the **Husbandmen,** and Day-Labourers in England. An Overseer is a Man, that having served his time, has acquired the Skill and Character of an experienced Planter, and is therefore intrusted with the Direction of the Servants and Slaves.

But to **compleat** this account of Servants, I shall give you a short **Relation** of the care their Laws take, that they be used as tenderly as possible.

By the Laws of their Country

1. All Servants whatsoever, have their Complaints heard without Fee, or Reward; but if the Master be found Faulty, the charge of the Complaint is cast upon him, otherwise the business is done **ex Officio.**

2. Any **Justice of Peace** may receive the Complaint of a Servant, and order every thing relating thereto, till the next County-Court, where it will be finally determin'd.

3. All Masters are under the Correction, and **Censure** of the County-Courts, to provide for their Servants, good and wholsome Diet, Clothing, and Lodging.

4. They are always to appear, upon the first Notice given of the Complaint of their Servants, otherwise to **forfeit** the Service of them, until they do appear.

5. All Servants Complaints are to be receiv'd at any time in Court, without **Process,** and shall not be delay'd for want of **Form;** but the Merits of the Complaint must be immediately inquir'd into by the **Justices;** if the Master cause any delay therein, the Court may remove such Servants, if they see Cause, until the Master will come to **Tryal.**

6. If a Master shall at any time disobey an Order of Court, made upon any Complaint of a Servant; the Court is **impower'd** to remove such Servant forthwith to another Master, who will be kinder; Giving to the former Master the produce only, (after Fees deducted) of what such Servants shall be sold for by **Publick Outcry.**

Forbear: Resist

Do's: Does

Husbandmen: Farm workers

Compleat: Complete

Relation: Account

Ex officio: Unofficially

Justice of peace: A judge who administers justice in minor offenses

Censure: An official reprimand

Forfeit: Give up

Process: Court order

Form: Procedure

Justices: Judges

Tryal: Trial

Impower'd: Empowered

Publick outcry: Public sale or auction

Faln: Fallen

Church-wardens: In the Anglican Church, unordained officials who oversee parish property

Boarded: Sent to live

Levy: Collect a fee

Chattels: Person items

Parish: An area of church jurisdiction, like a county

Intituled: Entitled

Privity: Knowledge

Over-reaching: Going to extremes

Complyance: Compliance; obedience

Thither: In the direction of

Intirely: Entirely

Freedom: Released from the indenture contract

Unpatented: Unowned

Piece of eight: A Spanish coin

Imputed: To lay responsibility or blame, often falsely or unjustly

Abhor: Loathe or hate

7. *If a Master should be so cruel, as to use his Servant ill [mistreat his servant], that is **faln** Sick, or Lame in his Service, and thereby render'd unfit for Labour, he must be remov'd by the **Church-Wardens** out of the way of such Cruelty, and **boarded** in some good Planters House, till the time of his Freedom, the charge of which must be laid before the next County-Court, which has power to **levy** the same from time to time, upon the Goods and **Chattels** of the Master; After which, the charge of such Boarding is to come upon the **Parish** in General.*

8. *All hired Servants are **intituled** to these Priviledges.*

9. *No Master of a Servant, can make a new Bargain for Service, or other Matter with his Servant, without the **privity** and consent of a Justice of Peace, to prevent the Master's **Over-reaching**, or scareing such Servant into an unreasonable **Complyance**.*

10. *The property of all Money and Goods sent over **thither** to Servants, or carry'd in with them; is reserv'd to themselves, and remain **intirely** at their disposal.*

11. *Each Servant at his **Freedom**, receives of his Master fifteen Bushels of Corn, (which is sufficient for a whole year) and two new Suits of Cloaths, both Linnen and Woollen; and then becomes as free in all respects, and as much intituled to the Liberties, and Priviledges of the Country, as any other of the Inhabitants or Natives are.*

12. *Each Servant has then also a Right to take up fifty Acres of Land, where he can find any **unpatented**: But that is no great Privilege, for any one may have as good a right for a **piece of Eight**.*

*This is what the Laws prescribe in favour of Servants, by which you may find, that the Cruelties and Severities **imputed** to that Country, are an unjust Reflection. For no People more **abhor** the thoughts of such Usage, than the Virginians, nor take more precaution to prevent it.*

What happened next . . .

During the eighteenth century indentured servants continued to be imported into the Chesapeake region, especially from Ireland. Manufacturing activity in the northern colonies also sparked the need of additional skilled workers like coopers, tanners, weavers, shipbuilders, printers, and clerks. In New England this demand was met through the local population, but the middle colonies (New York, New Jersey, Pennsylvania, and Delaware) continued to rely on indentured servants. Almost one hundred thousand were imported from the British Isles (England, Ireland, Scotland, and Wales) in the period of 1700–75, while another thirty-five thousand came from Germany. About half of all servants went to Pennsylvania, which became the main destination in the eighteenth century.

Did you know . . .

- Immigrant workers frequently arrived in America as redemptioners. These laborers were similar to indentured servants in that they agreed to work for a specific period in return for transatlantic passage. The difference was that redemptioners arranged a contract once they arrived in the colonies rather than agreeing to terms before beginning the trip. They could not leave the ships, however, until they found a colonist who was willing to pay for their voyage in return for labor. Whereas most indentured servants were unmarried men and women from England, redemptioners were usually families from Germany. In some cases an entire family would commit to a labor contract, or parents would obligate a child or children in return for payment of the family's passage to America.

- Most Africans were slaves, but many were also indentured servants. Black indentured servitude was prevalent in all colonies, especially in the North, and servants were even able to gain their freedom. In 1760 there were two thousand freed slaves (two to three percent of the African American population) in Virginia, and in the North about ten percent of the total African American population were freedmen (in Connecticut the figure was over twenty percent).

- Some women servants, blessed with exceptional health, married three or four times. The scarcity of women meant that many female servants did not have to complete their indenture, if an acceptable suitor was prepared to buy out their remaining period of service.

For more information

"Gottlieb Mittelberger, On the Misfortune of Indentured Servants" in *Documents Relevant to the United States Before 1700*. http://www.geocities. com/Athens/Forum/9061//USA/colonial/bef1700.html Available September 30, 1999.

Innes, Stephen, ed. *Work and Labor in Early America*. Chapel Hill, N.C.: University of North Carolina Press, 1988.

Kupperman, Karen Ordahl, ed. *Major Problems in American Colonial History*. Lexington, Mass.: D. C. Heath, 1993, pp. 98–100.

Middleton, Richard. *Colonial America: A History, 1585–1776*. Second edition. Malden, Mass.: Blackwell Publishers, 1996, pp. 112–13, 147–48, 224–25, 332–34.

Smith, Carter, ed. *Daily Life: A Sourcebook on Colonial America*. Brookfield, Conn.: Millbrook Press, 1991.

John Woolman

Some Considerations on the Keeping of Negroes

Reprinted in *Early American Writing*
Published in 1994
Edited by Giles Gunn

Slavery existed in Africa long before Europeans started an international slave trade off the western coast of the continent in the 1400s. For hundreds of years Africans had taken members of other tribes into slavery during wars or used slavery as punishment for crimes within their own groups. There were also enslaved craftsmen, warriors, and advisors to tribal chiefs and kings. While a small slave trade was conducted between Africa and Europe prior to the discovery of the Americas, it increased significantly when the Spaniards discovered that marketable products such as sugar could be grown in the Caribbean islands.

Initially the Europeans used Native Americans as workers on sugar plantations (large farms), but the native peoples quickly died from European diseases. As a result, plantation owners turned to Africa for slaves. Even at its height, the slave trade was not well organized, nor was it controlled by Europeans. Instead, African traders sold other Africans. They took their captives from an area that stretched three thousand miles south along the Senegambia River to the Congo River—a distance greater than that between present-day New York and California.

"If I purchase a Man who hath never forfeited his Liberty, the natural Right of Freedom is in him; and shall I keep him and his Posterity in Servitude and Ignorance?"

A Dutch ship arriving in Jamestown in 1619 with the New World's first African slaves. *Reproduced by permission of Archive Photos, Inc.*

The first slaves in North America arrived in 1619 at Jamestown, Virginia, when a Dutch trader exchanged twenty slaves for provisions (a stock of food). Soon Africans were essential to the American plantation economy. The slave trade became a booming business, not only in the South but also at busy ports in Massachusetts and Rhode Island. The trade route formed a triangle: ships loaded with European-made goods departed from British ports and landed on the west coast of Africa, where the goods would be exchanged for slaves. Then the slaves were transported to the American colonies or the Caribbean islands and traded for agricultural products. Finally, completing the triangle, the ships took this cargo back to England. Merchants made money only if the slaves were alive upon delivery in American ports, so they hired ship captains who kept Africans healthy during the long trip across the Atlantic Ocean.

Sailors referred to the shipboard experience of enslaved Africans as "the middle passage." During the voyage men were usually chained, while women and children were allowed some freedom of movement on the ship deck. Captains chose one of two methods for transporting slaves: tight packing or loose packing. Tight packing squeezed in as many slaves as possible, thus preventing them from moving about or even sitting up. Males lay in space six feet long, sixteen inches wide, and two and one-half feet high. Females occupied an area five feet long, fourteen inches wide, and two and one-half feet high. Captains who chose this method did not want to waste valuable space, since the more slaves they transported the more money they would get even if a higher percentage of slaves died. They also increased their profits by giving the slaves little food and hiring a minimum number of crewmen. Other captains chose loose packing. They believed that giving slaves more room, better food, and freedom to move about reduced the death rate. Many captains insured their slave cargo against drowning. Because insurance did not cover the loss of slaves who died during the voyage, some captains dumped dying slaves overboard and claimed they drowned in order to collect insurance benefits.

Once slave ships had docked, the goal of merchants was to make a profit from a quick sale. In some cases an entire group of slaves might be reserved for one planter (plantation owner), thus closing the sale to anyone else. A more common practice was to sell slaves at an auction where buyers would place bids (call out a price). Prior to the auction, slaves were exhibited before interested buyers (planters), who poked and prodded them. After the slaves had been examined, an auctioneer would sell them to buyers who had placed the highest bids. Another method involved merchants setting a price beforehand and then selling the slaves in groups as buyers scrambled into a holding pen to pick out the choicest slaves. Olaudah Equiano (c.1750–1797), a freed African slave, described the chaotic scene of such a sale in his autobiography, *The Interesting Narrative of the Life of Olaudah Equiano* (1789). "On a signal given," Equiano wrote, "the buyers rush at once into the yard where the slaves are confined, and make choice of that parcel (portion of land) they like best. The noise and clamor with which this is attended, and the eagerness visible on the countenances of the buyers, serve not a little to increase the apprehensions of terrified Africans."

After the mid-1600s slavery was legalized through a series of laws called slave codes. The Virginia legislature passed several such laws. A 1662 statute, for instance, made the child of a slave woman a slave (see "Servants and Slaves in Virginia")—even if the father was free and even if the father was a white master. A 1669 law declared that if a slave died while resisting his or her master, the master could not be charged with a felony. Slaves were worth large sums of money, so even harsher laws gave owners the right to demand the return of runaways, who were considered legal "property."

Although most slaves were put to work on tobacco and rice plantations in the South, all of the colonies used slave laborers. Whether slavery caused racism (prejudice because of race) or racism caused slavery might never be fully determined, but African slaves were generally considered unequal to white people. At first owners made an effort to keep slave families together. But gradually this practice changed and, as slaves were routinely bought and sold, families were broken apart. Husbands and wives tended not to live together, and children were often sold at a young age since they took time away from their mothers' work. By the 1740s the majority of African slaves remained in bondage throughout their lives. The number of slaves in a colony depended on economic factors. In areas where slavery was most profitable, there were more Africans—for instance, they comprised the majority of the population of South Carolina as early as 1708. Slaves had their own cabins in the South, whereas in the northern colonies they lived in cellars, attics, and sheds. Africans were frequently mistreated by white masters and overseers, who beat them for such infractions (violations) as not working hard enough or trying to run away.

By the late 1600s European colonists were interacting with Africans on a daily basis, and many masters even regarded their slaves as part of their own families. Historians have noted some improvements in the quality of life for slaves during this period. The Society for the Propagation of the Gospel, a religious organization in New England, advocated the education of blacks. Colonial leaders such as Massachusetts preacher Cotton Mather (1663–1728) taught Africans to read. There were also a few isolated protests against slavery. The first was voiced in 1688 by Francis Pastorius (1651–?1720), a German-born Quaker (member of a Christian Protestant group that advocated direct communication with God through an "inner light") who founded Germantown, Pennsylvania. In 1700 Samuel Sewall

(1652–1730), a Massachusetts merchant and judge, published a pamphlet titled *The Selling of Joseph* in which he attacked slavery as being un-Christian. Yet racism and mistreatment of blacks was still prevalent throughout the colonies, and whites rarely questioned the morality of slavery—it was too essential to the economy.

The movement against slavery did not gain momentum until nearly a half century later when Quaker pastor John Woolman (1720–1772) set out on the first of thirty annual excursions to attend Quaker meetings (religious services). From his home in Mount Holly, New Jersey, he journeyed around New England and down to the Carolinas. Wherever he went—in both the South and the North—he encountered slavery, and he was deeply troubled by the sight of people being owned as property. Woolman therefore resolved to mount a vigorous abolitionist (antislavery) campaign as he made his annual trips. When he traveled in the South, he preached his message to slave holders. In Rhode Island he tried to persuade ship owners not to transport slaves from Africa to North America. He refused to buy any products connected with the slave trade, and he would not accept hospitality from slave owners.

Quaker pastor John Woolman was the first to mount a vigorous anitslavery campaign in the colonies. *Reproduced by permission of The Granger Collection Ltd.*

Especially disturbing to Woolman was the fact that Africans were being held slaves by Christians, and even by Quakers. In fact, in the 1720s, the Society of Friends (the official name of the Quaker group) expelled at least one member who opposed the keeping of slaves. Finally Woolman decided to limit his abolitionist efforts to the Quaker community, writing essays on social injustices for Quaker publications. One of those essays was *Some Considerations on the Keeping of Negroes*, which was published in 1754.

Things to Remember While Reading *Some Considerations on the Keeping of Negroes:*

- Modern readers should be aware of *Some Considerations on the Keeping of Negroes* because it played a major role in starting the abolition movement, which gained full momentum in the nineteenth century. Largely as a result of the efforts of abolitionists, President Abraham Lincoln (1809–1865) issued the Emancipation Proclamation (1863), which freed all slaves during the Civil War (1861–65; also called the War Between the States, the Civil War was a conflict between the Northern states, or the Union, and the Confederacy, a group of Southern states that formed their own nation.)

- Nevertheless, Woolman's essay presents some difficulties for the modern reader. For example, he was addressing an eighteenth-century Quaker audience, so his writing style is typical of the period. He also made numerous references to the Bible (the Christian holy book). For those reasons, explanatory notes are included in the excerpts from *Some Considerations on the Keeping of Negroes*.

Some Considerations on the Keeping of Negroes

Woolman opened the essay by asserting that he had a duty to protest the mistreatment of African slaves in "an enlight'ned Christian Country." In the following two paragraphs he reminded his readers that all human beings, including Africans, share the same characteristics and that all people are members of "a general Brotherhood." As mere "Sojourners," (temporary travelers) in the world, they experience the same "Afflictions and Infirmities of Body, the like Disorders and Frailties in Mind, the like Temptations, the same Death." He went on to point out that over time Christians came to be "filled with fond Notions of Superiority," forgetting their duty to be caretakers of weaker fellow human beings.

When we remember that all Nations are of one Blood, **Gen. iii.20.** *that in this World we are but* **Sojourners,** *that we are subject to the like [same]* **Afflictions** *and Infirmities of Body, the like Disorders* **Frailties** *in Mind, the like Temptations, the same Death, and the same*

Gen. iii. 20: A book (Genesis), chapter, and verse in the New Testament of the Bible

Sojourners: A temporary resident

Afflictions: Inflict sufferings upon

Frailties: A fault due to weakness especially of moral character

Colonial America: Primary Sources

*Judgement, and, that the Alwise Being is Judge and Lord over us all, it seems to raise an Idea of a general Brotherhood, and a Disposition easy to be touched with a Feeling of each others Afflictions: But when we forget those Things, and look chiefly at our outward Circumstances, in this and some Ages past, constantly retaining in our Minds the Distinction **betwixt** us and them, with respect to out Knowledge and Improvement in Things divine, natural and artificial, our Breasts being apt to be filled with fond Notions of Superiority, there is Danger of **erring** in our Conduct toward them [mistreating them].*

*We allow them to be of the same Species with ourselves, the Odds is, we are in a higher **Station**, and enjoy greater Favours then they: And when it is thus, that our heavenly Father **endoweth** some of his Children with distinguished Gifts, they are intended for good Ends; but if those thus gifted are thereby lifted up above their Brethren, not considering themselves as Debtors to the Weak, nor behaving themselves as faithful **Stewards** none who judge impartially can suppose them free from Ingratitude [that is, they are not being properly grateful to God for the gifts they have been given]. . . .*

Woolman argued that Christians must imitate the impartial, "universal" love of God, which "begets a Likeness of itself, and the Heart is enlarged towards all Men." He warned that prejudice—considering "a People froward, perverse, and worse by Nature than others—is unworthy of Christians ("unbecoming the Excellence of true Religion"). Then he appealed to his readers to put themselves in the place of African slaves, "to make their Case ours." Suppose, he wrote, that white people had been held as slaves and received no education, no cultural advantages, no religious teachings, or no rewards for their own labor. Suppose further that they had been "treated as a contemptible, ignorant Part of Mankind." If that was the case, he asked, would white people be any different from Africans? Examining the case further, Woolman asserted that it is impossible for oppressed people to love their oppressors. The only result can be a miserable situation, which produces "Sloth and many other Habits appearing odious to us."

*To consider Mankind otherwise than **Brethren**, to think Favours are peculiar to one Nation, and exclude others, plainly supposes a Darkness in the Understanding: For as God's Love is universal, so where the Mind is inefficiently influenced by it, it **begets** a Likeness of itself, and the Heart is enlarged towards all Men. Again, to conclude a People **froward, perverse**, and worse by Nature than others (who ungratefully*

Betwixt: Between

Erring: To make a mistake

Station: Social status

Endoweth: To furnish with an income

Stewards: People who manage another's property

Brethren: Referring to the members of a profession, society, or sect

Begets: To produce especially as an effect or outgrowth

Froward: Frequently disobedient

Perverse: Corrupt

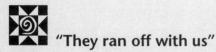

"They ran off with us"

In *The Interesting Narrative of the Life of Olaudah Equiano* (1789), freedman Olaudah Equiano described how, when he was eleven years old, he and his sister were kidnapped by African slave traders.

> One day, when all our people were gone out to their works as usual, and only I and my dear sister were left to mind the house, two men and a woman got over our walls, and in a moment seized us both; and, without giving us time to cry out, or to make resistance, they stopped our mouths, tied our hands, and ran off with us into the nearest wood, and continued to carry us as far as they could, till night came on, when we reached a small house, where the robbers halted for refreshment, and spent the night.
>
> We were then unbound, but were unable to take any food; and, being quite overpowered by fatigue and grief, our only relief was some sleep, which allayed [reduced] our misfortune for a short time. The next morning we left the house, and continued travelling all the day. For a long time we had kept to the woods, but at last we came into a road which I believed I knew. I now had some hopes of being delivered, for we had advanced but a little way before I discovered some people at a distance, on which I began to cry out for their assistance; but my cries had no other effect than to make them tie me faster, and stop my mouth, and then they put me into a large sack. They also stopped my sister's mouth, and tied her hands. And in this manner we proceeded till we were out of the sight of these people.
>
> When we went to rest the following night they offered us some victuals [food], but we refused them; and the only comfort we had was in being in one another's arms all that night, and bathing each other in our tears. But, alas! we were soon deprived of

Servile: Of or befitting a slave or a menial position

Destitute: Extremely poor

Pious: Marked by or showing reverence for deity and devotion to divine worship

Contemptible: Vile; despicable

Abject: Sunk to or existing in a low state or condition

receive Favours, and apply them to bad Ends) this will excite a Behaviour toward them unbecoming the Excellence of true Religion.

To prevent such Error, let us calmly consider their Circumstance; and, the better to do it, make their Case ours. Suppose, then, that our Ancestors and we had been exposed to constant Servitude in the more **servile** and inferior Employments of Life; that we had been **destitute** of the Help of Reading and good Company; that amongst ourselves we had had few wise and **pious** Instructors; that the Religious amongst our Superiors seldom took Notice of us; that while others, in Ease, have plentifully heap'd up the Fruit of our Labour, we had receiv'd barely enough to relieve Nature, and being wholly at the Command of others, had generally been treated as a **contemptible**, ignorant Part of Mankind: Should we, in that Case, be less **abject** than they now are? . . .

Although originally coming to American as a slave, Olaudah Equiano eventually gained his freedom and wrote about his experiences.
Reproduced by permission of the New York Historical Society.

even the smallest comfort of weeping together. The next day proved a day of greater sorrow than I had yet experienced; for my sister and I were then separated, while we lay clasped in each other's arms. It was in vain that we besought [begged] them not to part us: she was torn from me, and immediately carried away, while I was left in a state of distraction [mental confusion] not to be described. I cried and grieved continually; and for several days I did not eat anything but what they forced into my mouth.

Later Equiano's sister was brought to a house where he was working as a slave, and he was overjoyed to see her. But, he said, ". . . she was again torn from me forever! I was now more miserable, if possible, than before. . . ."

Reprinted in: Stiles, T. J., ed. In Their Own Words: The Colonizers. New York: Berkeley Publishing Group, 1998, pp. 352–53, 354.

When our Property is taken contrary to our Mind, by Means appearing to us unjust, it is only through divine Influence, and the Enlargement of heart from thence proceeding, that we can love our reputed Oppressors: If the Negroes fall short in this, an uneasy, if not a **disconsolate Disposition**, will be awak'ned, and remain like Seeds in their Minds, producing **Sloth** and many other Habits appearing **odious** to us, with which being free Men, they, perhaps, had not been chargeable. These, and other Circumstances, rightly considered, will lessen that too great Disparity, which some make between us and them. . . .

In the final excerpt from the essay, Woolman stated that it was time for white people to take responsibility for the situation they had created by owning slaves. He rejected the argument that slaves were a financial investment and

Disconsolate: Dejected, downcast

Disposition: Temperment

Sloth: Laziness

Odious: Exciting or deserving hatred or repugnance

owners were entitled to make a profit from them. Slavery is morally and logically wrong, he contended, and it is "better that there were none in our Country." In conclusion, he noted that continuing slavery would "not be doing as we would be done by [would not be treating others as we want to be treated]."

*It may be objected there is Cost of Purchase, and Risque of their Lives to them who possess' em, and therefore needful that they make the best Use of their Time: In a Practice just and reasonable, such Objections may have Weight; but if the Work be wrong from the Beginning, there's little or no Force in them. If I purchase a Man who hath never **forfeited** his Liberty, the natural Right of Freedom is in him; and shall I keep him and his **Posterity** in Servitude and Ignorance? How should I approve of this Conduct, were I in his Circumstances, and he in mine? It may be thought, that to treat them as we would willingly be treated, our Gain by them would be inconsiderable: And it were, in **divers** Respects, better that there were none in our Country.*

*We may further consider, that they are now amongst us, and those of our Nation the Cause of their being here; that whatsoever Difficulty **accrues** thereon, we are justly chargeable with, and to bear all Inconveniences attending it, with a serious and weighty Concern of Mind to do our Duty by them, is the best we can do. To seek a Remedy by continuing the **Oppression**, because we have Power to do it, and see others do it, will, I apprehend, not be doing as we would be done by.*

Forfeited: Forced to surrender

Posterity: Future generations

Divers: Several

Accrues: To come about as a natural growth, increase, or advantage

Oppression: Persecution

What happened next . . .

Woolman's abolitionist activities eventually produced results. He persuaded Quaker communities to make public protests against slavery, and he convinced owners to free their slaves. He was joined by others who shared his views, and in 1760 Quakers in New England, New York, and Pennsylvania ceased the buying and selling of slaves. The Society of Friends then moved to the forefront of the antislavery movement, which gained momentum in the nineteenth century.

Did you know . . .

- Between the sixteenth and nineteenth centuries, 10,000,000 to 11,000,000 African slaves crossed the Atlantic Ocean. Relatively few of them arrived in the American colonies. Most (eighty-five percent) went to Brazil and to British, French, Spanish, Danish, or Dutch colonies in the Caribbean. Nine percent of the slaves were sent to the Spanish mainland. Only six percent, or 600,000 to 650,000 Africans, went to the American colonies.

- Many former slaves owned farms. For instance, freedman freed slave Anthony Johnson (d. 1665) began acquiring his own plantation in Virginia during the 1640s. By 1651 he owned 250 acres of land, and he became known as the "black patriarch" of Pungoteague Creek (the area of Virginia where his estate was located).

- Gracia Real de Santa Teresa de Mose was founded as a town for freed blacks in 1738. Located in Spanish Florida two miles north of Saint Augustine, Mose was the only town of its kind in what would become the United States. The earliest settlers were escaped slaves from South Carolina. English attacks forced evacuation of the town from 1740 to 1752, and inhabitants moved to Saint Augustine.

For more information

Breen, T. H. and Stephen Innes. *"Myne Owne Ground": Race and Freedom on Virginia's Eastern Shore, 1640–1676*. New York: Oxford University Press, 1980.

Cady, Edwin Harrison. *John Woolman*. New York: Washington Square Press, 1965.

Dalglish, Doris N. *People Called Quakers*. Freeport, N.Y.: Books for Libraries Press, 1969.

Elliott, Emory, and others, eds. *American Literature: A Prentice-Hall Anthology*. Englewood Cliffs, N.J.: Prentice-Hall, 1991, pp. 399–401.

Gunn, Giles, ed. *Early American Writing*. New York: Penguin Books, 1994, pp. 391–95.

Johnson, Charles, Patricia Smith, and WGBH Research Team. *Africans in America: America's Journey through Slavery*. New York: Harcourt, Brace & Company, 1998, pp. 37–39, 42–46.

Middleton, Richard. *Colonial America: A History, 1585–1776.* Second edition. Malden, Mass.: Blackwell Publishers, 1996, pp. 311–34.

Wood, Peter H. *Strange New Land: African Americans, 1617–1776.* New York: Oxford University Press, 1995.

Thomas Morton

"The Maypole of Merry-Mount," an excerpt from
New English Canaan

Reprinted in *Eyewitness to America*
Published in 1997
Edited by David Colbert

Since the founding of the Plymouth Colony in 1620, Puritans dominated all aspects of life in New England, the northernmost region of the present-day United States. The Puritans were a Protestant Christian group who advocated radical reform of the Church of England (the official state religion) and stressed strict moral and religious codes. Also they objected to elaborate church rituals that were derived from Roman Catholicism (a Christian religion based in Rome, Italy, and headed by a pope who has absolute authority in all church affairs). Seeking religious freedom, the Puritans went to America in the early 1600s and founded two colonies—Plymouth and Massachusetts Bay—side by side in the southeastern part of New England. Within decades, however, serious social and political problems began to emerge when Puritans refused to grant others the freedom they had sought for themselves.

Leaders of the Plymouth Colony, who were called Pilgrims, had originally set out for Virginia, but a storm at sea forced them onto Cape Cod (off the coast of present-day Massachusetts). Since they were not on land that had been legally granted to them, the Pilgrims drafted and signed the Mayflower

"The setting up of this Maypole was a lamentable spectacle to the precise separatists that lived at new Plymouth."

193

The landing of the Pilgrims at Plymouth, Massachusetts in 1620. The Pilgrims were not tolerant of people whose views did not conform to their own.
Reproduced by permission of Archive Photos, Inc.

Compact, which gave them the right to establish a colony (see "The Pilgrims' Landing and First Winter"). In 1629 the Massachusetts Bay Company started a settlement to the north of Plymouth (see *John Winthrop's Christian Experience*), near Boston. After the arrival of a large group of Puritans in 1631, the settlement was reorganized as the Massachusetts Bay Colony.

Although the Plymouth and Massachusetts Bay colonists were Puritans, the colonies had different views of the Church of England. The Plymouth settlers were Nonconformists (also known as Separatists), who advocated complete separation from the church. The Massachusetts Bay colonists, however, wanted to reform the church and saw no reason to declare total independence. The Puritans sought religious freedom by moving to America, yet they generally did not tolerate the views of other groups. The Pilgrims were especially reluctant to admit anyone but Nonconformists to the Plymouth Colony.

Colonists in both Plymouth and Massachusetts Bay settled close together in towns that functioned as the center of government for surrounding farms and rural villages. These towns were organized around Puritan congregations (separate groups of church members) that controlled all aspects of life in the colony. Soon after arriving in New England the Puritans adopted covenants (laws), or solemn and binding agreements, which they believed were patterned upon covenants God had made with humans. In the covenant of works, for instance, Adam and Eve (the first man and woman on Earth, according to the Christian Bible) agreed to achieve salvation (the state of being saved from sin) by their own good works (moral behavior). Adam and Eve broke this covenant by sinning, however, and lost God's grace (goodwill).

Through the covenant of redemption, Jesus of Nazareth (the founder of Christianity; also called Christ) agreed to take upon himself the guilt and sins of all other human beings, thereby saving them from falling from God's grace. In the covenant of grace, God's spirit entered certain people, called the "elect," who had been predestined (chosen by God) for salvation. According to the Puritans, God also made covenants with groups of people, such as Abraham (an important Hebrew leader in the Old Testament of the Christian Bible) and his descendants. He looked upon these people with special favor if they tried to obey his will. The Puritans believed they were one of these favored groups, so they created their own covenants that regulated every function of society, including congregations, towns, government, and marriage. Taken together, these separate covenants formed society's covenant with God, and society was quick to punish anyone who violated these covenants.

Under Puritan covenants each congregation had authority to establish a town, form a government, and admit church members. Town leaders were a few "elect" men who had achieved salvation. Likewise, the Puritans accepted as members only those who could convince the leaders and the rest of the congregation that they had been saved. The Puritans believed that humans could reach salvation by hearing and understanding the word of God with the help of an ordained (officially appointed) minister.

The minister was therefore the most important person in a congregation. He had to be highly educated so he could explain the Bible and show how it related to daily life. The minister also led his congregation in performing good works, so people turned to him for advice on personal, economic, and political matters. Faced with these awesome responsibilities, neighboring ministers met in informal support groups to discuss common problems.

A Puritan church (also called a meeting house) was a plain, square building without a steeple (a tall structure, or tower, on the roof), stained-glass windows, or ornaments of any kind. The Puritans rejected these features, which could be found in Anglican churches (another name for the Church of England), as being too much like elaborate cathedrals built by the Roman Catholic Church. The Puritans strongly disapproved of both the Catholic Church and the Church of England, maintaining that they were corrupt and gave too much power to the pope and bishops. Puritan worshipers sat on hard, wooden benches (also called pews) facing the minister, who often stood on a raised platform. Later the benches were sectioned off into squares of family pews with partitions around them. This was an attempt to cut down on cold drafts and retain the heat from warmed bricks that people wrapped in cloths and placed on the floor. Pews were assigned according to a family's rank in society.

Although worship services were held throughout the week, the major service was on Sunday. It was a lengthy and formal event with a two-hour sermon (minister's lecture) that opened and closed with long prayers. Worshipers stood during the prayers and throughout much of the service. Sometimes the congregation would take a lunch break after the morning service and return for another session in the afternoon. Singing or chanting of psalms (song-poems from the Bible) was allowed, but with no musical accompaniment (an instrumental or vocal part designed to support a melody). A person called a "liner" would sing a line, and the congregation would repeat it in whatever tunes individuals chose to follow.

Since the Puritans lived close together, they were able to observe each other's behavior and make sure everyone obeyed the covenants. As a result, there was no privacy in Puritan communities. The cornerstone of the society was the family, which was carefully monitored by the townsfolk. If trouble arose in a family, church elders (leaders who were not ordained ministers) would take action. They were given the authority to remove children, apprentices, and servants from households that did not meet community standards.

A hierarchy (rank according to importance) existed within a family so that all members would know their places, thus avoiding competition and arguments. The husband was the head of the household and represented the family at public and church events. He was also responsible for raising the children in a strict manner to save them from the temptations of Satan (the devil, or the ultimate evil). A woman obeyed her husband and supervised private household affairs. The Puritans considered marriage a holy state blessed by God, viewing sexual relations between a man and a woman as a way to fulfill God's will in creating life. In fact, sexual activity was confined to this purpose alone. Since having sexual relations outside of marriage was sinful, the Puritans ostracized (banned from society) both unmarried women who became pregnant and married women who had children by men other than their husbands.

A hierarchy also existed in Puritan society. The most important institution was the church, with the minister at the top and the elders below him, followed by church members. At the bottom were nonchurch members. Government was in the hands of the "elect" because they alone could understand and follow God's will. Church membership was required of all adult males who wished to vote and hold political office. Since women were under the control of their husbands, they were excluded from holding office. Town government was strongly influenced by the church—although the Puritans held public meetings where all community members had a voice in resolving issues, decisions were based on obedience to God's will. The government of the colony was supposed to be separate from the church, but officials passed laws to insure that colonists adhered to Puritan covenants. Those who strayed would receive harsh punishment because God would punish the whole society if the government failed to maintain proper standards. The Puritans assumed that the Bible contained all necessary laws for a moral society, so they did not write a legal code (official set of laws) until 1641. The government also established schools to insure that everyone was able to read the Bible.

With religion at the center of their lives, the New England Puritans lived simply, dressed plainly, and worked constantly. Since they frowned on any activities that did not glo-

A Puritan family reading the Bible. All aspects of Puritan life centered on religion. *Reproduced by permission of The Granger Collection.*

rify God, they had strict rules against dancing, card playing, drinking alcohol, and other "immoral" or "frivolous" pastimes. The Puritans held special days of thanksgiving when they had good fortune, and they fasted (went without food) when they experienced widespread sickness or prolonged dry spells without rainfall. (They thought they had caused these misfortunes themselves by committing sins, so they fasted to seek God's forgiveness.)

The Puritans did not observe the holy days traditionally celebrated in the Catholic Church and the Church of England—not even Christmas (the celebration of the birth of Jesus of Nazareth) and Easter (the commemoration of Jesus's resurrection, or rising from the dead). The Puritans thought the Catholic Church had simply made up religious holidays to fit the dates of pagan (non-Christian) rituals so it would be easier to convert nonbelievers to Christianity. They also considered the popular holidays such as May Day to be mere superstitions. (May Day was a celebration held in England on May 1, in the tradition of the spring fertility rites of Egypt and India.)

In fact, Plymouth and Massachusetts Bay officials passed laws that prohibited any special observances of Christmas, Easter, and other holidays. They strictly enforced these laws by imposing stiff fines and other punishments on violators. Not surprisingly there were frequent conflicts between the Puritans and colonists who did not share their beliefs. The most famous was an incident at the town of Merry Mount in Massachusetts Bay. In 1627 Plymouth governor William Bradford (1590–1657) led a small party of Puritans into Merry Mount and disrupted a May Day celebration. The festivities had been organized by Thomas Morton (c. 1590–1647), the leader of the town. Morton had long been a nuisance to the Puritans because he not only ridiculed their way of life but he also encouraged rowdy behavior at a trading post he operated in Merry Mount.

Morton was an Englishman who arrived in New England in 1625 with a company headed by a Captain Wollaston. Wollaston founded a settlement called Mount Wollaston (now the city of Quincy, Massachusetts) and Morton set up a trading post, which he named Merry Mount. After Wollaston moved to Virginia, Morton took control of Mount Wollaston and renamed the town Merry Mount. He immediately had problems with the Puritans, particularly the Plymouth settlers, who lived nearby. Morton and his companions were Anglicans, who engaged in all of the "sinful" activities prohibited by the Puritans. Plymouth citizens objected to Morton's trading post, where he sold whiskey, guns, and ammunition to Native Americans in exchange for furs. Moreover, in violation of the law, he showed Native Americans how to use firearms (weapons). But Puritans were especially troubled because he had interfered with their fur trading activities. For instance, when the Plymouth settlers opened their first trade route in Maine in 1625, Morton followed them and established his own contacts with Native American traders.

Plymouth authorities claimed that Merry Mount undermined morality in New England. Bradford later wrote in his history of Plymouth, titled *Of Plymouth Plantation* (first published in 1857), that Merry Mount was a "den of iniquity [sin]." Morton's establishment attracted drunken carousers (people who drink liquor and engage in rowdy behavior) and men of questionable character—historians say it was a favorite meeting place for pirates (bandits who robbed ships at sea). Even worse, some Christians came there to drink rum and often socialized with Native Americans. Morton's troubles peaked on May Day 1627 when he built an eighty-foot Maypole (a flower-wreathed pole that is the center of dancing and games) at Merry Mount and hosted a noisy celebration. Colonists and Native Americans enjoyed a day of drinking and dancing. The Puritans were furious because Morton was violating their law against the celebration of holidays.

Things to Remember While Reading "The Maypole of Merry-Mount":

- "The Maypole of Merry-Mount" is Morton's account of his May Day confrontation with the Puritans. It appears as a chapter titled "Of the Revels of New Canaan" in *New English Canaan*, a history of New England that Morton published in 1637. It gives one of the few existing non-Puritan descriptions of early colonial life in Massachusetts.

- Details in "The Maypole of Merry-Mount" explain why the Puritans disrupted Morton's festivities. They were certainly upset by the dancing, drinking, and uninhibited (unrestrained) behavior, which broke Puritan laws, but they also objected to May Day itself as a sinful celebration of fertility (sexual reproduction). The Puritans strongly disapproved of any public references to sexual matters. They were offended by the buck's horns (a symbol of male sexuality) atop the Maypole, and they were uncomfortable with the pole, which was intended as another symbol of male virility (manliness).

- To the Puritans, May Day was a pagan (Greek and Roman) ritual that offended the Christian God. (Christians believe in only one god, whereas the Greeks and Romans worshipped many gods.) Note Morton's references to Jupiter, the chief Roman god, and Ganymede, the cupbearer to the gods (one who brings them mead, an intoxicating drink). Although May Day honored the Christian saints Philip and Jacob, the Puritans disapproved of saints as simply another form of paganism created by the Catholic Church. To make matters worse, Native Americans—themselves pagans—had helped Morton put up the Maypole, which the Puritans called the Calf of Horeb (a golden false god worshipped by the ancient Israelites, who were not Christians).

- The fertility celebration had particular significance because Merry Mount, like many frontier settlements, probably had mostly male inhabitants. In the early colonial years men came to America without women in order to prepare the way for future settlers by building towns and starting farms. Women arrived much later. In 1627, the time of the May Day incident, the Massachusetts colony had not yet been settled and Merry Mount was one of a few trading post villages along the frontier. Life was rough, and European women generally could not be found in these remote areas. The men at Merry Mount were therefore playfully honoring Hymen, the Greek god of marriage, so he might bring some women to the town. According to Morton, the young men "lived in hope to have wives brought over to them."

"The Maypole of Merry-Mount"

*The Inhabitants of **Pasonagessit** (having translated the name of their habitation from that ancient savage name to Merry-Mount) did devise amongst themselves to have it performed in a solemn manner with **revels** and merriment after the old English custom. They prepared to set up a **Maypole** upon the festival day of **Philip and Jacob**; and brewed a barrel of excellent beer, and provided a case of bottles*

Pasonagessit: Native American place name meaning "Little neck of land"; now part of Braintree, Massachusetts

Revels: A wild party or celebration

Maypole: A decorated pole around which people dance on May Day

Philip and Jacob: May Day is the feast day honoring Philip and James (Jacob in Latin), saints in the Roman Catholic Church

to be **spent**, with other good cheer, for all comers of that day. And because they would have it in a complete form, they had prepared a song fitting to the time and present occasion. And upon Mayday they brought the Maypole to the place appointed, with drums, guns, pistols, and other fitting instruments, for that purpose; and there erected it with the help of Savages, that came there to see the manner of our revels. A goodly pine tree, eighty feet long, was **reared** up, with a pair of **buck's horns** nailed on, somewhat near unto the top of it: where it stood as a fair **sea mark** for directions; how to find out the way to my host of Merry-Mount [Morton was referring to himself].

The setting up of this Maypole was a lamentable spectacle to the precise **separatists** that lived at new Plymouth. They termed it an Idol; yea they called it the **Calf of Horeb**, and stood at **defiance** with the place, naming it Mount Dagon; threatening to make it a woeful mount not a merry mount. . . .

There was likewise a merry song made, which (to make their revels more fashionable) was sung with a chorus, every man bearing his part; which they performed in a dance, hand in hand about the Maypole while one of the Company sung, and filled out the good liquor like **Ganymede** and **Jupiter**:

> Drink and be merry, merry, merry, boys,
> Let all your delight be in **Hymen**'s joys,
> Joy to Hymen now the day is come,
> About the merry Maypole take a room.
> Make greene **garlands**, bring bottles out;
> And fill sweet **Nectar**,
> freely about,
> Uncover thy head, and fear no harm,
> For here's good liquor to keep it warm. . . .

This harmless **mirth** made by young men (that lived in hope to have wives brought over to them . . .) was much distasted by the precise Separatists . . . troubling their brains more than reason would require about things that are **indifferent**, and from that time sought occasion against my honest host of Merry-Mount to overthrow his undertakings, and to destroy his plantation quite and clean [completely]. . . .

Spent: Consumed until empty

Reared: Erected

Buck's horns: The horns of a male sheep or deer; considered a symbol of virility (manliness)

Sea mark: An elevated object serving as a guide to sailors

Separatists: The Pilgrims

Calf of Horeb: An idol falsely worshipped by Israelites as their deliverer from slavery in Egypt

Defiance: Resistance to authority

Ganymede: In Roman myth, the cupbearer to the gods

Jupiter: The chief Roman god, the god of the skies

Hymen: The Greek god of marriage

Garlands: Ropes made of vines or flowers

Nectar: In Greek and Roman mythology, the drink of the gods

Mirth: Gladness or gaiety expressed with loud laughter

Indifferent: Unimportant

What happened next . . .

Resolving to shut down Merry Mount, Puritan officials tried unsuccessfully to reason with Morton over the next several months. In 1628 a company of men led by Plymouth colonist Miles Standish (1584–1656) arrested Morton, but he managed to escape. He was soon recaptured and charged with selling guns to Native Americans. He was then deported (forced to leave a country) to England for trial. After Morton's departure John Endecott (1588–1665), the extremely stern governor of Massachusetts Bay, took over Merry Mount, chopped down the Maypole, and changed the name of the place to Mount Dagon. Morton was finally acquitted (found innocent) of the charges in England, and he returned to Massachusetts. He resumed trading with Native Americans and stirred up opposition to Endecott.

Thomas Morton, leader of Merry Mount, had long been a nuisance to the Puritans because he ridiculed their way of life and encouraged rowdy behavior at a trading post he operated in Merry Mount. *Reproduced by permission of Archive Photos, Inc.*

In 1630 Morton was again arrested, more or less for being a public nuisance. Historians speculate that he may also have been a spy for Ferdinando Gorges (c.1566–1647), head of the Council of New England (a private organization that promoted trade and settlement in New England), who wanted to make Massachusetts a royal colony. (A royal colony would be under the direct control of the English king. Leaders of the Plymouth Colony and the Massachusetts Bay Company had been given private charters, or grants of land. They were permitted to form their own governments without interference from the king.)

Before deporting Morton to England a second time, Massachusetts authorities placed him in stocks (a device used for public punishment), took all of his property, and burned down his house. Morton was acquitted once again and remained in England for over a decade. He worked as a legal counsel for Gorges, who was trying to revoke the charter of the Massachusetts Bay Company. In the mid-1630s Morton wrote *New English Canaan,* in which he encouraged others to seek their fortune in New England. ("Canaan" in the title refers to the Promised Land, or destined home, of the Israelites in the Christian Bible. Likewise, New England was the promised land of the Puritans, who sought religious and political freedom.) Yet he also ridiculed Puritan manners and narrow-mindedness, depicting the Native Americans as being more Christian than the Puritans. Although he knew the Puritans would seek revenge for the book, Morton returned to Massachusetts in 1643. He was immediately arrested and jailed in Boston for two years. Upon his release in 1645, officials forced him to go to Maine, which was being colonized by Gorges. Morton died in poverty in 1647.

Did you know . . .

- Morton was unknown at the time of his death, but *New English Canaan* became a classic work of literature that influenced several American writers. Among them was Nathaniel Hawthorne (1804–1864), an author who was also harshly critical of the Puritans. In addition to such tales as *The Scarlet Letter,* Hawthorne wrote "The Maypole of Merrymount," a story based on Morton's celebration.

- The Pilgrims encountered numerous obstacles to making the Plymouth Colony a success. They had no luck in establishing a fur trade, which was thriving in other colonies, because they knew little about business. Pilgrim leaders paid attention to immediate needs rather than long-term plans, and they would admit only Nonconformists to the colony. In fact, they invited large numbers of Nonconformists from Europe even when there was a severe shortage of food. In 1692 the English government merged Plymouth with Massachusetts Bay under a royal charter that formed the colony of Massachusetts.

For more information

Colbert, David, ed. *Eyewitness to America.* New York: Pantheon Books, 1997, pp. 25–26.

Connors, Donald Francis. *Thomas Morton.* New York: Twayne Publishers, 1969.

Elliott, Emory, and others, eds. *American Literature: A Prentice-Hall Anthology.* Englewood Cliffs, N.J.: Prentice-Hall, 1991, pp. 105–06.

Johnson, Allen, and others, eds. *Dictionary of American Biography.* New York: Scribner, 1946–1958, p. 267.

Middleton, Richard. *Colonial America: A History, 1585–1776.* Second edition. Malden, Mass.: Blackwell Publishers, 1996, pp. 86–98.

Stephen, Leslie, and Sidney Lee, eds. *The Dictionary of National Biography.* London, England: Oxford University Press, 1917, pp. 1055–57.

Excerpt From the Trial of Anne Hutchinson

Reprinted in *Major Problems in American Colonial History*
Published in 1993
Edited by Karen Ordahl Kupperman

In the Massachusetts Bay Colony, which was founded as an ideal Puritan community, religious disputes often became legal problems. Although religion and government were supposedly separate, only men who were members of the Puritan church could vote or hold office. The Puritans expected some political debates, but they would not tolerate views that threatened the religious harmony of the colony. A few years after the initial settlement of Massachusetts Bay, several dissidents (those who question or oppose the laws of the church) engaged in activities that undermined Puritan society. One of the most prominent was Puritan minister Roger Williams (c.1603–1683), who advocated the complete separation of church and state. He argued that religion was corrupted by any government interference in spiritual affairs. In his view, magistrates (officials who administer laws) should have no power to use laws to enforce church doctrine (system of belief).

Williams went even further by challenging the legal basis of the colony itself. He claimed that the English king, Charles I (1600–1649), had had no right to grant a charter (legal agreement) for the founding of Salem, Massachusetts, in

"It is said, I will pour by Spirit upon your Daughters, and they shall prophesie. . . If god give me a gift of Prophecy, I may use it."

1629 because the land belonged to the Native Americans. After a prolonged struggle with Puritan officials, Williams was banished from (forced to leave) Massachusetts Bay. He then founded and governed Rhode Island, the first American colony to be based on separation of church and state. Williams also left the Puritan church and started the first Baptist church in the American colonies. (Baptist is a shortened form of Anabaptists, a Christian group who believed that infants should not be baptized, or inducted into the Christian faith through immersion in water).

Another famous dissident was Anne Marbury Hutchinson (1591–1643), who moved to Massachusetts Bay in 1636. Hutchinson was born in Alford, England, the oldest of thirteen children of Anglican (also known as the Church of England; the official state religion) clergyman Francis Marbury and his second wife, Bridget Dryden Marbury. Before Anne's birth Francis Marbury was imprisoned twice for rejecting church dogma (established opinion). Anne was baptized in the Anglican faith and received an education far superior to that provided to most young women in the seventeenth century. From an early age she was exposed to religious discussions in the family home, and she became familiar with church doctrine and Scripture (passages from the Bible). She was also influenced by her father's rebellious spirit and contempt for authority. In 1605 the family moved from Alford to London. Anne lived in London until 1612, when she married William Hutchinson, an affluent businessman. While living in Alford, Anne began attending services at St. Botolph's, a church headed by Puritan theologian John Cotton (1585–1652) in Boston, Lincolnshire. The Hutchinsons then moved to Alford, where they lived for the next twenty-two years.

At the time Hutchinson began attending St. Botolph's, Cotton was attempting to modify Puritan doctrine. One of the central doctrines of Puritanism was the belief that salvation (being saved from sin) could be earned only through good works (moral behavior). This was known to many as the covenant of works. Hutchinson was inspired by Cotton's emphasis upon the covenant of grace rather than the covenant of works. According to the covenant of grace, a Christian believer could gain salvation through revelation (direct communication with God). This doctrine became popular because it freed people from having to do good works in order to be saved from sin. Cotton insisted, however, that his followers continue doing good works whether or not they had received revelation from God. Hutchinson took the idea much further.

Hutchinson believed that Christians who had achieved grace actually became the spirit of God. Therefore, according to Hutchinson, the covenant of grace made the covenant of works unnecessary. That is, if people had this special connection with God, then they did not have to do good works to show that they had been saved. Hutchinson embraced the covenant of grace after the deaths of two of her daughters in 1630 and the later death of her father. She claimed to have received revelations from God during these experiences. Therefore, according to the covenant of grace, she was still saved despite the tragedies in her life. (Puritans believed that if they suffered misfortune they had done something to offend God and had to gain his forgiveness by doing good works. Hutchinson believed that if they had already been saved, however, they could not be held responsible for misfortunes.)

In 1633 Cotton was forced to resign his ministry because of his views. He then fled to the Massachusetts Bay Colony in America and took a position at the Puritan church in Boston. Soon afterward Hutchinson announced to her family that God had instructed her to follow Cotton to Massachusetts. William was a devoted husband who always supported her religious beliefs, so a year later the Hutchinsons left England on board the ship *Griffin.* In September 1634 they arrived in Boston, where William Hutchinson entered into the textile (fabric) trade. He eventually became quite successful and the Hutchinson family occupied a prominent position in the community. Anne Hutchinson's kind manner and her skills as a midwife (a person who assists women in childbirth) made her popular with affluent Boston women. During this time she became aware of the Massachusetts Puritans' belief in the covenant of works.

Determined to promote the covenant of grace, Hutchinson held private meetings for both men and women in her home. These gatherings usually began with a calm discussion of Cotton's sermons. Then, because Hutchinson possessed an intense intellect, people asked her to explain some of the more confusing aspects of Puritan doctrine. Finally, her

Anne Hutchinson preaching in her house in Boston, Massachusetts. *Reproduced by permission of The Library of Congress.*

religious fervor would take over, and she often became careless in advancing her own ideas and labeling them as Cotton's. Before long, Hutchinson had many followers who believed in her version of the covenant of grace.

Hutchinson conducted her meetings without interruption until 1635, when the prominent Puritan clergyman John Wilson returned to Boston from England. Hutchinson became increasingly troubled by Wilson's sermons, so she informed her followers that he was simply preaching another version of the covenant of works. In fact, she contended, most Massachusetts clergymen were promoting this doctrine. The only exceptions, she said, were Cotton and her brother-in-law, John Wheelwright (1592–1679), who both preached the covenant of grace. Not surprisingly, with these charges Hutchinson created a division between her followers and traditional Puritans, who charged that she was committing a form of heresy (a religious opinion contrary to church teachings) called antinomianism. Antinomianism was the belief that God had predetermined who would be saved from sin, so all people—including ministers—were powerless to change the situation by doing good works. Puritan leaders were especially angry because she challenged their authority to decide who was worthy of salvation. The rift rapidly spread through the entire colony, becoming a serious threat in 1637, when her male followers refused to fight in the Pequot War. (The Pequot War broke out when the Puritans, in retaliation for the murder of two English traders by Native Americans, nearly exterminated the Pequot tribe.) Puritan officials immediately charged Hutchinson with heresy.

Although Hutchinson was the principal agitator (one who stirs up public feeling) in the Puritan conflict, she was not the first to be punished. In March 1637 Wheelwright was brought before the Massachusetts General Court and charged with sedition (resistance against lawful authority). It was not until September 1637 that a church synod (advisory council) finally condemned Hutchinson for her religious beliefs. By this time, she had lost much of her support. After John Winthrop (1588–1649; see "John Winthrop's Christian Experience"), was reelected governor, several of Hutchinson's followers were removed from public office. Cotton even sided with church officials after making sure he would not get into trouble for teaching the covenant of grace. Wheelwright, Hutchinson's only remaining ally, was banished from the colony in November 1637.

Soon after Wheelwright was banished, Hutchinson was brought before the General Court and accused of defying the teachings of Puritan ministers. She was also charged with violating laws that forbade her, as a woman, to speak in public and to teach men or people older than herself.

Things to Remember While Reading excerpt From the Trial of Anne Hutchinson:

- The following excerpts were taken from a transcript of Hutchinson's trial in 1637. Puritan officials published the transcript in order to gain public support for their decision to banish her. Various officials, including Winthrop, questioned Hutchinson; all are referred to as "Court."

Excerpt From the Trial of Anne Hutchinson

*. . . [A] woman had been the breeder and nourisher of all these **distempers**, one Mistress Hutchi[n]son, the wife of Mr. William Hutchi[n]son of* Boston *(a very honest and peaceable man of good **estate**) and the daughter of Mr.* Marbury, *sometimes a Preacher in* Lincolnshire, *after of* London, *a woman of a very **haughty** and fierce **carriage** of a **nimble** wit and active spirit, and a very **voluble** tongue, more bold than a man, though in understanding and judgement, inferiour to many women. This woman had learned her skill in* England, *and had discovered some of her opinions in the Ship, as she came over, which had caused some jealousy of her, which gave occasion of some delay of her admission, when she first desired fellowship with the Church of* Boston, *but she **cunningly dissembled** and coloured her opinions, as she soon got over the block, and was admitted into the Church, then she began to go to work, and being a woman very helpful in the times of childbirth, and other occasions of bodily infirmities, and well furnished with means for those purposes, she easily **insinuated** herself into the affections of many, and the rather, because she was much **inquisitive** of them about their spiritual estates, and in discovering to them the danger they were in, by trusting to common gifts and graces. . . . [I]ndeed it was a wonder upon what a sudden the whole Church of* Boston *(some few excepted) were become her new **converts**, and **infected** with her opinions, and many also out of the Church, and of other Churches also, yea, many **profane** persons became of her opinion, for it was a very easy, and acceptable way to heaven, to see nothing, to have nothing, but wait for Christ to do all; . . . then she kept open house for all comers, and set up two Lecture days in the week, when they usually met at her*

Distempers: Disorders

Estate: Position, situation

Haughty: Proud

Carriage: Attitude

Nimble: Quick

Voluble: Talkative

Cunningly dissembled: Cleverly disguised

Insinuated: Manipulated

Inquisitive: Questioning

Converts: People persuaded to adopt a religion or belief

Infected: Affect people with an idea of belief

Profane: Irreligious

Threescore: Thirty

Fourscore: Forty

Hither: To this place

Broached: Addressed

Divulged: Revealed

house, **threescore** or **fourscore** persons, the pretence was to repeat Sermons, but when that was done, she would comment upon the Doctrines, and interpret all passages at her pleasure, and expound dark places of Scripture. . . .

When she appeared, the Court spoke to her to this effect.

Mistris Hutchi[n]son. You are called **hither** as one of those who have had a great share in the causes of our public disturbances, partly by those erroneous opinions which you have **broached** and **divulged** amongst us, and maintaining them, partly by **countenancing** and encouraging such as have sowed **seditions** amongst us, partly by casting **reproach** upon the faithful. Ministers of this Country, and upon their Ministry, and so weakening their hands in the work of the Lord, and raising prejudice against them, in the hearts of their people, and partly by maintaining weekly and public meetings in your house, to the offence of all the Country, and the **detriment** of many families, and still upholding the same, since such meetings were clearly condemned in the late general Assembly.

American religious leader Anne Hutchinson during her heresy trial which resulted in her banishment from the Massachusetts colony. *Reproduced by permission of The Bettmann Archive/ Corbis-Bettman.*

Now the end of your sending for [sending for you], is, that either upon sight of your errors, and other offences, you may be brought to acknowledge, and reform the same, or otherwise that we may take such course with you as you may trouble us no further. . . .

Court: Have you countenanced, or will you justify those seditious practises which have been **censured** here in this Court?

Hutchinson: Do you ask me upon point of conscience?

Court: No, your conscience you may keep to yourself, but if in this cause you shall countenance and encourage those that thus **transgress** the Law, you must be called in question for it, and that is not for your conscience, but for your practise.

Hutchinson: What Law have they transgressed? the Law of God?

Court: Yes, the fifth Commandement, which commands us to honour Father and Mother, which includes all in authority, but these

Countenancing: Acknowledging

Seditions: Acts inciting rebellion against authority

Reproach: Criticism

Detriment: Disadvantage

Censured: Forbidden

Transgress: Violate

seditious practices of theirs, have cast reproach and dishonour upon the Fathers of the Commonwealth [Massachusetts]. . . .

Court: . . . what say you to your weekly public meetings? can you show a warrant for them?

Hutchinson: I will show you how I took it up, there were such meetings in use before I came, and because I went to none of them, this was the special reason of my taking up this course, we began it but with five or six, and though it grew to more in future time, yet being tolerated at the first, I knew not why it might not continue.

*Court: There were private meetings indeed, and are still in many places, of some few neighbours, but not so public and frequent as yours, and are of use for increase of love, and mutual **edification**, but yours are of another nature, if they had been such as yours they had been evil, and therefore no good **warrant** to justify yours; but answer by what authority, or rule, you uphold them.*

Hutchinson: . . . where the elder women are to teach the younger.

*Court: So we allow you to do . . . privately, and upon occasion, but that gives no warrant of such set meetings for that purpose; and besides, you take upon you to teach many that are elder than your-self, neither do you teach them that which the **Apostle** commands [namely] to keep at home.*

Hutchinson: Will you please to give me a rule against it, and I will yield?

Court: You must have a rule for it, or else you cannot do it in faith, yet you have a plain rule against it; I permit not a woman to teach.

Hutchinson: That is meant of teaching men.

Court: If a man in distress of conscience or other temptation . . . should come and ask your counsel in private, might you not teach him?

Hutchinson: Yes.

Court: Then it is clear, that it is not meant of teaching men, but of teaching in public.

*Hutchinson: It is said, I will pour my Spirit upon your Daughters, and they shall **prophesie**. . . If God give me a gift of Prophecy, I may use it.*

Edification: Intellectual, moral, or spiritual improvement

Warrant: Evidence; proof

Apostle: One of the twelve followers Christ chose to preach the gospel

Prophesie: Prophesy; predict on the basis of mystical knowledge

What happened next . . .

At one point during the trial, Hutchinson was nearly cleared of all charges. Then she announced that she had received a direct revelation from God. This was clearly a heretical claim (a violation of church teachings) because Puritan leaders believed that God spoke to humans only through the Bible. The frightened judges immediately ruled that Hutchinson was to be banished from the colony. She would be allowed to remain through the winter, but she was to be placed in the custody of Joseph Weld of Roxbury. Despite Weld's attempts to persuade her to repent, (expressed regret for her behavior) Hutchinson continued to speak out against the church.

When Hutchinson was brought to trial again in March 1638, she failed to convince the judges that she had genuinely repented. She was therefore formally excommunicated (banished) from the church. Hutchinson left Massachusetts with her family and joined her husband at a settlement on the island of Aquidneck in Narragansett Bay, off the coast of Roger Williams' Rhode Island colony. She was followed by more than eighty families of supporters who had also been excommunicated. After William Hutchinson died in 1642, Anne Hutchinson moved with her six youngest children to the Dutch colony of New Netherland (now New York). They settled in Pelham Bay Park (now the Bronx section of New York City, near the Hutchinson River, which was named for Anne Hutchinson). The following year Hutchinson and five of her children were attacked and killed by Native Americans.

Did you know . . .

- Hutchinson gave birth to twelve children during her lifetime. Three of the children died. She also suffered an extremely difficult miscarriage (delivery of a dead fetus before the end of a nine-month term) after she and her family moved to Rhode Island. In a biographical sketch in *Notable American Women,* scholar Emery Battis wrote that the Puritan clergy and magistrates (a civil officer with the power to administer the law) ". . . solemnly pronounced a conclusive evidence" that the miscarriage was God's way of punishing Hutchinson for committing heresy. They therefore felt justified in banning her from the colony.

- One of Hutchinson's followers was Mary Dyer (?–1660), who also left the Massachusetts Bay Colony in 1638. Returning to England with her husband in 1652, Dyer became a Quaker (member of the Society of Friends, a Puritan group that believed in direct communication with God through an "inner light"). When she went back to New England five years later she was imprisoned because a recent law had imposed the death penalty on practicing Quakers. Although Dyer had been banished from Massachusetts Bay, she returned there twice in defiance (disobedience) of the law. After her second visit, in 1660, she was executed. Today Dyer is considered a symbol of religious freedom.

- Nathaniel Hawthorne (1804–1864), the great nineteenth-century American writer—and a harsh critic of Puritan society—used Hutchinson as the model for the character Hester Prynne in *The Scarlet Letter* (1850). Now a classic in American literature, *The Scarlet Letter* tells the story of Prynne, a woman who has a child out of wedlock (outside marriage) and is forced to wear the red letter "A" at all times as a sign of her sin of adultery.

For more information

Crawford, Deborah. *Four Women in a Violent Time: Anne Hutchinson (1591–1643), Mary Dyer (1591?–1660), Lady Deborah Moody (1660–1659), Penelope Stout (1622–1732)*. New York: Crown Publishers, 1970.

Faber, Doris. *Anne Hutchinson*. Champaign, Ill.: Garrard Publishing Co., 1970.

Kupperman, Karen Ordahl, ed. *Major Problems in American Colonial History*. Lexington, Mass.: D.C. Heath and Company, 1993, pp. 159–61.

Williams, Selma R. *Divine Rebel: The Life of Anne Marbury Hutchinson*. New York: Holt, Rinehart, and Winston, 1981.

Personal Narratives

American colonists had limited access to reading materials. Not only were most books still being published in Europe, but also Puritans forebade the reading of any literature except the Bible, religious poetry, and personal narratives. Although Puritans lived mainly in New England, their influence extended to the other colonies. Therefore the earliest form of American literature was autobiographical poetry, essays, and narratives in which people examined their souls and shared their experiences—much like participants in television "talk shows" today. One the best-known spiritual autobiographies was written by Puritan minister **John Winthrop.** Excerpts from his book, *John Winthrop's Christian Experience,* detail his struggle to lead a godly life. Perhaps the most popular narrative at the time was written by colonists who had been captured by Native Americans and survived to tell the tale. **Mary Rowlandson**'s *The Narrative of the Captivity and Restauration of Mrs. Mary Rowlandson* provided a description of her time in captivity and became a best seller.

The first published American poet was **Anne Dudley Bradstreet,** a Massachusetts housewife, whose poems gave a vivid account of colonial life and are still being read today. Another remarkable woman was **Sarah Kemble Knight,** who embarked on a trip alone through the New England wilderness. *The Journal of Madame Knight* provides a witty description of her journey. Bradstreet and Knight were liberated women by the standards of the colonial period, partly because they had supportive husbands. But most women had to abide by laws that made them the property of their husbands. An example was New Jersey housewife and teacher **Elizabeth Ashbridge,** who was abused by her husband because she disobeyed him and became a Quaker. Her moving autobiography, *Some Account of the Early Part of the Life of Elizabeth Ashbridge, . . . Written by Herself,* is a dramatic account of this abuse.

The most acclaimed autobiography in early American literature was written by inventor and statesman **Benjamin Franklin.** Franklin, who ran away from his home in Boston, Massachusetts, to seek his fortune in Philadelphia, Pennsylvania, is considered the model of the American self-made man. Another self-made man was **John Adams,** the second president of the United States, who left his family's Massachusetts farm to attend Harvard College. Excerpts from Adams's diary describe how a young man became a lawyer at a time when there were no law schools in the colonies.

John Winthrop

John Winthrop's Christian Experience
Reprinted in *Early American Writing*
Published in 1994
Edited by Giles Gunn

The Massachusetts Bay Colony was founded in 1630 by a group of Puritans (Protestant Christians who advocated strict moral and religious codes). Like the Pilgrims who settled the nearby Plymouth Colony in 1620 (see "The Pilgrims' Landing and First Winter"), they were fleeing persecution (punishment or discrimination because of their beliefs) they had faced in England. The Massachusetts Bay Puritans saw their venture as an opportunity to enjoy religious freedom and to establish an "ideal" community that would serve as a model for Puritans in England. In the ideal community, inhabitants would form separate congregations (groups who worship together) devoted to strict adherence to Puritan doctrines. Guided by ministers and members of the "elect" (certain people who had been chosen by God for salvation, or forgiveness of sins), they would live in harmony and glorify God. Within fifteen years, however, the ideal community was beset by political and religious turmoil, and by the late 1600s the Massachusetts Bay experiment was a failure.

The Massachusetts Bay Puritans were led by John Winthrop (1588–1649), a wealthy Englishman and member of

> "I had also a great striveing in my heart to draw others to God."

the elect, and the first governor of the colony. Winthrop was born into the aristocracy (upper or ruling class) in Suffolk, England. In 1603, at age fourteen, he entered Cambridge University. Although he left after two years without a degree, he was following the custom of most young gentlemen of the time. He also briefly attended Gray's Inn, where aristocrats studied law, but again he left without a degree. When Winthrop returned to the family estate, Groton Manor, in 1605, he had become a Puritan. Immediately he entered into an arranged marriage to Mary Forth of Great Stambridge, Essex. Over the next decade the couple had six children. Six months after Mary died in 1615, Winthrop wed Thomasine Clopton; unfortunately, she died within a year. He married for a third time in 1618, at the age of thirty. His new wife was Margaret Tyndal, a woman who shared his religious convictions, and they lived happily together for nearly thirty years.

By 1617 Winthrop had inherited Groton Manor. While serving as a justice of the peace (local judge who handles minor legal offenses), he began to study law more seriously. In 1627 Winthrop took a position as a government attorney. By this time, the Church of England (also known as the Anglican Church; the official state religion) began to promote good works as a means of salvation (forgiveness of sins). In other words, church members would perform good deeds and clergymen would then forgive their sins. Puritans were horrified at this new development, since they believed only God could determine who had earned salvation. Consequently, many Puritans felt so strongly about this issue that they left England for European countries such as the Netherlands. Others, including Winthrop, looked toward America.

In 1629 Winthrop joined the New England Company, a group of investors planning to start a settlement near the Plymouth Colony in Massachusetts. King Charles I (1600–1649) had granted the company a parcel (section) of land between the Charles and Merrimack rivers in Massachusetts, which was owned by the Council for New England (a private organization that promoted trade and settlement in New England). A small group of Puritans, under the leadership of John Endecott (1588–1665), had already gone to Massachusetts to pave the way for a "great migration" of Puritans. Winthrop and his associates, who would be part of that migration (moving from one country to settle in another), received a royal charter (the right to found a colony that would be ruled by the king) under the new name of "Governor and Company of the Massachusetts Bay in New England."

Although the Massachusetts Bay Company had initially planned to promote trade in the colony, their emphasis soon shifted to religion. Before leaving for America, Winthrop organized the signing of the Cambridge Agreement. It stated that, once they reached America, they would buy out the company, take over the charter, and govern the colony independently. Thus the Massachusetts Bay Company was the only colonizing venture that did not come under the control of governors in England—a situation that would lead to serious problems within only a few years. In 1629 Winthrop was chosen to head the company and he began assembling the fleet of eleven ships that would take the settlers to America. To help meet expenses he sold his estate. After arranging for his wife and children to join him in 1631, he set out with the first Massachusetts Bay settlers on the lead ship *Arbella*.

The Puritans arrived at Salem, Massachusetts, in 1630. As head of the Massachusetts Bay Company, Winthrop took over the position of governor from Endecott. The first order of business was to organize the Massachusetts Bay Colony on the basis of separate religious congregations that chose their own ministers. This decision led to diversity among congregations, which later became a severe problem in the colony. Winthrop also established a government, keeping power in his own hands with the aid of a few assistants. He gave some authority to freemen (men with the full rights of citizens; women had no rights), who served on a general assembly (law-making body). In 1634, when the freemen challenged Winthrop to show them the company's charter, they realized they were entitled to more power than he had allowed them. The freemen then formed a new assembly, elected members from each town, and voted Winthrop out of office in 1635. He was replaced by colonist John Haynes (1594–1654).

Winthrop's political fortunes over the next several years reflected the chaos in the Massachusetts Bay Colony. Although he was continually voted in and out of office during this time, he held his seat on the council (officials who administered the government) and continued to be a powerful force.

Along with Endecott and others, Winthrop supported a strict theocracy (control of the government by the church) and bitterly opposed the activities of religious dissidents (those who disagree with church practices). The Massachusetts Bay charter, which organized the colony on the basis of separate congregations, had opened the way for religious diversity. Many colonists were now refusing to conform to Puritan doctrines (established opinions). The problem was that the traditional Puritans (those who shared the vision of the founding fathers of the colony) would not tolerate any views but their own. Therefore, they were greatly disturbed by the protests of such dissidents as the Anabaptists, Presbyterians, and Quakers. All of these groups had their own Puritan congregations, but they followed different versions of Puritanism.

The Anabaptists (later called Baptists) opposed the baptism of infants, believing this ritual should be reserved only for adults who understood the meaning of religious conversion. (Baptism is a Christian ceremony in which a person is admitted to the church by being immersed in water or having water sprinkled on the head.) They also demanded complete separation of church and state. The Presbyterians asserted that church membership should be open to all people who agreed to live according to God's commandments rather than those who claimed to have achieved salvation (being saved from sin). But most threatening to the traditional Puritans were the Quakers (Society of Friends), who challenged not only the Puritan beliefs practiced in the colony but also its society and government. They advocated direct communication between the individual Christian and God, without the aid of ministers or a formal church, a belief that was the basis of the Massachusetts Bay community.

In 1636 the colony faced yet another crisis: Native American resistance to English settlement. As a result of the "great migration," the New England population was rapidly rising (it was four thousand in 1634 and would reach eleven thousand in 1638). The Puritans began to move west onto land that was controlled by the Pequots, a neighboring Native American tribe. For instance, the Hartford settlement (in present-day Connecticut) was established by Baptist minister Thomas Hooker (1586–1647), and nearby Fort Saybrook was built by the English Saybrook Company near the Pequot village of Mystic.

Native Americans attacking a colonial settlement during the Pequot War.
Reproduced by permission of Archive Photos, Inc.

The Puritans' main goal was to rid the area of all Native Americans. Even though the colonists had signed a treaty with the Pequots, they hoped to provoke the Native American group into breaking the agreement. Their opportunity came when Native Americans from an unknown tribe killed two English colonists, John Stone and John Oldham. The Puritans accused the Pequots of committing the murders, but the Pequots denied any involvement and even offered to negotiate with the colonists. The Puritans responded by demanding that the Pequots turn over the killers to prove they were not doing the work of the devil. (The Puritans believed that any disaster or misfortune was caused by the devil, or Satan, against whom they were constantly waging a battle.) The Pequots could not produce the killers. In September 1636, Endecott—now the military commander in Massachusetts—therefore led an attack on the Pequots and their allies on Block Island (off the coast of Rhode Island), thus beginning the Pequot War. After the Pequots retaliated by laying siege to Fort Saybrook, the conflict remained low-key for some time. When western settlers became worried that the Pequots would win the war, however, fighting soon escalated. The war finally ended at Mystic in 1637, after the settlers burned the village and exterminated nearly all the Pequots. The few survivors were either killed later by the Puritans or they fled to other parts of the country. (In 1638 the Treaty of Hartford declared the Pequot nation dissolved.)

Making matters even worse for Massachusetts Bay was the fact that the English government was trying to gain control of the colony. Fernando Gorges (1566–1647), head of the Council for New England, belatedly realized Charles I (1600–1649) had permitted the colonists to settle on land that was still in the possession of the council. Gorges did not approve of their independent charter and he wanted them to abide by the New England Council's plan of government. In 1634 William Laud (1573–1645), the Archbishop of Canterbury (the highest official in the Church of England), was appointed head of a committee to investigate the charter. Laud had been instrumental in removing Puritans from positions of power in England, so he was interested in keeping American congregations under the control of the English church. All Puritans, except the Nonconformists in the Plymouth Colony, had remained Anglicans, which ordained (officially appointed) Puritan ministers. (The Puritans were certain they could reform the church from within.)

When the committee discovered that the charter was not tied to any governing body in England, they began proceedings to terminate the Massachusetts Bay Company. In 1637 Charles I announced that he would rule Massachusetts through a royal governor and council, and Gorges would be his deputy (first representative). This was a victory for Gorges, who was supported by Massachusetts Bay trader and adventurer Thomas Morton (c. 1590–c. 1649; see "The Maypole of Merry-Mount"). The new royal government was never put in place, however, since England was also in turmoil at the time. Charles I had dismissed the Parliament in order to prevent Puritans from holding office and he was unsuccessfully trying to manage his empire alone. Gorges was left with wilderness territory in Maine, north of Massachusetts Bay.

In the meantime, Puritan leaders had been struggling to maintain harmony in Massachusetts Bay. They thought they might solve some of their problems by getting rid of religious dissidents (people who refuse to accept the beliefs or practices of an established religion). Their strategy involved trying to pressure the rebels into accepting traditional Puritan doctrine. If that method was a failure, they forced the troublemakers to leave the colony. For instance, in 1635 Haynes banished Roger Williams (1603–1683), an advocate of the separation of church and state, who later founded the Rhode Island colony. In 1636 Massachusetts officials also confronted Anne Hutchinson (1591–1643), a prominent figure in the community, who was challenging basic Puritan teachings (see Exerpt From the Trial of Anne Hutchinson). Some of Hutchinson's supporters were working for political as well as religious change. Among them were merchants who opposed tax and trade policies of the council. They scored a victory in the election of 1636, replacing Haynes with a new governor, Henry Vane (1613–1662), a member of Hutchinson's congregation.

Winthrop was again elected governor in 1637, and he immediately convened the Massachusetts General Court (a panel of judges that decided the laws of the colony) to review dissident cases. When the court ruled in favor of the traditional Puritans, government leaders moved to put Hutchinson and others on trial for sedition (resistance against lawful authority). Winthrop was actively involved in the trials. In 1637, at the height of the religious and political chaos in the colony, he wrote "John Winthrop's Christian Experience."

Things to Remember While Reading *John Winthrop's Christian Experience:*

- *John Winthrop's Christian Experience* is a famous spiritual autobiography (record of an individual soul's struggle between God and Satan). Puritan ministers encouraged church members to write about intense personal suffering, and Puritan leaders presented their own lives as models for the inspiration of others. By portraying himself as a flawed human being who struggled to resist the temptations of the world, Winthrop intended to help average Massachusetts Bay colonists overcome evil in their own lives. The goal was to achieve the Puritan ideal of moral and spiritual perfection.

• In his spiritual autobiography Winthrop traced his religious development from childhood to 1637 (the year he wrote the essay), when he was forty-nine years old. The excerpts included here begin with his student days at Cambridge, when he converted to Puritanism, then move on to his early marriage, his first encounter with the covenant of grace, and other significant events. (The covenant of grace was a Puritan belief that those who were willing to strictly obey God's laws were granted the state of being protected or sanctified by the favor of God.) Throughout *Christian Experience*, Winthrop portrayed an unrelenting struggle with evil, which frequently threatened to overwhelm him. Although he made no direct mention of the recent political and religious crises in Massachusetts Bay, he remarked that he had "gone under continuall conflicts between the flesh and the spirit, and sometimes with Satan himself (which I have more discerned of late then I did formerly)."

John Winthrop's Christian Experience

*About 14 years of age, being in Cambridge [University] I fell into a lingring feaver, which took away the comfort of my life. For being there neglected, and despised, I went up and down mourning with myself; and being deprived of my youthfull joyes, I **betook** my self to God whom I did believe to bee very good and mercifull, and would welcome any that would come to him, especially such a **yongue** soule, and so well qualifyed as I took my self to bee; so as I took pleasure in drawing neer to him. But how my heart was affected with my sins, or*

Betook: Caused to go or move

Youngue: Young

Christ: Jesus of Nazareth; founder of Christianity

Essex: A country in England

*what thoughts I had of **Christ** I remember not. But I was willing to love God, and therefore I thought hee loved mee. . . .*

*About 18 yeares of age (being a man in stature, and in understanding as my parents conceived mee) I married into a family under Mr. Culverwell his ministry in **Essex**; and living there sometimes I first found the ministry of the word [of God] to come to my heart with power (for in all before I found onely light) and after that I found the like in the ministry of many others. So as there began to bee some change which I perceived in my self, and others took notice of. Now I began to come under strong exercises of Conscience: (yet by fits only) I could no longer **dally** with Religion. God put my soule to sad tasks sometimes, which yet the flesh would shake off, and **outweare** still. . . .*

*Now came I to some peace and comfort in God and in his wayes, my chief delight was therein, I loved a Christian, and the very ground hee went upon. I honoured a **faythful** minister in my heart and could have kissed his feet: Now I grew full of zeal (which outranne my knowledge and carried mee sometimes beyond my calling) and very liberall to any good work. I had an **unsatiable** thirst after the word of God and could not misse a good sermon, though [even if it was] many miles off, especially of such as did search deep into the conscience. I had also a great strieving in my heart to draw others to God. It pittyed my heart to see men so little to regard their soules, and to despise that happines which I knew to bee better then all the world besides, which stirred mee up to take any opportunity to draw men to God, and by successe in my endeavors I took much encouragement hereunto. But those affections were not constant but very unsetled. . . .*

*But as I grew into employment and **credit** thereby; so I grew also in pride of my **guifts**, and under temptations which sett mee on work to look to my evidence more narrowly then I had done before (for the great change which God had **wrought** in mee, and the generall **approbation** of good ministers and other Christians, kept mee from makeing any great question of my good estate, though my secrett corruptions, and some tremblings of heart (which was greatest when I was among the most Godly persons) put me to some **plunges**; but especially when I perceived a great decay in my zeale and love, etc.).*

John Winthrop. His spiritual autobiography traced his religious development from childhood to middle age. *Reproduced by permission of The Library of Congress.*

Dally: Waste time

Outweare: Overcome

Faythful: Faithful

Unsatiable: Incapable of being satisfied

Credit: Honor

Guifts: Gifts

Wrought: Put together

Approbation: An act of officially approving

Plunges: Situations entered into suddenly

Eminent: Distinguished, well known

Hypocrite: A person who puts on a false appearance of virtue or religion

Intermissions: Temporary suspensions of activities

Yoake: Yoke; a collar put on work animals

Faine: Happy

Covenant of grace: The Puritan belief that those who were willing to strictly obey God's laws were granted the state of being protected or sanctified by the favor of God

Moses: In the Old Testament of the Bible, the Hebrew prophet who led the Israelites out of slavery from Egypt; significant to Winthrop because at Mount Sinai Moses also delivered to the Israelites the law establishing God's covenant with them

Affliction: To inflict suffering upon or to cause distress to

Weaned: Detached from a thing of dependence

Vile: Disgusting; unpleasant

Wretch: A miserable or unfortunate person

Discerned: Determined

Lyen: Lain

*. . . I was ashamed to open my case to any minister that knew mee; I feared it would shame my self and religion also, that such an **eminent** professour as I was accounted, should discover such corruptions as I found in my selfe, and had in all this time attained no better evidence of salvation; and I should prove a **hypocrite** it was too late to begin anew. . . .*

*While I wandred up and downe in this sad and doubtful estate (wherein yet I had many **intermissions**, for the flesh would often shake off this **yoake** of the law, but was still forced to come under it again) wherein my greatest troubles were not the sense of Gods wrath or fear of damnation, but want of assurance of salvation, and want of strength against my corruptions; I knew that my greatest want was fayth in Christ, and **faine** would I have been united to Christ but I thought I was not holy enough. . . .*

*Being in this condition it pleased the Lord . . . to manifest unto mee the difference between the **Covenant of grace**, and the Covenant of workes (but I took the foundation of that of workes to have been with man in innocency, and onely held forth in the law of **Moses** to drive us to Christ). This Covenant of grace began to take great impression in mee and I thought I had now enough. . . .*

*I was now about 30 yeares of age, and now was the time come that the Lord would reveale Christ unto mee whom I had long desired, but not so earnestly as since I came to see more clearly into the covenant of free grace. First therefore hee laid a sore **affliction** upon mee wherein hee laid mee lower in myne owne eyes then at any time before, and showed mee the emptines of all my guifts, and parts; left mee neither power nor will, so as I became as a **weaned** child. I could now no more look at what I had been or what I had done nor bee discontented for want of strength or assurance mine eyes were onely upon his free mercy in Jesus Christ. I knew I was worthy of nothing for I knew I could doe nothing for him or for my selfe. I could only mourn, and weep to think of free mercy to such a **vile wretch** as I was. . . .*

*Since this time I have gone under continuall conflicts between the flesh and the spirit, and sometimes with Satan himself (which I have more **discerned** of late then I did formerly) many falls I have had, and have **lyen** long under some, yet never quite **forsaken** of the Lord. But still when I have been put to it by any **suddaine** danger or fearefull temptation, the good spirit of the Lord hath not **fayled** to beare witnesse to mee, giveing mee comfort, and courage in the very **pinch**, when of my self I have been very fearefull, and dismayed. My usuall falls have been through dead heartedness, and **presumptuousnesse**,*

by which Satan hath taken advantage to wind mee into other sinnes.
*When the flesh **prevayles** the spirit withdrawes, and is sometimes so*
greived as hee seemes not to acknowledge his owne work. . . . .

What happened next . . .

Winthrop was elected governor for the final time in 1646, and he was still in office when he died three years later. Challenges to Puritan control of New England gained momentum. By 1660 more people were settling on isolated farms, away from churches and the guardians of strict morality. Merchants and laborers were putting their own individual needs above the community good. Non-Puritans arrived in greater numbers, seeking economic opportunity rather than joining the religious community. Church membership was declining rapidly, and soon there were few people who could claim to be saved. In desperation, some Puritan churches adopted the Half-Way Covenant, whereby children of any baptized person could be admitted to the church regardless of whether their parents were church members. Others took the Presbyterian position that anyone who led a moral life could join the church.

Meanwhile, Puritan officials were still fighting English threats to place them under royal control. Finally, in 1686, King James II (1633–1701) united Massachusetts Bay, Plymouth, Connecticut, Rhode Island, New Jersey, and New York into the Dominion of New England. He appointed Edmund Andros (1637–1714), an Anglican, as the royal governor. Andros was an unpopular leader who suppressed the rights of colonists. After James was overthrown in 1688 and the monarchs William III (1650–1702) and Mary II (1662–1694) took the throne in a transition called the Glorious Revolution. Now that Andros had no backing in England and could not defend himself against a rebellion, the colonists sent him and other officials to England as prisoners. Although the Dominion of New England had been dissolved, William and Mary did not restore the original charters to the colonies. Instead, in 1692,

Forsaken: To leave or abandon

Suddaine: Sudden

Fayled: Failed

Pinch: A difficult situation

Presumptuousness: Overstepping due bounds

Prevayles: Prevails; wins

Massachusetts Bay was placed under a royal charter with Plymouth, forming the single colony of Massachusetts.

Did you know . . .

- During the voyage to America, Winthrop delivered one of the most famous sermons in American history, "A Modell of Christian Charity." In his speech he compared the Puritans' new venture to "a Citty upon a Hill," and he proclaimed that the eyes of the world were upon them.

For more information

Dunn, Richard S. *Puritans and Yankees: The Winthrop Dynasty of New England 1630–1717.* Princeton, N.J.: Princeton University Press, 1962.

Gunn, Giles, ed. *Early American Writing.* New York: Penguin Books, 1994, pp. 113–18.

Middleton, Richard. *Colonial America: A History, 1585–1776.* Second edition. Malden, Mass.: Blackwell Publishers, 1996, pp. 81–89.

Morgan, Edward S. *The Puritan Dilemma: The Story of John Winthrop.* Boston: Little, Brown, 1958.

Mary Rowlandson

Excerpt from The Narrative of the Captivity and Restauration
of Mrs. Mary Rowlandson

Reprinted in *Eyewitness to America*
Published in 1997
Edited by David Colbert

New England Puritans were not allowed to read novels, plays, and many kinds of poetry. (The Puritans were a Protestant Christian group who observed strict moral and religious codes.) They disapproved of any kind of literature or entertainment that did not lead to spiritual improvement, so the only reading materials permitted by church leaders were the Bible (Christian holy book), sermons (ministers' lectures), and history books. Nevertheless Puritan clergymen (ministers) approved of captivity narratives (accounts written by colonists who had been captured by Native Americans) because they were true tales about suffering and triumph. The stories could also be read as sermons or as spiritual autobiographies (records of the individual soul's struggle with God and Satan, or the Devil). Many Puritan ministers even encouraged church members to write about intense personal suffering. One of the most famous spiritual autobiographies was written by John Winthrop (1588–1649), founder of the Massachusetts Bay Colony (see *John Winthrop's Christian Experience*). The captivity narrative was especially popular because Puritans believed that Native Americans were agents (helpers)

"I had often before this said, that if the Indians should come, I should choose rather to be killed by them than taken alive, but when it came to the trial, my mind changed";

of Satan, and that captives were being punished by God for failing to obey his will.

The first and best-known captivity narrative was *The Narrative of the Captivity and Restauration of Mrs. Mary Rowlandson* (also titled *The Soveraignty & Goodness of God*) by Mary White Rowlandson (1635 or 1637–c. 1711). The wife of a Puritan clergyman, Rowlandson lived with her family on the New England frontier during the late seventeenth century. The violent events of King Philip's War (1675–76; see "A Relacion of the Indyan Warre") transformed Rowlandson from a typical Puritan woman to a best-selling author.

On a night in February 1676, a Wampanoag raiding party kidnapped Rowlandson, her three children, and several other colonists. One of her children died in captivity. Three months later Rowlandson and the surviving children were released when her husband paid a ransom (payment made for release) to the Wampanoags. Rowlandson wrote about this experience in *The Narrative of the Captivity and Restauration of Mrs. Mary Rowlandson,* which she originally composed for her children. Rowlandson's account is valuable to historians because it describes life on the American frontier. The book also depicts the deep Christian faith of a Puritan woman and portrays the futile (unsuccessful) efforts of Native Americans to prevent colonists from taking over their land.

Rowlandson was born in Somersetshire, England, around 1635 (some sources report 1637), one of nine children of John and Joane (West) White. During Mary's early childhood the Whites migrated (moved from one country to another) to America and settled at Salem, a town in the Puritan colony of Massachusetts Bay. In 1653 the family moved to Lancaster, Massachusetts, a new village on the frontier, about thirty miles west of Boston. In 1656 Mary White married Joseph Rowlandson, a Puritan minister. The couple made their home on a hill overlooking Ropers Brook (a commemorative plaque now marks the site). For the next twenty years Mary Rowlandson led the life of a typical mother and minister's wife. From 1657 to 1669 she gave birth to four children, one of whom died in infancy. Then, in early 1676, Rowlandson was snatched from her frontier existence and thrust into a permanent place in early American history.

Mary Rowlandson. Her captivity narrative was the first and best-known in the colonies. *Reproduced by permission of The Granger Collection Ltd.*

A few years after the Rowlandsons were married, hostilities intensified between the Puritans and Native Americans. Tensions had been building since the death, in 1661, of the Wampanoag leader Massasoit (c.1580–1661), an ally of the Puritans. Massasoit's son and successor, Metacom (1640–1676; called King Philip), tried to maintain control of Wampanoag territory. Alarmed when the Puritans began taking more and more Native American land, Metacom feared the survival of his people was being threatened. War broke out in January 1675 when Puritan authorities in the town of Plymouth executed three Wampanoag warriors on the charge of murdering an Englishman. The conflict raged for eighteen months, mainly in towns along the western border of the Massachusetts colony and Native American territory.

The residents of Lancaster anticipated an attack at any moment, and Joseph Rowlandson went to Boston to obtain military aid. At dawn on February 10, 1676, while he was still in Boston, a party of four hundred Native Americans raided Lancaster. Burning houses and killing settlers, they attacked the Rowlandson home, where Mary, her three children, and thirty-two villagers were hiding. Twelve colonists died, including Rowlandson's sister and other relatives, and the warriors captured Rowlandson, her children, and the rest of the survivors. In the dead of winter the Wampanoags took the captives westward into Native American territory, subjecting them to cruel treatment along the way. When Joseph Rowlandson returned to Lancaster he found that his house had burned to the ground and his family had disappeared.

Rowlandson and her six-year-old daughter Sarah had been shot during the siege. Her older children, Joseph Jr. and Mary, were apparently unharmed, but on the trip through the wilderness Sarah was deprived of food and water. She died nine days later. Rowlandson was then separated from the two surviving children and sent to live as a slave with Sagamore (secondary chief) Quanopin, brother-in-law of Metacom, and his wife Wetamoo. Rowlandson was in captivity for nearly twelve weeks. She went with the Native Americans as they wandered around the New England region in search of food and game (wild birds) before returning to the Lancaster area.

Things to Remember While Reading an excerpt from *The Narrative of the Captivity and Restauration of Mrs. Mary Rowlandson:*

- In *The Narrative* Rowlandson used a simple but vivid style to describe the Wampanoag raid on her home and the harrowing ordeal of her captivity. She was taken to twenty "removes," or separate campsites, that the Native Americans set up on their journey. Usually she walked and carried heavy loads. She often suffered from hunger and loss of strength. She learned to tolerate Native American food such as nuts, grain meal, horsemeat, and game. Rowlandson described sleeping on the frozen ground and being sick, lonely, and frightened.

- A continuing theme in *The Narrative* is the possibility of violence and death that threatened both Rowlandson and the Native Americans on a daily basis. At first she was not treated well by her captors, who were frequently hungry and miserable themselves. Eventually she won them over with her sewing and knitting skills. Wetamoo in particular was charitable toward her. Rowlandson was allowed to see her two children on occasion, but they remained separated from her.

- Rowlandson was sustained throughout the ordeal by her Christian faith. She found great comfort in a Bible that was given to her by a Wampanoag warrior, who had stolen it during a raid. In her account, she cites passages from the Bible at least sixty-five times, and she asserts that her release was evidence of God's goodwill toward true Christians. Rowlandson generally depicts the Wampanoags as instruments of the Devil, yet she also reveals their tender, human side.

- The following excerpt is Rowlandson's description of the Wampanoag attack on her home.

Excerpt from The Narrative of the Captivity and Restauration of Mrs. Mary Rowlandson

On the 10th of February, 1675, came the Indians with great numbers upon Lancaster. Their first coming was about sunrising.

*Hearing the noise of some guns, we looked out; several houses were burning, and the smoke ascending to heaven. There were five persons taken in one house; the father and the mother and a **suckling** child they knocked on the head; the other two they took and car-*

Suckling: Still being fed from its mother's breast

ried away alive. There were two others, who, being out of their **garrison** upon some occasion, were set upon; one was knocked on the head, the other escaped. Another there was who, running along, was shot and wounded, and fell down; he begged of them his life, promising them money (as they told me), but they would not **hearken** to him, but knocked him in the head, and stripped him naked, and split open his **bowels.** Another seeing many of the Indians about his barn ventured and went out, but was quickly shot down. There were three others belonging to the same garrison who were killed; the Indians, getting up upon the roof of the barn, had advantage to shoot down upon them over their fortification. Thus these murderous **wretches** went on burning and destroying before them.

At length they came and beset our own house, and quickly it was the **dolefulest** day that ever mine eyes saw. The house stood upon the edge of a hill; some of the Indians got behind the hill, others into the barn, and others behind anything that could shelter them; from all which places they shot against the house, so that the bullets seemed to fly like **hail,** and quickly they wounded one man among us, then another, and then a third. About two hours (according to my observation in that amazing time) they had been about the house before they **prevailed** to fire it; they fired it once, and one ventured out and quenched it, but they quickly fired it again, and that took. Now is the dreadful hour come that I have often heard of, but now mine eyes see it. Some in our house were fighting for their lives, others wallowing in their blood, the house on fire over our heads, and the bloody **heathen** ready to knock us on the head if we stirred out. Now might we hear mothers and children crying out for themselves and one another, "Lord, what shall we do?" Then I took my children (and one of my sisters hers) to go forth and leave the house, but, as soon as we came to the door and appeared, the Indians shot so thick that the bullets rattled against the house as if one had taken a handful of stones and threw them, so that we were forced to give [move] back. We had six **stout** dogs belonging to our garrison, but none of them would stir, though another time if any Indian had come to the door, they were ready to fly upon him and tear him down. The Lord hereby would make us the more to acknowledge His hand, and to see that our help is always in Him. But out we must go, the fire increasing, and coming along behind us roaring, and the Indians gaping before us with their guns, spears, and hatchets to devour us.

No sooner were we out of the house but my brother-in-law (being before wounded in defending the house, in or near the throat) fell

Garrison: A military post

Hearken: To listen to

Bowels: Intestines in the digestive tract

Wretches: Mean people

Dolefulest: Full of grief

Hail: Small balls of icy rain or snow

Prevailed: To be victorious

Heathen: An uncivilized or irreligious person

Stout: Sturdy, vigorous

Colonial America: Primary Sources

Native Americans attacking settlers. Mary Rowland's account describes a scene similar to the one pictured here. *Reproduced by permission of Archive Photos, Inc.*

*down dead, whereat the Indians scornfully shouted and **hallooed**, and were presently upon him, stripping off his clothes. The bullets flying thick, one went through my side, and the same (as would seem) through the bowels and hand of my dear child in my arms. One of my elder sister's children (named William) had then his leg broke, which the Indians perceiving they knocked him on the head. Thus were we butchered by those merciless heathen, standing amazed, with the blood running down to our heels. My eldest sister being yet in the*

Hallooed: Yelled

Woeful: Mournful; sad

Infidels: One who is not a Christian or who opposes Christianity

Threshold:" Strip of wood under a door

Reaping: Receiving a reward

Daunted: Intimidated; discouraged

Ravenous: Very eager or greedy for food, satisfaction, or gratification

*house, and seeing those **woeful** sights, the **infidels** hauling mothers one way and children another, and some wallowing in their blood; and her elder son telling her that her son William was dead, and myself wounded, she said, "And, Lord, let me die with them"; which was no sooner said, but she was struck with a bullet, and fell down dead over the **threshold**. I hope she is **reaping** the fruit of her good labors, being faithful to the service of God in her place.*

*I had often before this said, that if the Indians should come, I should choose rather to be killed by them than taken alive, but when it came to the trial, my mind changed; their glittering weapons so **daunted** my spirit, that I chose rather to go along with those (as I may say) **ravenous** bears, than that moment to end my days.*

What happened next . . .

In early March, Metacom summoned Rowlandson to his "General Court" to discuss selling her back to her husband. Once they had agreed upon a ransom—two coats, half a bushel of seed corn, some tobacco, and twenty pounds (an amount of British money)—a message was sent to Boston. Joseph Rowlandson and several others, including John Hoar, a resident of Concord, engaged in negotiations with Metacom. Finally, on May 2, 1676, Hoar arrived unarmed at the Wampanoag camp with the ransom. When Rowlandson was released the Native Americans bid her a fond farewell, evidence that she had made friends among her captors. The Rowlandson children were freed from separate locations a few weeks later. King Philip's War ended a short time later.

The Rowlandsons lived in Boston until April 1677, when Joseph was appointed pastor of the church at Wethersfield, Connecticut. Upon his death in 1678, the town of Wethersfield voted to give Mary a pension of thirty pounds a year for the rest of her life. By 1682 Rowlandson had written *The Narrative*, an account of her experiences in captivity, which she had intended to give her children. The manuscript was published that year in Boston, however, and was immediately a commercial success. The date of Rowlandson's death is not certain, but she is believed to have died in 1711. Since 1682 *The Narrative* has appeared in at least thirty editions and has become a classic of frontier literature.

Did you know . . .

- Encouraged by the French, Native Americans continued to conduct raids on English colonists after King Philip's War, especially in sparsely populated areas. In 1677 Quentin Stockwell, a resident of Deerfield, Massachusetts, was taken prisoner and held for eight months. He wrote about his experience in "Quentin Stockwell's Relation of His Captivity and Redemption," which was first published in *An Essay for the Recording of Illustrious Providences* (1684) by Puritan minister Increase Mather.

- Ten-year-old John Gyles was captured in Pemaquid, Maine, in 1689 and was held for six years among Native Americans and nearly three years with the French. An account of his adventures was published as *Memoirs of Odd Adventures, Strange Deliverances, etc., in the Captivity of John Gyles, Esq.* in 1736.

- The outbreak of Queen Anne's War (a conflict involving the French and their Native American allies against the English in 1702) brought fresh trouble for settlements along the New England frontier. Many townspeople in Deerfield, Massachusetts, were killed during a raid in February 1704. Among the dead were two sons of John Williams, a minister. In his popular narrative, *The Redeemed Captive, Returning to Zion* (1707), Williams recounted how he and other survivors were forced to walk to Canada. His wife died during this long march. For three years Williams struggled to win freedom for his children and members of his congregation. He also tried to prevent them from being pressured by the French to convert to Roman Catholicism (a Christian religion based in Rome, Italy, and headed by pope who is the supreme authority in church affairs). Although Williams was eventually released, the Native Americans would not free his ten-year-old daughter Eunice. She not only became a Catholic but she also married a Native American and lived for the rest of her life with his tribe.

For more information

Colbert, David, ed. *Eyewitness to America.* New York: Pantheon Books, 1997, pp. 33–34.

James, Edward T., and others, eds. *Notable American Women,* Volume III. Cambridge, Mass.: Belknap Press of Harvard University Press, 1971, pp. 200–03.

"Hannah Duston," in *The Young Oxford History of Women in the United States: Biographical Supplement and Index.* Nancy F. Cott, ed. New York: Oxford University Press, 1995, p. 54.

Rowlandson, Mary. *The Narrative of the Captivity and Restoration of Mrs. Mary Rowlandson.* Excerpted in *American Literature: A Prentice-Hall Anthology.* Emory Elliott and others, eds. Englewood Cliffs, N.J.: Prentice-Hall, 1991, pp. 169–85.

Salisbury, Neal, ed. *Sovereignty and Goodness of God.* Boston: Bedford Books, 1997.

Anne Dudley Bradstreet

Poems by Anne Dudley Bradstreet
Reprinted in *Early American Writing*
Published in 1994
Edited by Giles Gunn

Throughout the colonial period, settlers in North America maintained close ties with their European homelands. The main connection was trade. All of the American colonies sent products such as fish, furs, lumber (wood used for buildings), tobacco (a leafy plant processed for smoking), rice, indigo (a blue dye), and livestock (animals raised for meat) to Europe. In exchange they received European-made weapons, ammunition, household items, and other necessities they could not produce themselves. The colonists also depended on Europe for news about recent world events.

Another strong link was culture. As the American colonies became more established, educated citizens increasingly relied on European books, pamphlets, and other publications. This was the only way they could stay in touch with scientific advances, political ideas, religious thought, literature, and drama. Soon colonists were thinking of themselves as members of a vast community or "Republic of Letters" that extended across the Atlantic to embrace both Europeans and Americans. Wealthy colonial leaders, merchants, and plantation owners traveled to Europe for their education, studying at

"We both are ignorant, yet love bids me/These farewell lines to recommend thee,/That when that knot's untied that made us one, I may seem thine, who in effect am none."

prestigious institutions. They took extensive tours, mingling with the most influential social circles to gain firsthand exposure to current achievements, manners, tastes, and learning.

In the 1600s and 1700s colonists began making contributions of their own, producing the early forms of American literature that are read today. Settlers issued books and pamphlets promoting settlement in North America, and leaders chronicled the histories of their colonies. Many colonists kept personal diaries or wrote their autobiographies. Religious reformers published essays on social issues and spiritual struggles. Colonists who had been kidnapped by Native Americans wrote captivity narratives, which became immensely popular. Prior to the late 1600s, works written by Americans were printed in England. The first American printing press was founded in Boston, Massachusetts, in 1638 for the publication of official documents and religious materials. Publishing books for literary purposes did not take place until much later. (In fact, many works from the colonial period did not appear in print until the nineteenth century.)

Nevertheless, a literary community was emerging, particularly in the Massachusetts Bay Colony in Puritan New England. (Puritans were members of a Protestant Christian group that observed strict moral and religious codes. They first settled in the Plymouth and Massachusetts Bay colonies, then dominated New England until the 1690s.) The Puritans were a well-educated society, as all church members had to learn to read at an early age so they could understand the Bible (the Christian holy book). Since Puritan leaders disapproved of any activities that did not lead to spiritual improvement, the only permissible reading materials were the Bible, sermons (ministers' lectures), and history books. Novels, plays, and many types of poetry were banned. Eventually Puritans encouraged both the writing and reading of captivity narratives, which they regarded as the ideal expression of the struggle between good and evil. (See *The Narrative of the Captivity and Restauration of Mrs. Mary Rowlandson.*) Early on Puritans urged church members to write spiritual autobiographies (accounts of personal struggles with good and evil based on passages from the Bible), which could be read by fellow Puritans or used as sermons by ministers. (See *John Winthrop's Christian Experience.*) The Puritans would have been surprised to learn that these spiritual autobiographies as well as captivity narratives eventually led their descendants to write novels in the nineteenth century.

During the colonial period Puritans also approved of poetry that communicated a spiritual message. Many religious leaders explained the Scriptures (passages from the Bible) or depicted their struggle between good and evil in poetry form. Several Puritans gained prominence as religious poets in both America and Europe. Among them was Michael Wigglesworth (1631–1705), a Massachusetts pastor who wrote *The Day of Doom* (1662), a book-length poem that is considered the first American best seller. His work was quite popular at the time, and his name was a household word. Edward Taylor (c. 1645–1729), another Massachusetts minister, is now regarded as an important Puritan poet, but his work was not discovered until the twentieth century. The honor of being the first published American poet, however, is reserved for a woman—Anne Dudley Bradstreet (1612–1672), a frontier Massachusetts housewife.

Bradstreet was born in Northampton, England. She was the second of six children of Thomas Dudley (1576–1653) and Dorothy Dudley. Her father was a clerk and a member of the gentry (upper or ruling class). In 1619, when he became steward (manager of a large estate) to Theophilus Clinton, Earl of Lincoln, he moved his family to the earl's estate in Sempringham. (An earl is an English nobleman, or member of the ruling class.) At the time the estate was a center of Puritan learning and activism (efforts to promote reform). Leading Puritan ministers often preached in the earl's chapel, and many of the Puritan gentry and nobility met there to have discussions.

As a child Anne received an excellent education. She had private tutors, and she read many books from the earl's extensive

Frontier housewife Anne Dudley Bradstreet became America's first published poet. *Reproduced by permission of vicar and church wardens of St. Botolph's Church, Boston, Lincolnshire.*

library. The ambitious young pupil studied theology (theory of religion), philosophy, and literature, and she learned to appreciate music and art. At nine years of age, she met her future husband, eighteen-year-old Simon Bradstreet (1603–1697), who was the son of a Puritan minister and a graduate of Cambridge University. He came to Sempringham to be an assistant to Thomas Dudley. The couple was married in 1628, when Anne was only sixteen and after she had recovered from smallpox (a potentially fatal virus disease that causes skin sores and scars). Historians speculate that their marriage was arranged, but Anne's poems suggest that she and Simon had a close and happy relationship during their forty-four years together.

The newlyweds moved to the estate of the dowager (a widow holding property or a title from her deceased husband) countess of Warwick, where Simon was appointed steward. Soon, however, political conditions turned against Puritans. King Charles I (1600–1649) favored William Laud (1573–1645), a bishop in the Church of England (also known as the Anglican Church, the official national religion), who used his influence to exclude Puritans from holding political office. As part of his effort to limit the role of Puritans in government, Charles I suspended Parliament (the supreme legislative body) in 1629. All Puritans in England, including the Bradstreets and Dudleys, realized they were losing influence in the country.

Puritan leaders therefore decided to promote religious reforms in England by establishing a Puritan settlement in America. In 1630 the Bradstreets and Dudleys joined other Puritans, including lawyer John Winthrop (1588–1649) and preacher John Cotton (1585–1652), and set out aboard the flagship *Arbella,* which led ten other vessels on the voyage to North America. Having begun their journey in April, they arrived at Salem, Massachusetts, harbor in June. Bradstreet was surprised by the harsh climate and rough surroundings in North America—a stark contrast with the privileged life she had known in England. After the families settled in Newtowne (now Cambridge), Massachusetts, Bradstreet joined the church in Boston. Since her husband and father held high positions in the Massachusetts Bay Company, the investment company of the colony, she led a relatively comfortable life. She apparently found time to write because the earliest of her surviving poems, "Upon a Fit of Sickness," dates from 1632. Composed while Bradstreet was ill and hovering near death, this poem reflects the somber reality of her new life.

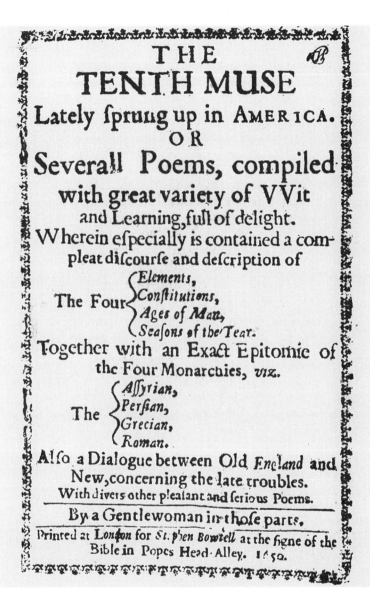

THE
TENTH MUSE
Lately fprung up in AMERICA.
OR
Severall Poems, compiled
with great variety of VVit
and Learning, full of delight.
Wherein efpecially is contained a com-
pleat difcourfe and defcription of

	Elements,
The Four	Conftitutions,
	Ages of Man,
	Seafons of the Year.

Together with an Exact Epitomie of
the Four Monarchies, viz.

	Affyrian,
The	Perfian,
	Grecian,
	Roman.

Alfo a Dialogue between Old England and
New, concerning the late troubles.
With divers other pleafant and ferious Poems.

By a Gentlewoman in thofe parts.

Printed at London for St. phen Bowtell at the figne of the
Bible in Popes Head-Alley. 1650.

The tile page for Anne Dudley Bradstreet's *The Tenth Muse Lately Sprung Up in America*. **Although it is the first book of poetry written in America, there is little mention of the New World in it.** *Reproduced by permission of Corbis-Bettmann.*

The Bradstreet family moved several times over the next two decades. During this period Bradstreet devoted herself to domestic life and gave birth to eight children. She had her first child, Simon, in 1633. Later she wrote in a poem titled "In Reference to Her Children"(1678): "I had eight birds hatched in one nest/Four Cocks [boys] there were, and Hens [girls] the rest." In 1635 the Bradstreets moved from New-towne to Ipswich, Massachusetts. Despite her domestic responsibilities and the hardships of frontier life, Bradstreet began to write poetry in earnest. In 1645 the Bradstreets moved to North Andover, Massachusetts. Finally settled, Bradstreet lived there for the rest of her life.

Even though it was unusual for women to pursue creative or intellectual pursuits at the time, Bradstreet's family took great pride in her work. They encouraged her to continue writing, and in 1647 her brother-in-law, John Woodbridge, carried a manuscript of thirteen poems to England. The book was published in 1650 without Bradstreet's knowledge. Titled *The Tenth Muse Lately Sprung Up in America,* it was the first collection of poetry written in America. Although *The Tenth Muse* is an important contribution to American literature, there is little mention of the New World (European term for North America and South America) in the work. In fact, the numerous classical allusions (references to great literature from previous eras) in the poetry are a reminder of the days when Bradstreet studied in the comfort of the earl's library in England. *The Tenth Muse* is not considered to be her best work, as she did not find her true poetic voice until later in life. Bradstreet continued to write both poetry and prose, but nothing else was published during her lifetime. Her last known poem was "As Weary Pilgrim," which she wrote in 1669 (it was published in 1876). Bradstreet died in North Andover in 1672.

Things to Remember While Reading Poems by Anne Bradstreet:

- *The Tenth Muse* was concerned primarily with history and politics, but Bradstreet's later poems are about everyday life in New England. The private poems reveal that she had difficulty submitting to the strict beliefs of Puritanism. The Puritans believed every moment spent on Earth was merely a preparation for life in Heaven after death. They preferred the wilderness because they believed that the more they suffered in their Earthly life, the higher the reward would be in the afterlife. Some of Bradstreet's poetry suggests that she was unhappy in the New World, and she missed the luxury of her previous existence in England.

- Bradstreet frequently depicted hardships such as the fear of death in childbirth, which she described in "Before the

Birth of One of Her Children." Written for her unborn child, to whom she expressed her love in case she did not live through the birth or died shortly after the child was born. Published in 1678, "Before the Birth of One of Her Children" was written sometime between 1640 and 1652.

- A favorite of modern readers is "The Author to Her Book," which Bradstreet possibly wrote in 1650. In this poem she expressed dismay and embarrassment over the shortcomings of *The Tenth Muse,* which she compared to a disobedient child whom she had to abandon ("And for thy Mother, she alas is poor,/Which caus'd her thus to send thee out of door"). Yet the publication of *The Tenth Muse* inspired her to continue writing poetry.

- Bradstreet composed several poems about her relationship with her husband, who was often away from home on business. One of the best known is "To My Dear and Loving Husband," which she wrote sometime between 1641 and 1643. It was published in 1678. The Bradstreets had a strong marriage, and in this poem she described their love as being richer than any material wealth and enduring long after death: "That we may live no more, we may live forever."

- "Here Follows Some Verses upon the Burning of Our House" was written by Bradstreet when the family home burned on July 10, 1666. Copied from a loose piece of paper by her son Simon, it was published in 1867. Like many of Bradstreet's poems, this one expressed her reliance on spiritual values instead of material possessions. She said the fire was the will of God, which she must accept: "My hope and treasure lies above."

"Before the Birth of One of Her Children"

All things within this fading world hath end,
***Adversity** doth still our joys attend;*
No ties so strong, no friends so dear and sweet,
But with death's parting blow is sure to meet.
*The sentence past is most **irrevocable**,*
*A common thing, yet oh, **inevitable**.*

Adversity: Misfortune

Irrevocable: Unalterable

Inevitable: Unavoidable

How soon, my Dear, death may my steps attend,
How soon't [it] may be thy **lot** to lose thy friend,
We both are ignorant, yet love bids me
These farewell lines to recommend thee,
That when that knot's untied that made us one,
I may seem **thine**, who in effect am none.
And if I see not half my days that's due,
What nature would, God grant to yours and you;
The many faults that well you know I have
Let be **interred** in my **oblivious** grave;
If any worth or **virtue** were in me,
Let that live freshly in thy memory
And when thou feel'st no grief, as I no harms,
Yet love thy dead, who long lay in thine arms.
And when thy loss shall be repaid with gains
Look to my little babes, my dear remains.
And if thou love thyself, or love'st me,
These O protect from **step-dame's** injury.
And if chance to thine eyes shall bring this verse,
With some sad sighs honour my absent **hearse**:
And kiss this paper for thy love's dear sake,
Who with salt tears this last farewell did take.

"The Author to Her Book"

Thou ill-form'd **offspring** of my **feeble** brain,
Who after birth did'st by my side remain,
Till **snatcht** from **thence** by friends, less wise than true
Who thee abroad, expos'd to publick view,
Made thee in raggs, halting to the' press to **trudge**,
Where errors were not lessened (all may judge)
At thy return my blushing was not small,
My rambling brat (in print) should mother call,
I cast thee by as one unfit for light,
Thy **Visage** was so **irksome** in my sight;
Yet being mine own, at length affection would
Thy blemishes amend, if so I could:
I wash'd thy face, but more defects I saw,
And rubbing off a spot, still made a flaw.
I stretcht thy joynts to make thee even feet,
Yet still thou run'st more hobling then is meet;
In better dress to **trim** thee was my mind,
But nought save home-spun Cloth, i'th' [in the] house I find

Lot: Fate

Thine: Mine

Interr'd: Interred; to deposit (a dead body) in the earth or in a tomb

Oblivious: Lacking memory or awareness

Virtue: Goodness

Step-dame: Step-mother

Hearse: Funeral carriage

Offspring: Child

Feeble: Markedly lacking in strength

Snatcht: Snatch

Thence: From that place

Trudge: A long, tedious walk

Visage: Face

Irksome: Annoying

Trim: Put on (clothing)

In this array, 'mongst **Vulgars** mayst thou roam
In **Critick's** hands, beware thou dost not come;
And take thy way where yet thou art not known,
If for thy Father askt, say, thou hadst none:
And for thy Mother, she alas is poor,
Which caus'd her thus to send thee out of door.

"To My Dear and Loving Husband" (1678)

If ever two were one, then surely we.
If ever man were lov'd by wife, then thee;
If ever wife was happy in a man,
Compare with me ye women if you can.
I prize thy love more then whole Mines of gold,
Or all the riches that the East doth hold.
My love is such that Rivers cannot quench,
Nor ought but love from thee, give **recompence.**
Thy love is such I can no way repay,
The heavens reward thee **manifold** I pray.
Then while we live, in love let's so **persever,**
That when we live no more, we may live ever.

"Here Follows Some Verses upon the Burning of Our House" (July 10th, 1666)

Copied Out of a Loose Paper

In silent night when rest I took
For sorrow near I did not look
I wakened was with thund'ring noise
And **piteous** shrieks of dreadful voice.
That fearful sound of "Fire!" and "Fire!"
Let no man know is my desire.
I, starting up, the light did spy,
And to my God my heart did cry
To strengthen me in my distress
And not to leave me **succorless.**
Then, coming out, beheld a space
The flame consume my dwelling place.
And when I could no longer look,
I blest His name that gave and took [God],
That laid my goods now in the dust.
Yea, so it was, and so 'twas just.

Vulgars: Of or relating to the common people

Critck's: Critic's

Recompence: In return for something done, suffered, or given

Manifold: Multiple times

Persever: Persevere; to persist

Piteous: Of a kind to move to pity or compassion

Succorless: Without aid or relief

It was His own, it was not mine,
*Far be it that I should **repine**;*
*He might of all justly **bereft***
But yet sufficient for us left.
When by the ruins oft I past
My sorrowing eyes aside did cast,
And here and there the places spy
Where oft I sat and long did lie:
Here stood that trunk, and there that chest,
*There lay that **store** I counted best.*
My pleasant things in ashes lie,
And them behold no more shall I.
Under thy roof no guest shall sit,
Nor at thy table eat a bit.
No pleasant tale shall e'er be told,
Nor things recounted done of old.
No candle e'er shall shine in thee,
Nor bridegroom's voice e'er heard shall be.
In silence ever shall thou lie,
***Adieu**, Adieu, all's **vanity**.*
*Then straight I 'gin my heart to **chide**,*
And did thy wealth on earth abide?
Didst fix thy hope on mold'ring dust?
The arm of flesh didst make thy trust?
Raise up thy thoughts above the sky
*That **dunghill** mists away may fly.*
Thou hast an house on high erect,
Framed by that mighty Architect, [God]
With glory richly furnished,
Stands permanent though this be fled.
It's purchased and paid for too
By Him who hath enough to do.
A price so vast as is unknown
Yet by His gift is made thine own;
There's wealth enough, I need no more,
*Farewell, my **pelf**, farewell my store.*
The world no longer let me love,
My hope and treasure lies above.

Repine: To long for something

Bereft: Deprived or robbed of something needed

Store: Supply put away for future use

Adieu: Farewell

Vanity: Worthless

Chide: Voice disapproval

Dunghill: Something (as a situation or condition) that is repulsive or degraded

Pelf: Money, riches

What happened next . . .

John Foster, who set up the first printing press in Boston, Massachusetts, released *Several Poems* in 1678, six years after Bradstreet's death. It was the first American edition of her poetry. In 1867 John Harvard Ellis published *The Works of Anne Bradstreet in Poetry and Prose*.

Did you know . . .

- Ruth Belknap (dates unknown) was another American colonial poet. Like Bradstreet, Belknap was a member of a privileged family. Being the wife of a minister in Dover, New Hampshire, kept Belknap from poverty. However, like Bradstreet, she still had a difficult life. In her poem "The Pleasures of a Country Life" (see box) she described in detail all the chores she had to accomplish as a typical housewife. In the same poem, Belknap went on to describe the difference between people who lived in the country and those who lived in town. She portrayed the latter as lazy and much less industrious than colonists who were forced to labor on the farm.

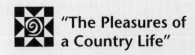

"The Pleasures of a Country Life"

The following poem was written by American colonial poet Ruth Belknap. Like Bradstreet, Belknap used her poetry to describe her life as a colonial housewife.

> All summer long I toil & sweat,
> Blister my hands, and scold & fret.
> And when the summer's work is o'er,
> New toils arise from Autumn's store.
> Corn must be husk'd, and pork be kill'd.
> The house with all confusion fill'd.
> O could you see the grand display
> Upon our annual butchering day,—
> See me look like ten thousand sluts,
> My kitchen spread with grease & guts.

For more information

Dunham, Montrew. *Anne Bradstreet; Young Puritan Poet.* Indianapolis, Ind.: Bobbs-Merrill, 1969.

Elliott, Emory, and others, eds. *American Literature: A Prentice Hall Anthology.* Englewood Cliffs, N.J.: Prentice-Hall, 1991, pp. 115–19.

Gunn, Giles. *Early American Writing.* New York: Penguin Books, 1994, pp. 178–92.

James, Edward T. and others, eds. *Notable American Women, 1607–1950,* Volume I. Cambridge, Mass.: Belknap Press of Harvard University Press, 1971, pp. 222–23.

White, Elizabeth Wade. *Anne Bradstreet, "The Tenth Muse."* New York: Oxford University Press, 1971.

Sarah Kemble Knight

Excerpt from The Journal of Madame Knight

Reprinted in *Early American Writing*
Published in 1994
Edited by Giles Gunn

Historians have learned quite a bit about the colonial period from records kept by explorers, settlers, and travelers. European explorers recorded their impressions of the New World (a European term for North America and South America) in reports they sent back to their home countries to encourage future exploration or colonization (see "Christopher Columbus Reports to Ferdinand and Isabella"; "Alonso de Benavides Reports New Mexico Indians Eager for Conversion"; and "Jolliet and Marquette Travel the Mississippi"). Founders of colonies tried to attract new settlers with books and pamphlets that promoted the benefits of living in America (see Thomas Harriot's *A Brief and True Report of the New Found Land of Virginia* and William Penn's *The Propriety of Pennsylvania*). Frequently Europeans went to America on business and later published their impressions of the colonies (see Per Kalm's "Impressions of New Jersey and New York").

Private journals and diaries also offer glimpses of how people lived—and how they managed to travel long distances—in various parts of America. One of the most popular works of travel literature from the colonial period is *The Jour-*

"This Rode was poorly furnished with accommodations for Travellers, so that we were forced to ride 22 miles by the post's account, but neerer thirty by mine, before we could bait so much as our Horses. . . ."

nal of Madame Knight by Sarah Kemble Knight (1666–1727). Published in 1825, nearly a century after Knight's death, it is an account of her journey through New England in 1704. This remarkable diary provides a detailed portrait of the landscape and culture of early colonial Massachusetts, Connecticut, and New York. It also reveals Knight's strong personality, which enabled her to overcome the limitations placed on women. At that time many women could not read or write, let alone take on a difficult journey through the wilderness. In addition to writing the journal, Knight was a successful businesswoman and legal advisor.

Knight was born on April 19, 1666, in Boston, Massachusetts, to Thomas Kemble and Elizabeth (Trerice) Kemble. Her mother was the daughter of Nicholas Trerice, a shipowner in Charlestown, Massachusetts. Knight's father was a merchant who owned land in the area that is now Maine. As a young woman, Knight acquired the education that enabled her to write her famous diary and to participate in business and legal activities. Before her father died in 1689, she married Richard Knight, a widower (a man whose wife has died) and shipowner who was much older than herself. The couple had one child, Elizabeth.

Upon the death of her father, Knight took over as head of his household and ran a boarding house (a lodging house where meals are provided), where many of her relatives lived. In addition she engaged in legal activities such as assisting in settling estates (the property of deceased persons) and recording public documents. Historians have found hundreds of official papers that bear her signature as well as court records presumably written by her. There is little evidence, however, to support the popular claim that Knight taught the future scientist and statesman Benjamin Franklin (see *Benjamin Franklin: A Biography in His Own Words*) at the writing school she operated after her husband died in 1706.

Because of her legal skills, Knight was able to take on many business responsibilities. In 1704 one of the boarders at her Boston residence married her cousin, Caleb Trowbridge, who lived in New Haven, Connecticut. Trowbridge died within two months after the marriage. In October of that year, Knight set out for New Haven to help Trowbridge's widow with legal matters. The trip through the wilderness from Boston to

New Haven was extremely difficult and hazardous. For a woman to undertake such a journey alone—and on horseback—was considered unthinkable.

Things to Remember While Reading an excerpt from *The Journal of Madame Knight:*

- Knight made her trip at a time when land travel between colonies was extremely difficult. The number and condition of roads depended on the population of towns and villages and funds provided by colonial legislatures. As a result, in many places roadbeds (the foundations laid for railroad tracks or roads) were poor and there were few bridges. Often travelers had to wade through fords (shallow places in streams and rivers) that became deep and dangerous during heavy rainstorms. Roads turned into mud holes. Even in dry weather traveling was rough and became rougher when routes went inland. Since there were very few roads or bridges, Knight had to seek the help of guides during her journey from Boston to New Haven. (She followed the route now used by the Pennsylvania Central Railroad.)

- Despite encountering hardships, Knight gave lighthearted, humorous impressions of the trip in her diary. She recorded all the "Bugbears [problems] to a fearful female travailer," such as "Bridges which were . . . very tottering and of vast Length." When there were no bridges she crossed rivers in canoes (long, narrow boats) or on horseback. Knight described farmhouses and inns, she wrote about country people and their local dialects (speech pat-

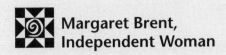

Margaret Brent, Independent Woman

Like Sarah Kemble Knight, Margaret Brent (c.1601–c.1671) was unique because she was one of few independent women living during the colonial period. Never marrying, Brent was actively involved in the legal and political affairs of the colony at a time when women had little or no power. Brent is remembered today as a feminist because she demanded the right to vote in Maryland, even though she knew she would be denied the privilege because of her gender. It is believed that she was the first practicing female attorney in America. Some historians point out, however, that Brent was not actually advocating equality for women in general, and she was never licensed as a lawyer. Nonetheless, she was an exceptional woman for her day: she owned and managed a large estate, she was the executor (one appointed to carry out a will) of the Maryland governor's estate, and at one point she managed the supply and payment of an army.

terns), and she commented on food and lodging. Knight rose above the dangers of her journey by mocking obstacles, and she provided a vivid account of the culture in New Haven, where she remained for two months. During this time, she met Thomas Trowbridge, who was probably Caleb' father, and decided to accompany him to New York City. They arrived at their destination in three days, and Knight once again wrote about the local culture. After finishing their business in New York, she and Trowbridge returned to New Haven. She then proceeded on to Boston in late February, arriving in early March.

- The following excerpt is taken from Knight's account of the Boston-New Haven trip. (Knight often used unusual spellings of words, which are clarified in the margin.)

Excerpt from The Journal of Madame Knight:

MONDAY, OCTB'R THE SECOND, 1704

About three o'clock afternoon, I begun my Journey from Boston to New-Haven; being about two Hundred Mile. My **Kinsman**, Capt. Robert Luist, waited on me as farr as Dedham [Massachusetts], where I was to meet the Western **post**.

WEDNESDAY, OCTOBER 4TH.

About four in the morning, we set out for Kingston (for so was the Town called) with a french Docter in our company. Hee and the Post put on [rode their horses] very furiously, so that I could not keep up with them, only as now and then they'd stop till they see mee. This Rode was poorly furnished with accommodations for Travellers, so that we were forced to ride 22 miles by the post's account, but neerer thirty by mine, before wee could **bait** so much as our Horses, which I exceedingly complained of. But the post encourag'd mee, by saying wee should be well accommodated **anon** at mr. Devills, a few miles further. But I questioned whether we ought to go to the Devil [Knight was associating the man's name with Satan, or the Devil] to be helpt out of **affliction**. However, like the rest of **Deluded** souls that post to the Infernal denn [go to the Devil's den, or hell], Wee made all possi-

Kinsman: A male relative

Post: Mail carrier

Bait Give food or drink

Anon: Soon, presently

Affliction: Suffering

Deluded: Deceived

Alliting: Alighting; dismounting from a horse

Importunity: Pleading

Sophister: Wise man

Bin: Been

*ble speed to this Devil's Habitation; where **alliting** in full assurance of good accommodation, wee were going in. But meeting his two daughters, as I suposed twins, they so neerly resembled each other, both in features and habit, and look't as old as the Divel himselfe, and quite as Ugly, We desired entertainm't, but could hardly get a word out of 'um, till with our **Importunity**, telling them our necesity, &c. [etc.] they call'd the old **Sophister**, who was as sparing of his words as his daughters had **bin**, and no, or none, was the reply's hee made us to our demands. Hee differed only in this from the old fellow in to'ther [the other] Country: hee let us depart. . . .*

Finally the travelers found rooms at a boarding house. Knight gave a humorous account of the elderly landlady, who spent the evening complaining about her aches and pains to the French doctor. The next day Knight parted from her companions and continued the journey alone. When she came to a deep river she met an old man who said he would help her across after the water level went down. He invited her to his house, where she met his family, who were "the picture of poverty," and a strange guest.

*. . . . This little Hutt was one of the **wretchedest** I ever saw a habitation for human creatures. It was suported with **shores** enclosed with **Clapbords**, laid on Lengthways, and so much **asunder**, that the Light come throu' every where; the doore tyed on with a cord in the place of hinges; The floor the bear earth; no windows but such as the thin covering afforded, nor any furniture but a Bedd with a glass Bottle hanging at the head on't [on it]; an earthen cupp, a small pewter **Bason**, A Bord with sticks to stand on, instead of a table, and a block or two in the corner instead of chairs. The family were the old*

Early American literature

In the 1600s and 1700s colonists produced the earliest forms of American literature. Pioneering settlers issued books and pamphlets promoting settlement in North America (see *A Brief and True Report of the New Found Land of Virginia* and *The Propriety of Pennsylvania*). Others wrote histories of their colonies (see "The Founding of Jamestown" and "The Pilgrims' Landing and First Winter"). Religious leaders published essays on social issues (see *Some Considerations on the Keeping of Negroes*) or spiritual matters (see *John Winthrop's Christian Experience*). Many colonists kept personal diaries, such as the "The Journal of Madame Knight," or wrote autobiographies (see *Some Account of the Early Part of the Life of Elizabeth Ashbridge* and *Benjamin Franklin: A Biography in His Own Words*). Several wrote captivity narratives, which became one of the first types of popular American literature (see *A Narrative of the Captivity and Restauration of Mrs. Mary Rowlandson*). Colonists also wrote poetry. Anne Dudley Bradstreet, a housewife on the Massachusetts frontier, became the first published American poet.

Wretchedest: Extremely bad

Shores Props

Clapbords: Wood shingles

Asunder: Far apart

Bason: Metal basin

man, his wife and two Children; all and every part being the picture of poverty. Notwithstanding both the Hutt and its Inhabitance were very clean, and tydee. . . .

I had scarce done thinking, when an Indian-like Animal come to the door, on a creature very much like himselfe, in **mien** and feature, as well as Ragged cloathing; and having 'litt, makes an Awkerd Scratch with his Indian **shoo**, and a **Nodd**, sits on the block, fumbles out his black **Junk**, dipps it in the Ashes, and presents it piping hott to his muscheeto's, [mustache] and fell to sucking like a calf, without speaking, for near a quarter of an **hower**. At length the old man said how do's Sarah do? who I understood was the wretches wife, and Daughter to the old man: he Replyed—as well as can be expected, &c [etc.] . . . as ugly as hee was, I was glad to ask him to show me the way to Saxtons, at Stoningtown; which he promising, I ventur'd over with the old mans assistance . . . I Ridd on very slowly thro' Stoningtown, where the Rode was very Stony and uneven. I asked the fellow, as we went, **divers** questions of the place and way, &c. I being arrived at my country Saxtons, at Stoningtown, was very well accommodated both as to **victuals** and Lodging, the only Good of both [the best so far] I had found since my setting out. Here I heard there was an old man and his Daughter to come that way, bound to N. London; and being now **destitute** a Guide, gladly waited for them, being in so good a harbour. . . .

THIRSDAY, OCTOBER THE 5TH,

about 3 in the afternoon, I sat forward with neighbor Polly [Polly sat behind Knight on the horse] and Jemima, a Girl about 18 Years old, who hee said he had been to fetch out of the **Narragansetts**, and said they had Rode thirty miles that day, on a **sory** lean **Jade**, with only a Bagg under her for a **pillion**, which the poor Girl often complain'd was very uneasy.

Wee made Good speed along, which made poor Jemima make many a **sow'r** face, the **mare** being a very hard trotter; and after many a hearty and bitter Oh, she at length **Low'd** out: Lawful Heart father! this bare mare hurts mee [she was sitting behind her father on his horse] . . . I'me **direfull** sore I vow; with many words to that purpose: poor Child **sais Gaffer**—she us't to serve your mother so. I don't care how mother us't to do, quoth Jemima, in a passionate tone. At which the old man Laught, and **kik't** his Jade o' [on] the side, which made her Jolt ten times harder.

About seven that Evening, we come to New London [Connecticut] Ferry: here, by reason of a very high wind, we mett with great diffi-

Mien: Manner

Shoo: Shoe

Nodd: To nod the head as a form of greeting

Junk: Smoking pipe

Hower: Hour

Divers: Diverse; various

Victuals: Food

Destitute: Lacking

Narragansetts: Native American tribe

Sory: Sorry

Jade: Broken-down horse

Pillion: Saddle cushion

Sow'r: Sour

Mare: Female horse

Low'd: Lowed; moaned

Direfull: Dreadful

Sais: Says

Gaffer: An old man

Kik't: Kicked

*culty in getting over—the Boat **tos't** exceedingly, and our Horses **cap-per'd** at a very surprizing Rate, and set us all in a fright. . . .*

*Being safely arrived at the house of Mrs. Prentices in N. London, I treated neighbour Polly and daughter for their **divirting** company, and bid them farewell; and between nine and ten at night waited on the Rev Mr. Gurdon Saltonstall, minister of the town, who kindly Invited me to Stay that night at his house, where I was very hand-somely and plentifully treated and Lodg'd; and made good the Great Character I had before heard concerning him: . . . that hee was the most **affable**, courteous, **Genero's** and best of men.*

Tos't: Tossed

Capper'd: Capered; scampered

Divirting: Entertaining

Affable: Friendly

Genero's: Generous

What happened next . . .

Although Knight did not receive fame for her journal during her lifetime, she became a known for her other accomplishments. Her mother died in 1712, and her daughter Elizabeth was married the following year to John Livingston of New London, Connecticut. When the newlyweds moved to Connecticut, Knight sold her property in Boston and went with them. She bought property in Norwich and New London. From 1714 until her death, she operated a shop and a house of entertainment, managed many farms, and conducted business with Native Americans. When Knight died in 1727 in New London, her estate was apparently inherited by Elizabeth.

After Knight's death her journal passed into private hands and remained in manuscript form. About a hundred years later the diary was discovered by Theodor Dwight, Jr., who had it published as *The Journal of Madame Knight* (1825). Over the years the book was reprinted a number of times and read by generations of new readers. *The Journal of Madame Knight* provides a more realistic portrait than most literature of the period. Presenting the vivid contrasts between wilderness and civilization, the diary gives accounts of a variety of cultures as well as the author's own cheerful personality in the face of hardship.

Did you know . . .

- In 1718 Knight and several other Connecticut business owners were accused of selling liquor to local Native Americans. (Many colonies had passed laws prohibiting the sale of rum and brandy to Native Americans because they had become highly addicted to alcohol, which had been introduced to them by Europeans.) Although Knight blamed a servant for the deed, she was still forced to pay a fine. However, the incident did not affect her standing in society.

- When Knight died, she left an estate worth 1800 pounds (an amount of British money), which was more than one hundred times the wealth of the average property owner in Connecticut at the time.

For more information

Elliott, Emory, and others, eds. *American Literature: A Prentice Hall Anthology.* Englewood Cliffs, N.J.: Prentice-Hall 1991, pp. 235–36.

Gunn, Giles, ed. *Early American Writing.* New York: Penguin, 1994, pp. 269–73.

Johnson, Allen, and others, eds. *Dictionary of American Biography.* New York: Scribner's, 1946–1958, pp. 340–41.

James, Edward T. and others, eds. *Notable American Women, 1607–1950,* Volume II. Cambridge, Mass.: Belknap Press of Harvard University Press, 1971, pp. 340–41.

Motion: A Travel Journal—Time Travelers: Sarah Kemble Knight (1666–1727). (Contains the only known portrait of Sarah Kemble Knight) http://www.nearbycafe.com/motion/motionmenu/timetravel/knight.html Available September 30, 1999.

Sigerman, Harriet, ed. *Young Oxford History of Women in the United States: Biographical Supplement and Index.* New York: Oxford University Press, 1994, pp. 92–93.

Elizabeth Ashbridge

Excerpts from **Some Account of the Early Part of the Life of Elizabeth Ashbridge,... Written by Herself**

Reprinted in *Early American Writing*
Published in 1994
Edited by Giles Gunn

Elizabeth Ashbridge (1713–1755) was born in England and brought up a member of the Anglican faith (Church of England, the official state church). At the age of fourteen she eloped (ran away and got married), but her husband died within five years. Soon after his death she went to America as an indentured servant. (An indentured servant was an immigrant who signed a contract to work for an employer, or master, in the colonies for four to seven years). Ashbridge had a cruel master, so she married a second time in order to escape a desperate situation. (A female indentured servant could be released from her contract if an acceptable suitor was prepared to buy out her remaining period of service.) She reported that her new husband, a school teacher named Sullivan, "fell in love with me for my dancing." Ashbridge was attracted by his worldliness. One day she set out from their home in New Jersey to visit relatives in Pennsylvania. Once she arrived, she immediately learned that they were Quakers. (Quakers were members of a Puritan group called the Society of Friends, which was outlawed in England until 1689. William Penn founded the colony of Pennsylvania in

"Once he came up to me, took out his penknife, and said 'If you offer to go to meeting tomorrow, with this knife I'll cripple you, for you shall not be a Quaker.'"

1681 so they could have religious freedom; see "The Propriety of Pennsylvania.")

At first Ashbridge was shocked because she had no idea her relatives had joined this religion, which was not accepted by Anglicans or even other Puritan groups. Like traditional Puritans, Quakers advocated a strict moral and spiritual life. Unlike Puritans, however, they believed in direct individual communication with God through an "inner light." Both the Quakers and the Puritans considered the Church of England corrupt and in need of reform. The Puritans were trying to make reforms from within the church, however, and all of their ministers were ordained (officially appointed) in the church. Quakers refused to have anything to do with an established church. They held their meetings (religious services) in private homes, and anyone who felt especially inspired could lead a meeting or become a traveling minister. Puritans were therefore highly suspicious of the Quakers, who rejected the very basis of Puritan society—officially appointed ministers and an organized church. Since the Puritans dominated New England and parts of surrounding colonies, Quakers frequently encountered persecution (punishment or ridicule for their beliefs). They were also shunned by Anglicans, who found them troublesome and a threat to the basis of English society. By the mid-1700s, when Ashbridge went to Pennsylvania, other religious groups had settled in the colony and Quakers were sometimes harassed.

During her visit, Ashbridge became interested in Quakerism and converted to the faith. She decided to stay in Pennsylvania and took a teaching position at a nearby school. She was afraid to let anyone know she was a Quaker, however, and was careful not to wear the plain clothing that would identify her as a Friend (another name for Quaker). When she found a teaching job for her husband she wrote and asked him to join her. By the time Sullivan reached Pennsylvania he had learned about her conversion. Once again Ashbridge found herself in a miserable situation. Sullivan was extremely abusive toward her because he did not approve of Quakers (he himself was an Anglican). Ashbridge's autobiography tells the story of her struggle to remain a Quaker in spite of mistreatment from an alcoholic husband.

Some Things to Remember While Reading Excerpts from *Some Account of the Early Part of the Life of Elizabeth Ashbridge,. . .Written by Herself:*

- Ashbridge's autobiography gives the modern reader insight into the position of women in the eighteenth century. In both Europe and America women were considered morally, intellectually, and physically inferior to men—an attitude that had existed for hundreds of years. Men thought women were silly and helpless, and therefore in need of protection. Regardless of social class, a woman was totally dependent on her husband, and her first duty was to obey him. She was even required to get his approval to pursue another religion. Note that Ashbridge had to ask Sullivan's permission to go to meetings or visit Friends.

- Keep in mind that a woman had no way out of an unhappy marriage. A husband had a legal right to beat his wife if she displeased him, and mental cruelty was not recognized by the courts. Therefore, Ashbridge was forced to endure physical and verbal abuse from Sullivan. She could not hope to get a legal separation or divorce because marriage was a sacred bond that was never broken, except in extreme circumstances (such as desertion or lack of financial support on the part of the husband). Most women, like Ashbridge, could escape an abusive husband only if he happened to die.

- Sullivan was embarrassed and confused by his wife's religion, and he felt she brought dishonor on him by attending Quaker meetings. Although he tried to be understanding, he could not deal with a disobedient wife. Notice that in spite of their differences, Ashbridge tried to think the best of Sullivan. She maintained this attitude because Quakers taught that misfortune must be endured with patience.

- Ashbridge frequently used "thee" and "thou," which were Quaker words for "you."

- The excerpts from Ashbridge's autobiography open at the point when Sullivan forced her to leave Pennsylvania and return to New Jersey. She insisted on attending meetings, however, and he continued to treat her cruelly.

Excerpts from Some Account of the Early Part Life of the Life of Elizabeth Ashbridge,. . .Written by Herself

*When meeting-time came, I longed to go, but dared not to ask my husband's leave. As the Friends were getting ready themselves, they asked him if he would accompany them, observing, that they knew whose who were to be his employers, and, if they were at meeting, would speak to them. He consented. The woman Friend then said, "And wilt thou let thy wife go too;" which request he denied; but she answered his objections so **prudently** that he could not be angry, and at last consented. I went with joy, and a heavenly meeting it was. . . .*

*By the end of the week, we got settled in our new **situation**. We took a room, in a friend's house, one mile from each school, and eight from the **meeting-house**. I now **deemed** it proper to let my husband see I was determined to join with friends. When first day came, I directed myself to him in this manner: "My dear, art thou [are you] willing to let me go to meeting? He flew into a rage, and replied "No you sha'n't [shall not]." Speaking firmly, I told him, "That, as a dutiful wife, I was ready to obey all his lawful commands; but, when they imposed upon my conscience, I could not obey him. I had already wronged myself, in having done it too long; and though he was near to me, and, as a wife ought, I loved him, yet God, who was nearer than all the world to me, had made me sensible that this was the way in which I ought to go. I added, that this was no small cross to my own will; but I had given up my heart, and I trusted that He who called for it would enable me, for the remainder of my life, to keep it steadily devoted to his service; and I hoped I should not, on this account, make the worse wife." I spoke, however, to no purpose;—he continued inflexible. . . .*

*Finding that all the means he had yet used could not alter my **resolutions**, he several times struck me with severe blows. I endeavoured to bear all with patience, believing that the time would come when he would see I was in the right. Once he came up to me, took out his penknife, and said, "If you offer to go to meeting to-morrow, with this knife I'll cripple you, for you shall not be a Quaker." I made him no answer. In the morning, I set out as usual; he did not attempt to harm me. Having **despaired** of **recovering** me himself, he fled, for help, to*

Prudently: Wisely

Situation: Position of employment

Meeting-house: Place where Quaker services are held

Deemed: Considered

Resolutions: Determinations

Despaired: Loss of all hope

Recovering: Getting back

In order to prevent
Elizabeth Ashbrigde from
attending Quaker meetings
like the one pictured here,
her husband often
physically abused her.
*Reproduced by permission of
Archive Photos, Inc.*

*the **priest**, whom he told, that I had been a very religious woman, in
the way of the Church of England, of which I was a member, and had
a good certificate from Long Island; that I was now **bewitched**, and
had turned Quaker, which almost broke his heart; and, therefore, he
desired that, as he was one who had the care of souls, he would come
and pay me a visit, and use his **endeavours** to reclaim me, which he
hoped, by the blessing of God, would be done. The priest consented,
and fixed the time for his coming, which was that day two weeks, as*

Priest: Anglican minister

Bewitched: Possessed by
an evil spirit

Endeavours: Attempt; strive

he said he could not come sooner. My husband came home extremely pleased, and told me of it. I replied, with a smile, I trusted I should be enabled to give a reason for the hope within me; yet I believed, at the same time, that the priest would never trouble himself about me, which proved to be the case. . . .

. . . . My husband still went to no place of worship. One day he said to me, "I would go to meeting, only I'm afraid I shall hear your **clack**, which I cannot bear." I used no persuasions. When meeting-time came, he got the horse, took me behind him, and went. For several months, if he saw me offer to rise, he went out; till, one day, I rose before he was aware and then, as he afterwards owned, he was ashamed to do it.

From this time, he left off the practice, and never hindered me from going to meeting. Though he did not take up the cross [convert to Quakerism], yet his judgement was convinced; and, sometimes, melting into tears, he would say to me, "My dear, I have seen the beauty there is in the truth, and that thou hast followed the right way, in which I pray God to preserve thee." I told him, that I hoped He who had given me strength would also favour him, "O," said he, "I cannot bear the **reproach** thou dost, to be called **turn-coat**, and become a laughing-stock to the world; but I'll no longer hinder thee." This I considered a favour, and a little hope remained that my prayers, on his account, would be heard.

We lived in a small house by ourselves, which, though **mean**, and though we had little to put in it, our bed being no better than **chaff**, I was truly content. The only desires I had were for my own preservation, and to be blessed with the reformation of my husband. He was connected with a set of men whom he feared would **make game** of him, which indeed they already did; asking him when he designed to commence preacher, for they saw he intended to turn Quaker, and seemed to love his wife better since she became one than before. They used to come to our house, and provoked him to sit up and drink with them, sometimes till near day, while I have been sorrowing in a stable. Once, as I sat in this condition, I heard him say to his company, "I can't bear any longer to **afflict** my poor wife in this manner; for, whatever you may think of her, I do believe she's a good woman." He then came to me and said, "Come in, my dear, God has given thee a deal of patience: I'll put an end to this practice." This was the last time they sat up at night.

Ashbridge's husband decided they would be happier if they went to a place where no one knew him, but she did not want to move.

Clack: Preach

Reproach: Disgrace

Turn-coat: Traitor

Mean: Not valuable

Chaff: Seed coverings left after the threshing of grain; used for stuffing mattresses

Make game: Make fun

Afflict: To cause suffering

Colonial America: Primary Sources

*All I could say would not **avail**. Hearing of a place at Bordentown, he went **thither**, but was not suited. He next removed to Mount Holly [New Jersey], where he settled. We had each of us a good school; we soon got our house pretty well furnished, and might have done very well. Nothing seemed wanting to complete my happiness, except the reformation of my husband, which I had much reason to doubt I should not see soon. It fell out according to my fears. He addicted himself much to drinking, and grew worse than before. Sorrow was again my lot, I prayed for patience to bear my afflictions, and to submit to the **dispensations** of **Providence**. I murmured not; nor do I recollect that I ever uttered any harsh expressions except on one occasion. My husband coming home a little intoxicated, (a state in which he was very **fractious**,) and, finding me at work by a candle, he put it out, fetching me, at the same time, a **box** on the ear, and saying, "You don't earn your light." At this unkind usage, which I had not been used to for the last two years, I was somewhat angry, and said, "Thou art a **vile** man." He struck me again; but my anger had cooled, and I received the blow without so much as a word in return. This also displeased him, and he went on in a **distracted** like manner, uttering such expressions of despair as, he believed he was **predestined to damnation**, and he did not care how soon God struck him dead. I said very little, till, at length, in the bitterness of my soul, I broke out into these expressions: "Lord, look down on my afflictions, and deliver me by some means or other." My prayer was granted, but in such a manner that I thought it would have killed me. He went to Burlington, where he got drunk, and inlisted to go as a common soldier to Cuba, in the year 1740. I had drunk many bitter cups, but this seemed the bitterest of them all. A thousand times I blamed myself for making such a request, which I was afraid had displeased God, who had, in displeasure, granted it for my punishment.*

*I have since had cause to believe that he was benefitted by his rash act, as, in the army, he did what he could not at home;—he suffered for the testimony of truth [converted to Quakerism]. When they came to prepare for an **engagement**, he refused to fight; he was whipt, and brought before the general, who asked him, why he inlisted if he would not fight. "I did it," said he, "in a drunken **frolic**, when the devil had the better of me; but now my judgment is convinced I ought not to fight, neither will I, whatever I suffer. I have but one life, and you may take that if you please, for I'll never take up arms." [Quakers are pacifists; that is, they do not believe in war.] He adhered to this resolution. By their cruel usage of him in consequence, he was so much disabled [he was beaten so badly] that the general*

Avail: Assist

Thither: There

Dispensations: A general state or ordering of things

Providence: God

Fractious: Unruly

Box: Blow; hit

Vile: Disgusting; unpleasant

Distracted Mentally confused

Predestined to damnation: Doomed to hell

Engagement: Battle

Frolic: A playful or mischievous

sent him to Chelsea Hospital, near London. Within nine months afterwards, he died at his place, and I hope made a good end.

Having been obliged to say much of his ill usage to me, I have thought it my duty to say what I could in his favour. Although he was so bad, I never thought him the worst of men. If he had suffered [allowed] religion to have had its perfect work, I should have been happy in the lowest situation of life. I have had cause to bless God, for enabling me, in the station of a wife, to do my duty, and now that I am a widow, I submit to his will. . . .

What happened next . . .

In 1746, two years after Sullivan's death, Ashbridge married her third husband, Aaron Ashbridge. They were happy together, and he helped her prepare her autobiography. Elizabeth died in 1755, and her story was published in 1807, under the full title *Some Account of the Early Part of the Life of Elizabeth Ashbridge, . . . Written by Herself.*

Did you know . . .

- Ashbridge was not typical of former indentured servants. Most women continued to work as domestic servants, whereas she became a teacher. Few indentured servants, male or female, had a formal education, but Ashbridge apparently had enough schooling to qualify her to teach others to read and write.

- By the early 1700s laborers comprised the majority of new arrivals in America, and most of them were indentured servants. According to some estimates, one-half to two-thirds of all Europeans who traveled to the American colonies were committed to some form of labor contract. The majority were men because employers wanted male workers to do heavy labor. Women tended to be house servants, a luxury only the wealthiest American settlers could afford. Consequently, there were far fewer women than men in all of the colonies. This meant that women had their choice of husbands, and many married three or four times. Ashbridge, who had three husbands, was therefore typical of eighteenth-century colonial women.

- Unlike other European immigrant groups, the Dutch (former inhabitants of the Netherlands) treated women as near-equals of men in many respects. Women of the upper and merchant classes in the Netherlands were considered the most liberated in Europe. This was a result of their being educated and trained to manage household accounts in good times and to take over financial matters if they were ever widowed. Dutch women in the New Netherland colony (later New York) were also expected to hold onto family property so that their children would have an inheritance. An example was Maria van Cortlandt van Rensselaer (1645–1689). When her husband died she became the overseer (manager or supervisor) of Rensselaerswyck, his family estate. She was able to keep secure one of the largest estates in New York for her children.

For more information

Berkin, Carol. *First Generations: Women in Colonial America.* New York: Hill & Wang, 1996.

Elgin, Kathleen. *The Quakers; The Religious Society of Friends.* New York: D. McKay Company, 1968.

Gunn, Giles, ed. *Early American Writing.* New York: Penguin Books, 1994, pp. 380–86.

Middleton, Richard. *Colonial America: A History, 1585–1776.* Second edition. Malden, Mass.: Blackwell Publishers, 1996, pp. 263–82.

Benjamin Franklin

Excerpt from **Benjamin Franklin: A Biography
in His Own Words**

**Reprinted in *In Their Own Words: The Colonizers*
Published in 1998
Edited by T. J. Stiles**

In the eighteenth century the Enlightenment (a movement that stressed rational analysis and observation) was sweeping Europe, and influential thinkers were looking at the world in a different way. The Enlightenment had an impact on science, religion, philosophy, politics, and the arts, as traditional views were being questioned and replaced with radically new theories. One of the most important changes was the idea that God was not an all-powerful force that controlled every aspect of human life. This insight was introduced by scientists and then adopted by theologians (religious philosophers), who began to teach that God had given humans the ability to understand their environment through reason.

Upper-class, educated American colonists were especially intrigued by the latest innovations coming from Europe. Full of enthusiasm, they welcomed these theories, which ideally suited their own social experiment in the New World (the European term for North America and South America).

Philadelphia, Pennsylvania, was emerging as the center of scientific thought and experimentation in the colonies. This was a logical development because Pennsylvania was founded by

"... I found myself in New York, near 300 miles from home, a boy of but 17, without the least recommendation to or knowledge of any person in the place, and with very little money in my pocket. ..."

Although he was the best known scientist of the eighteenth century, Benjamin Franklin was also a printer, writer, inventor, politician, and ambassador. *Reproduced by permission of The Library of Congress.*

Quakers, who believed that God had granted humans the gift of intellect so they could understand the world around them. (Quakerism, or the Society of Friends, was a branch of Puritanism that stressed direct communication between the individual and God through an "inner light.") The American Philosophical Society, the first scientific institution in the colonies, was established in Philadelphia, Philadelphia, in 1743. Among the mostly Quaker founders of the society was a famous non-Quaker, Benjamin Franklin (1706–1790). Franklin moved to Philadelphia in 1723, and by the 1740s he had gained international recognition for his experiments and writings on electricity.

Franklin pursued a wide range of interests during his long life. A printer, writer, civic leader, inventor, politician, and ambassador, he was also the best-known scientist of the eighteenth century, in both Europe as well as America. Before he conducted his experiments, electricity was considered a bizarre force that was of interest mainly for entertainment. As a result of his discoveries, the study of electricity was established as a valid scientific pursuit.

A native Bostonian, Franklin ran away to Philadelphia at the age of seventeen. He started his own printing business and retired a rich man in 1748. His annual *Poor Richard's Almanack* provided a wealth of information about stars and planets, advice about medicine, weather predictions, and rhymes and witty sayings for the teaching of morals. In 1771, after he had embarked on a career as a statesman—which would lead to his becoming one of the "founding fathers" of the United States—he began writing his life story. Franklin's autobiography is considered one of the greatest personal narratives ever written in the English language.

Things to Remember While Reading an Excerpt from *Benjamin Franklin: A Biography in His Own Words:*

- The excerpt below covers the first seventeen years of Franklin's life. Because his family was poor—there were seventeen children altogether—the young Franklin did not receive a proper education. For instance, he attended the Boston Grammar School for only one year because his parents could not afford the tuition (instruction fees). Later he spent a year at George Brownell's English School, where he failed arithmetic. Luckily, because Franklin's parents encouraged reading, thinking, and discussion, he grew up in an educational environment. At the age of ten, he began working as an apprentice (one who learns by practical experience) in his father's chandlery shop (a place where candles are made).

• Since Franklin enjoyed reading, his parents eventually decided he should enter the printing trade. Therefore, at the age of twelve, he became an apprentice for his brother James, who ran a Boston newspaper, *The New England Courant.* James's printing shop was a center of social activity, which provided the young Franklin with a constant flow of new ideas. Customers would often linger to discuss politics or religion, and they also brought books for him to borrow. During this time the ambitious young man improved his writing and editing talents. At the age of seventeen Franklin left Boston to seek his fortune in Philadelphia.

Excerpt from Benjamin Franklin: A Biography in His Own Words

Josiah, my father, married young, and carried his wife with three children unto New England, about 1682. . . . By the same wife he had four children more born there, and by a second wife ten more, in all 17, of which I remember 13 sitting at one time at his table, who all grew up to be men and women, and married. I was the youngest son [born in 1706], and the younger child but two, and was born in Boston, N. England. My mother, the second wife, was Abiah Folger, a daughter of Peter Folger, one of the first settlers of new England. . . .

*My elder brothers were all put **apprentices** to different trades. I was put to the grammar school at eight years of age, my father*

Apprentices: One who is learning by practical experience under skilled workers of a trade

intending to devote me as the **tithe** of his sons to the service of the Church [of England]. My early readiness in learning to read (which must have been very early, as I do not remember when I could not read) and the opinion of all his friends that I should certainly make a good scholar, encouraged him in this purpose of his. My uncle Benjamin too approved of it, and proposed to give me all his **shorthand** volumes of **sermons**, I suppose as a stock to set up with, if I would learn his character [shorthand].

I continued however at the grammar school not quite one year, tho' in that time I had risen gradually from the middle of the class of that year to be the head of it, and farther was removed into the next class above it, in order to go with that into the third at the end of the year. But my father in the meantime, from a view of the expense of a college education which, having so large a family, he could not well afford, and the mean living many so educated men were afterwards able to obtain, reasons that he gave to his friends in my hearing, altered his first intention, took me from the grammar school, and sent me to a school for writing and arithmetic kept by a then famous man, Mr. Geo. Brownell. . . . Under him I acquired fair writing pretty soon, but I failed in the arithmetic, and made no progress in it.

At ten years old, I was taken home to assist my father in his business which was that of a **tallow chandler** and soap boiler. A business he was not bred to, but had assumed on his arrival in New England and on finding his dying trade would not maintain his family, being in little request. Accordingly I was employed in cutting wick for the candles, filling the dipping mold, and the molds for the cast candles, attending the shop, going of errands, etc.

I disliked the trade and had a strong **inclination** for the sea; but my father declared against it. However, living near the water, I was much in and about it, learned early to swim well, and to manage boats, and when in a boat or canoe with other boys I was commonly allowed to govern, especially in any case of difficulty; and upon other occasions I was generally a leader among the boys, and sometimes led them into **scrapes**. . . .

To return. I continued thus employed in my father's business for two years, that is till I was 12 years old; and my brother John, who was bred to that business, having left my father, married and set up for himself at Rhode Island. There was all appearance that I was destined to supply his place and be a tallow chandler. But my dislike to the trade continuing, my father was under **apprehensions** that if he did not find one for me more agreeable, I should break away and get

Tithe: A voluntary contribution for the support of the church

Shorthand: A system of handwriting using symbols for words, phrases, and letters

Sermons: A religious speech delivered as part of a church service

Tallow chandler: A maker of the white solid produced from the fat of cattle and sheep used chiefly in soap, candles, and lubricants

Inclination: Preference

Scrapes: A scuffle; fight

Apprehensions: Suspicions or fears

Colonial America: Primary Sources

to sea, as his son Josiah had done to his great **vexation**. He therefore sometimes took me to walk with him, and see **joiners**, bricklayers, **turners**, **braziers**, etc., at their work, that he might observe my inclination, and **endeavor** to fix it on some trade or other on land. . . .

From a child I was fond of reading, and all the little money that came into my hands was ever laid out in books. Pleased with the Pilgrim's Progress, my first collection was of John Bunyan's works, in separate little volumes. I afterwards sold them to enable me to buy R. Burton's Historical Collections; they were small Chapmen's Books, and cheap, 40 or 50 in all. . . . This bookish inclination at length determined my father to make me a printer, tho' he had already one son (James) of that profession.

In 1717 my brother James returned from England with a press and letters to set up his business in Boston. I liked it much better than that of my father, but still had a hankering for the sea. To prevent the **apprehended** effect of such an inclination, my father was impatient to have me bound to my brother. I stood out some time, but at last was persuaded and signed the **indentures**, when I was yet but 12 years old. I was to serve as an apprentice till I was 21 years of age, only I was to be allowed **journeyman**'s wages during the last year.

In a little time I made great **proficiency** in the business, and became a useful hand to my brother. I now had access to better books. An acquaintance with the apprentices of booksellers enabled me sometimes to borrow a small one, which I was careful to return soon and clean. Often I sat up on my room reading the greatest part of the night, when the book was borrowed in the evening and to be returned early in the morning, lest it should be missed or wanted. . . .

My brother had in 1720 or 21 begun to print a newspaper. It was the second that appeared in America, and was called The New England Courant. The only one before it was The Boston News Letter. I remember his being **dissuaded** by some of his friends from the **undertaking**, as not likely to succeed, one newspaper being in their judgment enough for America. . . . He went on, however, with the undertaking, and after having worked in composing the types and printing off the sheets I was employed to carry the papers thro' the streets to meet customers.

He had some **ingenious** men among his friends who amused themselves by writing little pieces for this paper, which gained it credit, and made it more in demand; and these gentlemen often visited us. Hearing their conversations, and their accounts of the **appro-**

Vexation: Trouble or distress

Joiner: A person whose occupation is to construct articles by joining pieces of wood

Turner: A person who forms articles with a machine which work is rotated about a horizontal axis and shaped by a fixed tool

Braziers: One that works in brass

Endeavor: Attempt; strive

Apprehended: Mental grasp

Indentures: A contract binding one person to work for another for a given period of time

Journeyman: A workman who had completed his apprenticeship

Proficiency: Advancement in knowledge or skill

Dissuade: To advise (a person) against something

Undertaking: Venture

Ingenious: Marked by originality, resourcefulness, and cleverness in conception

A young Benjamin Franklin working as a printer's apprentice. *Reproduced by permission of Archive Photos, Inc.*

bation *their papers were received with, I was excited to try my hand among them. But being still a boy, and suspecting that my brother would object to printing anything of mine in his paper if he knew it to be mine, I **contrived** to disguise my hand [handwriting], and writing an anonymous paper I put it in at night under the door of the printing house.*

It was found in the morning and communicated to his writing

Approbation: Praise

Contrived: Planned

friends when they called in as usual. They read it, commented on it in my hearing, and I had the exquisite pleasure of finding it met with their approbation, and that in their different guesses at the author, none were named but men of some character among us for learning and **ingenuity**. I suppose now that I was rather lucky in my judges, and that perhaps they were not really so very good ones as I them esteemed them.

Encouraged however by this, I wrote and conveyed in the same way to the press several more papers, which were equally approved, and I kept my secret till my small fund of sense for such performances was pretty well exhausted, and then I discovered [revealed] it; when I began to be considered a little more by my brother's acquaintances, and in a manner that did not quite please him, as he thought, probably with reason, that it tended to make me too **vain**.

And perhaps this might be one occasion of the differences that we frequently had about this time. Tho' a brother, he considered himself as my master, and me as his apprentice; and accordingly expected the same services from me as he would from another; while I thought he demeaned me too much in some he required of me, who from a brother expected more **indulgence**. Our disputes were often brought before our father, and I **fancy** I was either generally in the right, or else a better pleader, because the judgment was generally in my favor. But my brother was passionate and had often beaten me, which I took extremely amiss; and thinking my apprenticeship very **tedious**, I was constantly wishing for some opportunity of shortening it, which at length offered in a manner unexpected.

One of the pieces in our newspaper, on some political point which I have now forgotten, gave offense to the Assembly. He [Franklin's brother] was taken up, **censured**, and imprisoned for a month by the Speaker's Warrant, I suppose because he would not discover his author. I too was taken up and examined before the Council; but tho' I did not give them any satisfaction, they contented themselves with **admonishing** me, and dismissed me; considering me perhaps as an apprentice, who was bound to keep his master's secrets.

During my brother's confinement, which I resented a good deal, notwithstanding our private differences, I had the management of the paper, and I made bold to give our rulers some rubs with it, which by brother took very kindly, while others began to consider me in an unfavorable light, as a young genius that had a turn for **libelling** and **satire**. My brother's discharge was accompanied with an order of the House (a very odd one) that James Franklin should no longer print the

Ingenuity: Cleverness

Vain: Having or showing undue or excessive pride in one's appearance or achievement

Indulgence: Tolerance; lenient treatment

Fancy: To form a conception of

Tedious: Boring

Censured: To find fault and criticize as blameworthy

Admonishing: To express warning or disapproval in a gentle manner

Libelling: To make published statements without just cause and tending to expose another to public contempt

Satire: A literary work holding up human faults to ridicule or scorn

paper called the New England Courant.

There was a consideration held in our printing house among his friends what he should do in this case. Some proposed to **evade** the order by changing the name of the paper, but my brother, seeing the inconveniences in that, it was finally concluded on as a better way, to let it be printed for the future under the name of Benjamin Franklin. And to avoid the censure of the Assembly that might fall on him, as still printing it by his apprentice, the **contrivance** was that my old indenture should be returned to me with a full discharge on the back of it, to be shown on occasion; but to secure to him the benefit of my service I was to sign new indentures for the remainder of the term, which were to be kept private.

A very flimsy scheme it was, but however, it was immediately executed, and the paper went on accordingly under my name for several months. At length a fresh difference arising between my brother and me, I took upon me to assert my freedom, presuming that he would not venture to produce the new indentures. It was not fair in me to take this advantage, and this I therefore reckon one of the first **errata** of my life. But the unfairness of it weighed little with me. . . .

When he found I would leave him, he took care to prevent my getting employment in any other printing house of the town, by going round and speaking to every master, who accordingly refused to give me work. I then thought of going to New York as the nearest place where there was a printer; and I was rather inclined to leave Boston, when I reflected that I had already made myself a little **obnoxious** to the governing party; and from the **arbitrary** proceedings of the Assembly in my brother's case it was likely I might if I stayed soon bring myself into scrapes; and farther that my **indiscreet disputations** about religion begun to make me pointed at with horror by good people, as an **infidel** or **atheist.**

I determined on the point; but my father now siding with my brother, I was sensible that if I attempted to go openly, men would be used to prevent me. My friend Collins therefore undertook to manage a little for me. He agreed with the captain of a New York **sloop** for my passage, under the notion of my being a young acquaintance of his that had got a naughty girl with child. . . . So I sold some of my books to raise a little money, was taken on board privately, and as we had a fair wind in three days I found myself in New York, near 300 miles from home, a boy of but 17, without the least recommendation to or knowledge of any person in the place, and with very little money in my pocket. . . .

Evade: To avoid facing up to

Contrivance: An artificial arrangement or development

Errata: Errors

Obnoxious: Highly offensive

Arbitary: Not limited by law

Indiscreet disputations: Unwise arguments

Infidel: One who is not Christian or who opposes Christianity

Atheist: One who denies the existence of God

Sloop: A rigged boat with one mast and a single sail

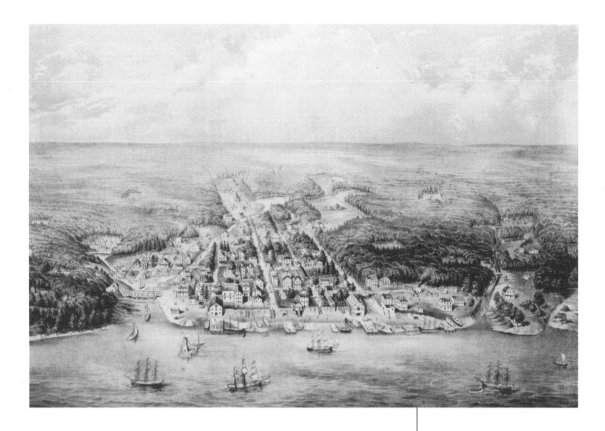

An illustration of Philadelphia in the 1700s. Benjamin Franklin came to Philadelphia to escape working as his brother's apprentice. *Reproduced by permission of The Granger Collection.*

I offered by service to the printer of the place, old Mr. William Bradford (who had been the first printer in Pennsylvania, but removed from thence upon the quarrel of [Governor] George Keith). He could give me no employment, having little to do, and help enough already. But, says he, my son at Philadelphia has lately lost his principal hand, Aquila Rose, by death. If you go thither I believe he may employ you. . . .

*[I] arrived there [in Philadelphia] about 8 or 9 o'clock, in the Sunday morning, and landed at the Market Street **wharf**. . . . I was in my working dress, my best clothes being to come round by sea. I was dirty from my journey; my pockets were stuffed out with shirts and stockings; I knew no soul, nor where to look for lodging. I was fatigued with travelling, rowing, and want of rest. I was very hungry, and my whole stock of cash consisted of a Dutch dollar and about a **shilling** in copper. The latter I gave the people of the boat for my passage, who at first refused it on account of my rowing; but I insisted in their taking it, a man being sometimes more generous when he has but a little money than when he has plenty, perhaps thro' fear of being thought to have but little.*

Wharf: a structure built along navigable waters so ships could receive and discharge cargo and passengers

Shilling: A former monetary unit

Then I walked up the street, gazing about, till near the Market House I met a boy with bread. I had made many a meal on bread, and inquiring where he got it, I went immediately to the baker's he directed me to in Second Street; and asked for biscuit, intending such as we had in Boston, but they it seems were not made in Philadelphia. Then I asked for a three-penny loaf, and was told they had none such; so not considering or knowing the difference of money and the greater cheapness nor the names of his bread, I bad him give me three penny worth of any sort. He gave me accordingly three great puffy rolls. I was surprised at the quantity, but took it, and having no room in my pockets, walked off, with a roll under each arm, and eating the other. . . .

Thus refreshed I walked again up the street, which by this time had many clean dressed people in it who were all walking the same way. I joined them, and thereby was led into the great Meeting House of the **Quakers** *near the Market. I sat down among them, and after looking round a while and hearing nothing said, being very drowsy thro' labor and want of rest the preceding night, I fell asleep, and continued to till the meeting broke up, when one was kind enough to rouse me. This was therefore the first house I was in or slept in, in Philadelphia. . . .*

I began now to have some acquaintance among the young people of the town, that were lovers of reading, with whom I spent my evenings very pleasantly. And gaining money by my industry and **frugality***, I lived very agreeably, forgetting Boston as much as I could. . . .*

Quaker: A member of the Society of Friends, a Protestant Christian group that believes in direct communication with God through an "inner light"

Frugality: Thriftiness

What happened next . . .

Franklin finally settled in Philadelphia in 1726. Three years later he purchased a failing newspaper, *The Pennsylvania Gazette,* which eventually reached a high circulation. In 1733 he also began publishing *Poor Richard's Almanack,* a collection of witty sayings and pieces of advice that he wrote under the pseudonym (pen name) of Richard Saunders.

During the 1730s Franklin branched out into other projects. In 1736 he founded the Union Fire Company in Philadelphia. The industrious young man also started a police force and promoted the paving and lighting of city streets.

Reflective of his lifelong love of reading, Franklin founded what was probably the first circulating library in America. Established in 1731, it was originally a subscription library to which members contributed an annual fee in return for the full use of books and pamphlets. In 1736 Franklin was appointed clerk (official in charge of records) of the Pennsylvania Assembly (legislative body), where he gained valuable political experience over the next fifteen years.

During the 1740s scientists around the world were investigating static (accumulated) electricity. Franklin first witnessed this new force in a demonstration of the Leyden jar (a device used for producing electrical energy) in 1743. Franklin was so inspired by the Leyden jar that he conducted his own experiments, thus beginning his career as an amateur scientist.

Through further experiments, Franklin discovered that electricity is an independent force, which he called "electrical fire." The idea that the overall electrical energy in a system does not increase or decrease is now a fundamental law in science. Franklin introduced many other terms that still pertain to electricity, including battery, conductor, charge, and discharge. He also invented the lightning rod (a metallic rod with one end embedded in the ground, which diverts electricity to the earth and protects buildings against fire caused by lightning). By 1782, there were four hundred lightning rods in Philadelphia.

While waiting for the lightning rod to be installed on Christ Church, Franklin came up with an idea for a faster way to get a conductor into the sky. He made a kite by tying a large silk handkerchief to two crossed wooden sticks. Next, to the kite he attached a long silk thread that had a metal key tied at the end. Then he waited for a thunderstorm. During the storm the rain soaked the thread, making it an excellent conductor (an item that permits flow of electric current) that transmitted a static charge from the sky down to the key. When Franklin touched his knuckle to the key, a spark jumped from the key to his hand, thus proving the existence of electricity in the sky.

Although Franklin was best known for his work with electricity, he investigated other areas as well. His interest in the weather led him to notice that weather patterns usually travel from west to east. Another of Franklin's interests was the sea. During his diplomatic career he journeyed across the Atlantic Ocean eight times, and on these trips he took notes of his observations of ocean waters. With the help of a sea captain, he created the first chart of the Gulf Stream (a warm current in the Atlantic Ocean). Franklin also devised a method of using a thermometer to gauge water temperature to determine if a ship was on course in the Gulf Stream.

Franklin introduced several innovations in the field of medicine. He was a strong supporter of regular exercise, particularly swimming. He believed in the importance of fresh air for good health, even though at the time many people thought night air and drafts caused disease. Expanding on his electrical studies, he used electric shocks to treat people with paralysis (loss of body movement). He determined, however, that the treatment did not have any permanent benefits. When the smallpox inoculation was first introduced, Franklin warned against the practice. (Smallpox is a highly contagious, often fatal disease. Inoculation is the introduction of the disease-causing agent into the body in order to create immunity.) After his own son died of the disease, however, he reversed his opinion and published a pamphlet on the importance of inoculation.

In 1748 Franklin retired from business and science to devote the rest of his life to politics and diplomacy. Three years later he was elected to the Pennsylvania Assembly. In 1757 Franklin began his diplomatic career when he was sent to England as a lobbyist (one who represents a particular group in attempting to influences public officials). Franklin's experiments with electricity brought him great fame in America and Europe. Not only was he respected by the scientific community, he was popular with the general public. He spread his ideas through a number of writings, including articles in the leading scientific journal of the time, *Philosophical Transactions of the Royal Society.* In 1751 Franklin's papers on electricity were gathered and published in a ninety-page book in London. The Royal Society, a British scientific organization, awarded him the Copley Medal in 1753 for his accomplishments and made him a member of the society in 1756. (In 1744 Franklin had modeled the American Philosophical Society on the prestigious Royal Society.)

Franklin was a member of the Second Continental Congress (the governing body of the Thirteen Colonies). He helped to draft the Declaration of Independence (a document that stated the American colonists' reasons for demanding freedom from Great Britain), which was completed in 1776. Two years later he signed treaties with France that may have helped America win the Revolutionary War (1775–83; a conflict in which the American colonies won independence from Great Britain).

During his lifetime, Franklin began a long union with Deborah Reed, whom he never officially married because she was never divorced from her husband. Franklin already had one son, William, born to an unknown mother, who joined the family. Franklin and Reed also had two children of their own, a son Francis (who died of smallpox) and a daughter Sarah. During the last few years of his life, Franklin lived with Sarah and numerous grandchildren in a large house on Market Street in Philadelphia. He spent his time completing his autobiography (first published in 1868), which became a classic work in American literature. Franklin died in Philadelphia on April 17, 1790, at the age of eighty-five. His funeral was attended by approximately twenty thousand people, who came to mourn the passing of a great man.

Did you know . . .

- One of Franklin's first major inventions was the Pennsylvania fireplace, now known as the Franklin stove, which he developed around 1740. Improving on an existing design, he equipped the stove with a flue (heat channel) that heats the air around it. The stove was highly efficient, and Franklin claimed it made a room twice as warm as other stoves even though it used only twenty-five percent of the usual amount of wood. Another popular Franklin invention was bifocal eyeglasses, in which the lower part of the lens is designed for near vision and the upper for distant vision. Franklin is also credited with creating the rocking chair.

For more information

Benjamin Franklin Citizen of the World. A&E Home Video, 1994. Videocassette recording.

Benjamin Franklin Scientist and Inventor. Living History Productions, 1993. Videocassette recording.

Franklin, Benjamin. *Benjamin Franklin: A Biography in His Own Words.* Thomas Fleming, ed. New York: Newsweek, 1972.

McFarland, Philip James. *The Brave Bostonians: Hutchinson, Quincy, and The Coming of the American Revolution.* Boulder, Colo.: Westview Press, 1998.

Rudy, Lisa Jo, ed. *The Benjamin Franklin Book of Easy and Incredible Experiments.* New York: Wiley, 1995.

Stiles, T. J., ed. *In Their Own Words: The Colonizers.* New York: Berkeley Publishing, 1998, pp. 314–418.

John Adams

Excerpt from **The Diary and Autobiography of John Adams**
Reprinted in *Major Problems in American Colonial History*
Published in 1993
Edited by Karen Ordahl Kupperman

America was the first nation to provide free education to all citizens. The importance of an educated population dated to the earliest years of the colonial period. New England Puritans were the first to establish schools, but solely for the purpose of giving religious education and training ministers. (Puritans were a Protestant Christian group that observed strict moral and religious codes.) Adults and children were expected to be able to read the Bible and to understand the laws of the colony, which were based on the Bible.

For instance, in 1647 the Massachusetts Bay legislature passed a law stating that parents must educate their children. If they failed to do so, community leaders would assume the responsibility. Three years later a similar law was enacted in Connecticut. Boys and girls in rural communities were sent to "dame" schools where they were taught grammar by female members of the church. In towns, male teachers called masters headed schools that admitted only boys. Within fifty years New England had an exceptionally high literacy rate for the time—seventy percent of men and forty-five percent of women could read and write.

"The Difficulties that attend the study may discourage some, but they never discouraged me. . . ."

Education was given less priority in the other colonies during the seventeenth century, mainly because churches did not stress learning as a way to comprehend the will of God. Anglicans (followers of the Church of England) in the southern colonies, for instance, relied on ministers to guide them with sermons, worship services, and parish visits. Baptists and Quakers in the middle colonies, such as Pennsylvania, New Jersey, New York, and Delaware, saw little value in literacy, since they relied on individual inspiration rather than the Scriptures for an understanding of God. Nevertheless schools had been started throughout the colonies by 1700, and all were affiliated with a church. The first school in New York was established by the Dutch Reformed church (a branch of Puritanism based in the Netherlands), and in Philadelphia the first educational institution was founded by Quakers in 1689. Families living in rural areas or small towns—especially in the South—usually hired private tutors to teach their children.

By the early eighteenth century, however, schools were established with no church affiliation (connection). Colonists had become aware that learning was necessary to prepare for everyday life. For example, governments, businesses, and legal systems required literate officials and employees. Also many colonists saw education as a route to prosperity and moral improvement. In Maryland and South Carolina there was a movement to provide schooling for the poor, and throughout the colonies the wealthy were leaving money for schools in their wills.

This upsurge in learning had produced significant trends by 1760. Many people were pursuing teaching careers, which had previously been limited to ministers. The literacy rate increased dramatically. Nevertheless the education of women was still a low priority, since women could not participate in public life and therefore needed only to know how to read. The exceptions were daughters of wealthy families, who were taught social graces such as painting, singing, or playing musical instruments.

Higher education was also emphasized during the colonial period. In 1636 Harvard College opened its doors in Cambridge, Massachusetts, becoming the first institution of higher learning in the colonies. (Harvard was named for John Harvard, a Puritan minister who donated a large sum of money and his private library.) Courses in the classics and philosophy were offered in addition to religion, but men who wished to study law or medicine had to go to Europe. For half a century Harvard was the only college in America, and it served mainly to educate the sons of Puritans.

Finally, in 1693, the College of William and Mary (named for English monarchs William III and Mary II) was established in Williamsburg, Virginia, to train Anglican ministers and to provide a college for the sons of Virginia plantation owners. Within fifteen years William and Mary had added courses in law and medicine.

In the meantime, Harvard had been influenced by educational trends in Europe. The college expanded its curriculum (program of study) to include the liberal arts (grammar, rhetoric, logic, arithmetic, geometry, astronomy, and music) as well as science, philosophy, politics, and other subjects. Harvard also added another year of study at the freshman level, dropping the average age at entry to between fifteen or sixteen. The basic requirement for admission was a solid background in the Latin language.

Eventually some Harvard graduates became concerned that the college had strayed from Puritan teachings because fewer graduates were going into the ministry. In 1701 the group started a college to educate ministers in a traditional Puritan curriculum. For several years the school was moved among various locations in Connecticut. Finally in 1720 a permanent building was constructed in New Haven, Connecticut, and the college was named Yale College for Elihu Yale, who had contributed a large sum of money to the enterprise. Yet by 1760 Yale had also adopted European trends.

Colleges were established much later in the middle colonies. Unlike New England and the southern colonies, New York was populated by numerous religious groups, and no church had gained enough dominance to open an institution of higher learning. The Quakers still controlled Pennsylvania, but they had no interest in starting a divinity (religious) school because they did not have ordained ministers. Yet Presbyterians (a branch of Puritanism) were arriving in Pennsylvania in increasing numbers. At first their ministers attended Harvard, but they soon saw a need for their own college. In 1746 the Presbyterians founded the interdenominational (open to all

" . . . I said, this is certainly a tavern."

In 1680 New York colonists Jasper Danckaerts and Peter Sluyter paid a visit to Harvard. They expected to see an impressive institution, but instead they found that only ten students were enrolled and the college barely had enough funds to stay open. Danckaerts and Sluyter were also surprised that the students were heavy smokers and could not even speak Latin (which was supposed to be one of the basic requirements for admission to Harvard).

We started out to go to Cambridge, lying to the northeast of Boston, in order to see their college, and printing office. We reached Cambridge, about eight o'clock. It is not a large village, and the houses stand very much apart. The college building is the most conspicuous [noticeable] among them. We went to it, expecting to see something curious, as it is the only college, or would-be academy of the Protestants in all America, but we found ourselves mistaken. In approaching the house, we neither heard nor saw anything mentionable; but, going to the other side of the building, we heard noise enough in an upper room, to lead my comrade to suppose they were engaged in disputation [argument].

We entered, and went up stairs, when a person met us, and requested us to walk in, which we did. We found there, eight or ten young fellows, sitting around, smoking tobacco, with the smoke of which the rooms was so full, that you could hardly see; and the whole house smelled so strong of it, that when I was going up stairs, I said, this is certainly a tavern. We excused ourselves, that we could speak English only a little, but understood Dutch or French, which they did not. However, we spoke as well as we could. We inquired how many professors there were, and they replied not one, that there was no money to support one. We asked how many students there were. They said at first, thirty, and then came down to twenty; I afterwards understood there are probably not ten. They could hardly speak a word of Latin, so that my comrade could not converse with them. They took us to the library where there was nothing particular. We looked over it a little. They presented us with a glass of wine. This is all we ascertained [found out] there. The minister of the place goes there morning and evening to make prayer, and has charge over them. The students have tutors or masters.

Colbert, David, ed. *Eyewitness to America*. New York: Pantheon Books, 1997, pp. 37–38.

religious groups) College of New Jersey at Elizabethtown. The school was moved to Princeton, New Jersey, in 1754 and was officially named Princeton College in the 1760s. In 1754 King's College (now Columbia University) was started in New York City as a nondenominational institution.

The first institution that abandoned religious requirements was the Academy of Philadelphia, founded in 1751 with the support of Benjamin Franklin (see *Benjamin Franklin: A Biography in his Own Words*). His goal was to provide a "useful" education, with courses in astronomy, arithmetic, accounting, and geometry, as well as English, history, botany, agriculture, mechanics, Greek, and Latin. In 1755 the academy was renamed the Academy and College of Philadelphia (now the University of Pennsylvania), and is now regarded as the basis for the public education system that was later adopted in the United States.

By the end of the colonial period six colleges had been established in America, all of them admitting only male students. With fewer men entering the ministry, the colleges were increasingly offering nonreligious courses of study. Yet there were still no professional schools, and young men who wanted to become doctors or lawyers had to earn their degrees in Europe. Those who could not afford a European education attended colonial colleges and then practiced for two or three years with a qualified professional. The autobiography of John Adams, a Harvard student and future president of the United States, gives the modern reader insight into the experiences of a young man who found himself in this situation.

John Adams (1735–1826) was born on a farm near Braintree, Massachusetts, the oldest of three sons of John Adams and Susannah Boylston Adams. Young John Adams grew up in a Puritan community, going to church twice on Sundays and working hard on the farm the rest of the week. His family valued education, so he learned to read at an early age. He began attending a dame school run by a neighbor, Mrs. Belcher, and he also excelled in arithmetic. But he lost interest in education once he had moved to a public school, where he studied Latin grammar under an uninspiring master. By the age of ten he was skipping school, and he spent his time playing at nearby beaches and bogs. When the elder John Adams found out he was furious. An uneducated man himself, he had placed great hopes in his son's studying for the ministry at nearby Harvard College and escaping the drudgery of the farm. The boy announced that he wanted to be a farmer and had no desire to go to college, but his father won out. Adams remained bored with school, so when he was fourteen his father agreed to let him study with a tutor named Mr. Marsh. Marsh taught him to love learning, and within a year he had passed the Harvard entrance exams.

Adams entered Harvard in 1751, two months before his sixteenth birthday. Life at the college was very strict. The ninety students got up each morning at five o'clock, attended chapel at six, and had breakfast at seven. Classes started at eight, then the afternoon was set aside for study until supper at six. Students had some free time until curfew, when they snuffed their candles, put out fires in fireplaces, and went to bed. In addition to following this rigid schedule, students were forbidden to tell a lie, drink alcohol, or play cards. They could not go skating without permission, and they were required to observe the Sabbath (Sunday), a day set aside for church services and religious contemplation. All violators were fined ten shillings (a sum of British money equal to about $1.20) for each offense. No one was allowed to leave the college grounds without a good reason and permission from his tutor.

Adams thrived at Harvard in spite of the rules. He enjoyed spending time in the library, where he discovered many new ideas. He had been studying for the ministry, but he soon had doubts about narrow Puritan beliefs and decided to become a teacher. After graduating in 1755, when he was almost twenty years old, Adams took a job as a schoolmaster at a grammar school in Worcester, Massachusetts. Within a year he realized he was interested in learning law, so he arranged to study with James Putnam, a prominent Worcester lawyer. For two years Adams lived with Putnam, teaching school during the day and working in Putnam's office at night. He copied deeds and wills, prepared briefs, discussed cases, and studied law. In 1758 Adams went to Boston, where he was introduced into the legal profession by the prominent lawyers Jeremiah Gridley and James Otis.

Things to Remember While Reading an Excerpt from *The Diary and Autobiography of John Adams:*

- This excerpt from Adams's diary begins just after his arrival in Boston, when he met Gridley and Otis and other members of the legal profession. At this point Adams had not been admitted to the bar (an association of lawyers who are permitted to represent clients and try cases in court), and he was seeking advice about how to become a lawyer.

- Adams felt out of place in Boston. As the son of a farmer, he was dazzled by the elite social world—the "Spacious and elegant" court room, the "gayest Company of Gentlemen and the finest Row of Ladies." On his first visit to the court house, he also found the assembled lawyers to be a "sour" group. During his time in Boston, Adams made contacts that enabled him to join the ranks of the elite and become one of the great leaders of the American Revolution (1775–83).

- Keep in mind that there were no law schools in the colonies, and Adams had to obtain his legal education by studying with practicing lawyers. His diary gives the modern reader a glimpse into the process a young colonial American went through in order to enter the legal profession. One step was to submit to a review of his education and credentials. For instance, in the entry for October 26, Adams described his meeting with Mr. Prat. Prat questioned him extensively about such matters as his academic studies, his work with Putnam in Worcester, and the status of his legal studies. Notice that Adams did not like Prat, finding him "ill natured" in comparison to Gridley, who was "good natured."

- Gridley gave Adams numerous tips and bits of advice. At one point he cautioned Adams not to practice law for profit, or "the Gain of it," but for the pursuit of law itself. He also told the aspiring attorney not to marry early because he would slow his progress ("obstruct your Improvement") and take on too many financial responsibilities ("involve you in Expence"). In addition, Gridley warned against socializing too much ("not to keep much company") because a lawyer must constantly apply himself to his work. Adams appears to have taken Gridley's last piece of advice. In his diary he showed that he was very conscientious; for example, he reminded himself to pay better attention to small details and become more organized. He was already acquiring the habits of a lawyer.

- On the recommendation of Gridley, Adams was admitted to the bar and qualified to practice law. Adams was an outsider (he was "unknown" in Boston). He was certain that Samuel Quincy, another aspiring lawyer, would be admitted to the bar because he already knew everyone in the Boston legal community. At this point Adams was without a patron (sponsor), so he was sure his own request for admission would be turned down. At the last minute Gridley spoke up for him.

Excerpt from The Diary and Autobiography of John Adams

Tuesday [24 October]

*Rode to Boston. Arrived about after 10. Went into the Court House, and sett down by Mr. Paine [Robert Treat Paine; a fellow student] att the Lawyers Table. I felt Shy, under Awe and concern, for Mr. Gridley, Mr. Prat, Mr. Otis, Mr. Kent, and Mr. Thatcher were all present and looked sour. I had no Acquaintance with any Body but Paine and Quincy [Samuel Quincy; a student also seeking admission to the bar] and they took but little Notice. However I attended Court Steadily all Day, and at night, went to **Consort** with Samll [Samuel] Quincy and Dr. Gardiner. There I saw the most Spacious and elegant Room, the gayest Company of Gentlemen and the finest Row of Ladies, that ever I saw. But the weather was so dull and I so **disordered** that I could not make one half the observations that I wanted to make.*

Wednesday [25 October]

Went in the morning to Mr. Gridleys, and asked the favour of his Advice what Steps to take for an Introduction to the Practice of Law in this County. He answered "get sworn" [admitted to the bar].

Ego [I; Adams]. But in order to that, sir, as I have no Patron, in this County.

*G. [Gridley] I will recommend you to the Court. Mark the Day the Court **adjourns** to in order to make up Judgments. Come to Town that Day, and in the mean Time I will speak to the Bar for the Bar must be consulted, because the Court always inquires, if it be with Consent of the Bar.*

*Then Mr. Gridley inquired what Method of Study I had pursued, what Latin Books I read, what Greek, what French. What I had read upon **Rhetorick**. Then he took his Common Place Book [a guide to law] and gave me Ld. [Lord] Hales Advice to a Student of the **Common Law**, and when I had read that, he gave me Ld. C[hief]*

Consort: Conjunction or association

Disordered: Lack of order

Adjourns: Suspend until a later stated time

Rhetorick: The study or writing or speaking as a means of communication or persuasion

Common law: The body of law which is the basis for the United States legal system, except in Louisiana

Civil law: The law of civil or private rights

Admiralty law: Law relating to the sea

Natural law: The law derived from nature

Sollicitor Lawyer who represents clients in lower courts

Scrivener: A professional or public copyist or writer

Colonial America: Primary Sources

*J[ustice] Reeves Advice [to] his Nephew, in the Study of the common Law. Then He gave me a Letter from Dr. Dickins, Regius Professor of Law at the University of Cambridge, to him, pointing out a Method of Studying the **civil Law.** Then he turned to a Letter He wrote himself to Judge Lightfoot, Judge of the Admiralty in Rhode Island, directing to a Method of Studying the **Admiralty Law.** Then Mr. Gridley run a Comparison between the Business and studies of a Lawyer or Gentlemen of the Bar, in England, and that of one here. A Lawyer in this Country must study common Law and civil Law, and **natural Law,** and Admiralty Law, and must do the duty of a Counsellor, a Lawyer, an Attorney, a **sollicitor,** and even of a **scrivener,** so that the Difficulties of the Profession are much greater here than in England.*

The Difficulties that attend the study may discourage some, but they never discouraged me. . . .

*I have a few Pieces of Advice to give you Mr. Adams. One is to pursue the Study of the Law rather than the Gain of it. Pursue the Gain of it enough to keep out of the **Briars,** but give your main Attention to the study of it.*

The next is, not to marry early. For an early Marriage will obstruct your Improvement, and in the next Place, twill involve you in Expence.

*Another Thing is not to keep much Company. For this application of a Man who aims to be a lawyer must be **incessant.** His Attention to his Books must be constant, which is inconsistent with keeping much Company.*

*In the study of Law the common Law be sure deserves your first and last Attention, and He has conquered all the Difficulties of this Law, who is Master of the **Institutes.** You must conquer the Institutes. The Road of Science is much easier, now, than it was when I sett out. I began with Co. Litt. and broke thro.*

*I asked his Advice about studying Greek. He answered it is a matter of meer Curiosity.-After this long and familiar Conversation we went to Court. Attended all Day and in the Evening I went to ask Mr. Thatchers **Concurrence** with the Bar. Drank Tea and spent the whole Evening, upon **original sin,** act of disobedience*

Origin of Evil, the Plan of the Universe, and at last, upon Law. . . .

Since there were no law schools in the colonies, John Adams obtained his legal education by studying with practicing lawyers.
Reproduced by permission of the National Archives and Records Administration.

Briars: Debt

Incessant: Continuing without interuption

Institutes: Major areas of academic study

Concurrence: Cooperation or agreement or union in action

Orginal sin: The sin that marks all human beings as a result of Adam's first

Thursday [26 October]

Went in the morning to wait on Mr. Prat. He inquired if I had been sworn at Worcester? No. Have you a Letter from Mr. Putnam [James Putnam, the lawyer with whom Adams studied in Worcester] to the Court? No. It would have been most proper to have done one of them things first. When a young Gentleman goes from me into another County, I always write in his favour to the Court in that County, or if you had been sworn, there, you would have been intitled to be sworn here. But now, no Body in this County knows any Thing about you. So no Body can say any Thing in your favour, but by hearsay. I believe you have made a proper **Proficiency** *in science, and that you will do very well from what I have heard, but that is only hearsay. [How different is this from Gridleys Treatment? Besides it is weak, for neither the Court nor the Bar will question the* **Veracity** *of Mr. Gridly and Mr. Prat, so that the only Uncertainty that can remain is whether Mr. Putnam was in* **Earnest**, *in the Account he gave of my Morals and Studies to them Gentleman, which cannot be removed by a Line from him, or by my being sworn at Worcester, or any other Way than by getting Mr. Putnam sworn.] After this, he asked me a few, short Questions about the Course of my studies which I answered, and then came off as full of Wrath as [I] was full of Gratitude when I left Gridley the morning before. Prat is infinitely harder of Access than Gridley. He is ill natured, and Gridley is good natured.-Attended Court all Day, and at night waited on Otis at his office where I conversed with him and he, with great Ease and familiarity, promised me to join the Bar in recommending me to the Court. . . .*

Let me remarke here on important neglect of the last Week. I omitted **minuting** *the Names of the Cases at Trial in my Ivory Book, and I omitted to keep Pen, Ink, and Paper at my Lodgings, in order to comitt to Writing, at Night, the Cases and Points of Law that were argued and* **adjudged** *in the Day.*

Let me remember to mark in my Memorandum Book, the Names of the Cases, and the Terms and Points of Law that occur in each Case, to look these Terms and Points in the Books at Otis's, Prats or any other office, and to digest and write down the whole in the Evening at my Lodgings. This will be **reaping** *some real Advantage, by my Attendance on the Courts, and, without this, the Observations that I may make will lie in total Confusion in my mind.*

Friday, Saturday, Sunday, Monday [27-30 October]

All Spent in absolute **Idleness***, or what is worse,* **gallanting** *the Girls.*

Proficiency: Advancement in knowledge or skill

Veracity: Truthfulness

Earnest: Deep sincerity

Minuting Keeping track of

Adjudged: To pronounce judicially

Reaping: Obtaining

Idleness: Laziness

Gallanting: To pay court to ladies

Colonial America: Primary Sources

Thursday [2 November]

*Rode as far as Smelt Brook. Breakfasted, made my fire and am now set down to Van Muyden [a book written by Van Muyden] in Earnest. His latin is easy, his deffinitions are pretty clear, and his Divisions of the subject, are **judicious.***

Monday [6? November]

*Went to Town. Went to Mr. Gridleys office, but he had not returned to Town from Brookline [a town near Boston]. Went again. Not returned. Attended Court till after 12 and began to grow uneasy expecting that Quincy would be sworn and I have no Patron, when Mr. Gridly made his Appearance, and on sight of me, whispered to Mr. Prat, Dana, Kent, Thatcher &c. about me. Mr. Prat said no Body knew me. Yes, says Gridley, I have tried him, he is a very sensible Fellow.-At last He rose up and bowed to his right Hand and said "Mr. Quincy," when Quincy rose up, then bowed to me, "Mr. Adams," when I walked out. "May it please your Honours, I have 2 young Gentlemen Mr. Q. and Mr. Adams to present for the Oath of an Attorney. Of Mr. Q it is sufficient for me to say he has lived 3 Years with Mr. Prat. Of Mr. Adams, as he is unknown to your Honours, It is necessary to say that he has lived between 2 and 3 Years with Mr. Put[nam] of Worcester, has a good Character from him, and all others who know him, and that he was with me the other day several Hours, and I take it he is qualified to study the Law by his scholarship and that he has made a very considerable, a very great Proficiency in the Principles of the Law, and therefore that the Clients Interest may be safely intrusted in his Hands. I therefore recommend him with the Consent of the Bar to your Honors for the Oath." Then Mr. Prat said 2 or 3 Words and the Clerk was ordered to swear to us. After the Oath Mr. Gridly took me by the Hand, wished me much Joy and recommended me to the Bar. I shook Hands with the Bar, and received their Congratulations, and invited them over to Stones [a pub] to drink some Punch. Where the most of us **resorted**, and had a very cheerful [Chat].*

Judicious: Having, exercising, or characterized by sound judgment

Resorted: A place frequented by people for relaxation

John Adams's wife Abigail was one of the most outstanding first ladies in American history.
Reproduced by permission of Archive Photos, Inc.

What happened next . . .

Adams returned to the family farm in Braintree and set up his own law practice. In 1764 he married Abigail Smith. Adams moved on to a brilliant career as a lawyer, statesman, and revolutionary leader. He entered politics as an opponent of repressive British measures such as the Stamp Act, which led to the American Revolution (1775–1783). (The Stamp Act of 1765 was the first direct tax levied by Britain on the American colonies. It required that a stamp be placed on all documents, newspapers, commercial bills, and other published materials issued in the colonies. The revenues from the stamp tax would be used for defense. The act produced intense opposition.) In 1774 Adams was a delegate to the First Continental Congress (the newly formed legislature of the thirteen colonies). He was one of the principal drafters of the Declaration of Independence (a document that declared American independence from Britain; adopted July 4, 1776). The thirteen colonies then became known as the United States of America.

At the end, a difficult term as United States ambassador (official representative of a government) to France, Adams helped draw up the Treaty of Paris (1783), which ended the American Revolution. From 1789–1797 he served as vice president under George Washington, the first president of the new nation. Adams was elected the second United States president, serving one term (1797–1801). After leaving office he retired to Quincy, Massachusetts, where he wrote and received many letters. His most notable correspondence was with Thomas Jefferson, another revolutionary leader and third United States president. Adams died in Quincy at the age of ninety–one.

Did you know . . .

- Abigail Adams was one of the most outstanding first ladies in American history. She was instrumental in the success of her husband as president and political leader. She was a productive letter writer, and her correspondence provides a rich source of information about life in colonial and revolutionary America.

- Abigail and John Adams's son, John Quincy Adams, was the sixth president of the United States.

- John Adams and Thomas Jefferson died on the same day—July 4, 1826—the fiftieth anniversary of American independence. Just before dying Adams reportedly said, "Thomas Jefferson survives." He was unaware that Jefferson had died only a few hours earlier at Monticello, in Virginia.

- In 1721 John Adams's maternal grandfather, Zabdiel Boylston, was persuaded by amateur scientist Cotton Mather to administer the first smallpox inoculation (vaccination) in America. (Smallpox is a deadly viral disease; inoculation involves introducing a microorganism of the virus into the body to produce immunity.) Smallpox inoculation was unproven at the time, so the procedure was considered by some to be dangerous. Threats were even made against the lives of both Boylston and Mather. Boylston inoculated 240 persons, including his son and two of his slaves, and all but six survived.

For more information

Brill, Marlene Targ. *Encyclopedia of Presidents: John Adams*. Chicago: Children's Press, 1986.

Ellis, Joseph S. *Passionate Sage: The Character and Legacy of John Adams*. New York: Norton, 1994.

Ferling, John E. *John Adams: A Life*. New York: Henry Holt & Company, 1996.

John Adams. http://www.studyworld.com/John_Adams.htm Available September 30, 1999.

Kupperman, Karen Ordahl, ed. *Major Problems in American Colonial History*. Lexington, Mass.: D. C. Heath, 1993, pp. 411–14.

Middleton, Richard. *Colonial America: A History, 1585–1776*. Second edition. Malden, Mass.: Blackwell Publishers, 1996, pp. 291–95.

Nagel, Paul C. *Descent from Glory: Four Generations of the John Adams Family*. Cambridge, Mass.: Harvard University Press, 1999.

Index

Bold type indicates
main entries and their page
numbers. Illustrations are
marked by (ill).